ROMANCING
THE
ROADS

ROMANCING THE ROADS

A DRIVING DIVA'S FIRSTHAND GUIDE

Volume II: West of the Mississippi

- - - - - - - - - - - - - - - - - - - -

GERRY HEMPEL DAVIS

TAYLOR TRADE PUBLISHING

Lanham • New York • Boulder • Toronto • Plymouth, UK

Published by Taylor Trade Publishing
An imprint of The Rowman & Littlefield Publishing Group, Inc.
4501 Forbes Boulevard, Suite 200, Lanham, Maryland 20706
http://www.rlpgtrade.com

Estover Road, Plymouth PL6 7PY, United Kingdom

Distributed by NATIONAL BOOK NETWORK

British Library Cataloguing in Publication Information Available

Library of Congress Cataloging-in-Publication Data
Davis, Gerry Hempel.
Romancing the roads : a driving diva's firsthand guide, volume II :
weat of the Mississippi / Gerry Hempel Davis.
p. cm.
Includes index.
ISBN 978-1-58979-639-3 (pbk. : alk. paper) — ISBN 978-1-58979-640-9
(electronic)
1. Automobile travel—West (U.S.) 2. Women automobile drivers—West (U.S.)
3. Women travelers—West (U.S.) 4. West (U.S.)—Description and travel. I. Title.
GV1024.D39 2011
917.8—dc23
2011023161

917,8
DAV

Printed in the United States of America

CONTENTS

ACKNOWLEDGMENTS

As with every book I write, I must first acknowledge my family: sons, Clint and Mark; daughters-in-law, Chris and Michelle; grandchildren, Olivia, Sawyer, Heyden, and Alex. I thank them for their enthusiasm, their queries, and for being there.

Thanks also to Rick Rinehart, publisher, who is receptive to my ideas even though some are loopy or truly not feasible. He is tactful and thoughtful. I thank him for believing in my literary pursuits. We have had some interesting times and have books to show for our endeavors.

To each person—and there are a hundred or so from coast to coast—who helped me: Thank you. I could not have accumulated so much data without your support. I enjoyed each and every one of you and look forward to keeping in touch.

Thanks and appreciation go to Janice Braunstein, Flannery Scott, and Jennifer Kelland Fagan. These talented and dedicated females do so much in getting a book in hand.

INTRODUCTION

West of the Mississippi is very different than east of that same body of water. Not that one is better—indeed no—but different, yes. One must do the West at least once. You will not forget it.

I have either been to every place included in this volume or I inform the reader if I have not. Whether you are driving miles on the straightest road imaginable or standing on the rim of the Grand Canyon or buying a trinket at a truck stop or seeing something you had only read about, I promise you will not be disappointed, and you will definitely be enriched. There have been changes and closings, and I wish you all well.

Ultra hotels, bed-and-breakfasts, restaurants of every variety, shops (consignment too), and so much more are all included. Several national parks are described, but it is hard to put into words these totally awesome places. "Awesome" is an understatement; add unbelievable. Towns—medium, large, tiny, or just a dot—are described, and there is a megalopolis or two.

Whether you actually take a drive or just see via the words the places I describe, I hope you enjoy. This book is not only for the road warrior but for the armchair traveler. Let us start our trip. . . . Repeat: *Even if you can't go, you can know*. Enjoy!

LOUISIANA

NEW ORLEANS

One hears so much about New Orleans and its famous **French Quarter**, but even before the devastating hurricanes of 2005, it didn't seem to me to be particularly well managed. A simple thing like cleaning up the streets would have been a step in the right direction, and following Katrina, it took far too long to clean up the debris. Everybody should have pitched in more vehemently and with more enthusiasm and determination. The French Quarter escaped a lot of Katrina's fury.

Soniat House
1133 Chartres St.
800-544-8808
www.soniathouse.com

I'm happy to report this special property is alive and well. The Soniat House is actually in two parts—one on each side of the street—distinguished by green shutters and filigreed wrought iron accents. It was created over twenty years ago by combining three historic Creole townhouses. Owners Rodney and Frances Smith developed this fabulous property. Their good taste, creativity, and respect for old-world charm have made the Soniat House the very admirable and distinguished place that it is today.

It is easy to see how this charming property came to receive accolades from such disparate sources as *Time* magazine and *Architectural Digest*. The main building has two large green doors that open onto a courtyard that extends to the middle of the property. Slightly down and off to the side is a small room where you check in. Adjacent is a living room where you can sit and enjoy a drink from the honors bar.

My room (or suite, rather) was in the building across the street behind a locked gate and toward the middle of the back courtyard. From the moment I entered, I found the living room, bedroom, and bath pleasant, relaxing, and very attractive.

One cannot mention the Soniat House without mentioning (1) Calvin, who helped me with my bags and gave me general information about the Soniat as well as where to eat; (2) Jessie, a porter, and (3) Clarice the Cat.

Once settled, I headed out for a brief tour of the French Quarter, ending up at the French Market.

French Market
Decatur and Saint Peter's streets
504-522-2621
www.frenchmarket.org

At the French Market, I saw a lot of people trying to sell the same things: beads upon beads, sunglasses, and stacks of trinkets. Somehow it must work, because no one looks to be starving.

Driving Diva Alert: You won't want to wear thin heels, or perhaps any heels, in the French Quarter. The streets aren't cobblestone, they're just plain uneven.

A Travel Serendipity: The gentleman who helped me with my bags at the hotel, Calvin, recommended a nearby restaurant for dinner. When I couldn't find it, I stopped a woman laden with several large boxes. I think she was delighted to have a reason to stop and put the boxes down. I asked her for directions, and as we continued to talk, we introduced ourselves. She, Carole Lovelace, is founder and president of *Ladies Day Fund Inc.* (www.ladiesdayfund.com), which gives financial aid to Delta Flight attendants who are seriously ill. It turns out that the boxes were full of flower pocketbooks that were to be sold at the next event to raise money for the charity. Right there, on the corner, she showed me one. I couldn't resist buying several! Our conversation then led to plans to get together the following morning, and we have kept in touch ever since. Ah, a serendipity of travel.

Verti Marte
1201 Royal St.
504-525-4767
www.vertimarte.com

This eatery at first looked like a questionable deli. But Calvin had recommended it, so I walked in and was greeted by a woman in casual attire. A few people were waiting in line in the back by the deli case. The place advertises "Real Food for Real People at Real Prices." Yes! I ordered a sandwich called "All That Jazz" and a piece of pie to go.

The sandwich was huge. Back at the hotel, Calvin greeted me and asked if I had found the place. Indeed! I offered to give him half of my All That Jazz, which he eagerly accepted. Just so you know, it was probably one of the best sandwiches I've ever had and a bargain, too! The most expensive item on the Verti Marte menu was $6.95 (then).

Back in my suite, I took note of a few accommodation details such as the glass-topped tables (which I think are a necessity), the roomy bathroom (though more hooks would be nice), and the sheer curtains. A bathroom window looks out onto the garden, and given the sheer curtains, when it's is dark outside, it's possible someone could follow your au natural shadow climbing into and out of the tub. It's probably unlikely, but I think a shade would be appropriate. The tub knobs are labeled in French: *chaud* and *froid*—a nice touch. The lighting in general could be better.

Overall, the suite's antique furnishings are excellent, and the Frette Egyptian cotton bed linens are fantastic to your bod, your psyche, and your dreams. The bright-red wooden hangers are terrific. (Can hangers be terrific?) They can be purchased.

The next morning I had breakfast in the main courtyard amid the garden's variegated foliage, hanging baskets, singing birds, and the occasional cat that checked me out. I sat at a round table with a crisp white tablecloth and enjoyed a glass of freshly squeezed orange juice, Creole café au lait (jolt!), and delicious hot biscuits with Soniat House strawberry preserves. What a way to start the day! Thank you!

The main commercial street in the French Quarter is **Royal**, where shops of every variety can be found. One of my first discoveries was Royal Pharmacy, which had been serving the French Quarter for over one hundred years.

Royal Pharmacy
1101 Royal St.
504-523-5401

This is a true old drugstore, with ceiling fans, small tiles on the floor, and a very congenial pharmacist.

Royal Street's other shops offered a little bit of everything, from fine lingerie, to custom millinery, to outstanding antiques and works of art, to jewelry—you name it.

A sudden downpour drove me into Brennan's, the famous Royal Street eatery that's been around since 1947.

Brennan's Restaurant
417 Royal St.
504-525-9711
www.brennansneworleans.com

The menu was a bit pricey, but, of course, you are paying not only for food but also for atmosphere and history. Maybe on the next trip I will indulge.

Driving Diva Tip: Get the "French Quarter Self-Guided Walking Tour" brochure.

For visitor information, call 504-566-5003 or visit www.new orleanscvb.com. At the end of Royal, you leave the French Quarter and enter downtown New Orleans.

Bourbon Street

There is only one Bourbon Street, New Orleans. This famous and infamous street has a whole lot going on. You don't have to wait until Mardi Gras to get the vibes, the beat, the noise, the smells, the laugher, the yells—they are always there, just more so during Mardi Gras. Be sure to visit this street—even if it is just to walk and look and hear.

Places of Note

K-Paul's
416 Chartres St.
504-524-7394
www.kpauls.com

Those who eat have, of course, heard of Paul Prudhomme, the Louisiana chef with the big smile and culinary creativity. I enjoyed eating at K-Paul's, but I did not have enough room to taste all that I wanted to try.

The turtle soup was excellent, as was the classic shrimp étouffée. A little less smothering with brown gravy would have been my preference for my midriff. The K-Paul's delicious house salad—which was created twenty-two years ago—has definitely remained a winner. The sweet potato pecan pie served with Chantilly cream was sinfully scrumptious.

I was given a great tour of the restaurant by Sandy Crowder, the customer service manager. The restaurant is attractive and the food is *so* Paul Prudhomme.

The menu changes daily. Appetizers start at approximately $6.95; main courses at $25.95 approximately; dessert at about $6. Attire is casual.

Tip: Wear loose-fitting clothes, because you need space for all you will eat.

You might see "debris sauce" on the menu. What is it? It is a reduction of twenty gallons of liquids down to five gallons! It takes seventy-two hours to make. That's three days!

How many restaurants star you? At K-Paul's they do just that. When you finish your meal, you get a gold star if you cleaned your plate, a green star if you ate your vegetables, and a red star if you were rowdy. A paper cover on the table has cartoons informing you of the preparations for shepherd's pie for six, a Cajun martini, and chicken and andouille gumbo. This is a good souvenir, which you are welcome to take.

Muriel's

801 Chartres St.
504-568-1885
www.muriels.com

Muriel's is a must-see, and that is just what I did. To me, it seemed like a real original French Quarter spot. As the advertising states, "Decadence, Opulence, Mystery." There are five different areas: the bistro, the balcony, the soiree, the séance lounge, and the courtyard bar. As you walk around, you discover exposed-brick walls, gourmet aromas, and antiques. You quickly realize that Muriel's is not your usual restaurant.

I was delighted to look around this unique spot. I walked up the flight or two to the séance lounge, though no one was holding one at the time. I am not sure I am ready for a séance. I have read reviews of Muriel's, and if I am ever back in the French Quarter, a meal there is definitely on the agenda. I hear the pecan sweet potatoes are a must. Sounds good to me. I still do not think a séance is necessary.

French Quarter Discoveries

Muse Inspired Fashions
532 Saint Peter St. (Jackson Square)
504-522-8738
www.museinspiredfashion.com

This came highly recommended; then, when I looked it up, I had to include it. Go and see!

The following are some of the places I stopped in due to a rainstorm or simply because they had interesting, tempting displays.

Robinson's Antiques
329 Royal St.
504-523-8863

Ladies' Quarter
427 Royal St.
504-596-3000

Maximo's Italian Grill
1117 Decatur St.
504-586-8883
www.maximosgrill.com

Rumors
58 Royal St.
504-525-0292
www.rumors.com

Lazybug
600 Rue Royal
504-524-3649
www.lazybugshops.com

M. S. Rau Antiques
630 Royal St.
504-523-5660
www.rauantiques.com

This award-winning, third-generation antique dealership has been in business since 1912. Its reputation is exemplary, as is its antique collection.

Antiques, Art, & Collectibles
811 Royal St.
504-524-6918
www.antiquesartcollectibles.com

This shop offers rare coins, toys, and the like.

Fleur de Paris
523 Royal St.
504-525-1899
www.fleurdeparis.net

Here you will find fine lingerie, custom millinery, and contemporary and couture clothing.

Kabuki
1036 Royal St.
504-523-8004
www.kabukihats.com

Kabuki offers great, brightly colored hats and other accessories. Almost everything in shop is handmade by Tracy and Maria.

Objective Eye's Observation: As a female visitor to the French Quarter, I would go and enjoy—wearing comfortable shoes. I would not walk around late at night alone.

Downtown New Orleans

Windsor Court

300 Gravier St.
504-523-6000
www.windsorcourthotel.com

This superb downtown New Orleans property was not difficult to find, and the circular driveway was immediately welcoming. The doorman was attentive. I could see the garage was adjacent to the front. I explained that I might need to get into my car, and the attendant said he would put it where I could walk to it and pointed to an area just inside. How fortuitous to have the garage close by and a most amenable attendant.

The Windsor Court is beautiful in appearance, attitude, and attributes. It is grand and regal and almost incongruous in its positioning in downtown New Orleans, which is not quite so immaculate. As its name suggests, it is British in many ways. Instantly, you are impressed with the antique furnishings and art that decorates the various areas and adorns almost every wall.

Check-in was efficient and female friendly; the welcome was genuine, and I am sure it is given to each guest. As of this writing, there is a new general manager, David Teich, who previously was in Charleston, South Carolina. He brought several of his colleagues with him to the Windsor Court, and their expertise is evident in what they have done to this wonderful property.

I was shown to my accommodations, which were roomy and British in detail. In the bedroom, I immediately noticed a box at the foot of my king-size bed. (When you visit as many hotels as I do, you try to notice the details that make each different.) I noticed a major switch at the side of the bed. I flipped it, and out of the box came a large TV. Later I was to discover that British TV channels are part of the programming.

My bags were delivered, and decisions for the discoveries of the day were made.

The **Polo Club Lounge** (504-522-1994) is upscale and pleasant. The paneled walls are bold but welcoming and reflect in the long mirror behind the handsome bar. Inviting, cozy seating arrangements are well placed. Art masterpieces on the walls, as well as appropriate sculpture, all themed "polo," decorate the lounge. Piano music subtly fills the air. (This is not true in many lounges.) Have one drink, and you might think you are in London. The Polo Lounge is open for lunch, which, when I was there, included a complimentary glass of sparkling wine. It is cigar friendly, which I presume also includes cigarettes.

The New Orleans Grill is now the **Grill Room** (504-522-1994). The new general manager and his team have fine-tuned this exquisite room; the food is exceptional, and the ambiance superb. The *Times Picayune* states, "The Grill Room Reclaims Its Greatness."

When I was there, my dinner was very good and well served. I thought a few things needed attention, but they need not now be mentioned since all reports state that the Grill Room has been tweaked to perfection.

Windsor Court is an ideal focal point, even if you are not staying there. The New Orleans trolley is most convenient. It stops a couple of blocks from the Windsor Court.

Within walking distance from the Windsor Court is the New Orleans Riverwalk, where a bit of everything can be found.

New Orleans Riverwalk
500 Port of New Orleans Pl.
504-522-1555
www.riverwalkmarketplace.com

Harrah's, the gambling haunt, is here.

Harrah's New Orleans

Canal at the River
504-533-6000
www.harrahsneworleans.com

Like all casinos, Harrah's was noisy, with glaring lights, and sometimes sad. I say the latter because, as you watch the throngs of participants (at any casino) with their eternal look of hope, you know their chances of winning are slim. I am glad for the enjoyment they are having, but saving a few coins would make them real winners. I thought the prices at the restaurant were high.

Within a short distance of the Windsor Court, a shopping area has several upscale stores, like **Saks**, **Gucci**, **William Sonoma**, and more.

Speaking of shopping, the Windsor Court has a very special but pricey boutique.

Trolley Travel

I recommend trolley travel. New schedules and routes may have been implemented after the hurricane. The streetcar fare was $1.25 (then), and the trolley has comfortable wooden seats. The bus driver says, "Lay bill flat and put exact change in hole." Easy. The ride to my destination took about twenty minutes.

Objective Eye's Observations: Before the hurricane, from what I saw, New Orleans needed a good washing and garbage removal. It looked like these were being done piecemeal, with Band-Aid fixes.

Tip: Do one block thoroughly and then repeat the scrub on the next block until all are clean. This is a task everyone could participate in, even if done gratis. It's better than sitting and waiting, because moving the debris benefits all.

Discoveries in Downtown New Orleans

I had researched places to visit in the New Orleans area and added to my "collection" after reading the local paper and brochure. I took the **Canal Street trolley**—watching the neighborhoods as I went—to the New Orleans Museum of Art.

New Orleans Museum of Art
1 Collins C. Diboll Cir., City Park
504-658-4100
www.noma.org

The museum is about three long city blocks from the trolley stop. The walk would prove worth it, even though it had started to rain—again—and my walking apparatus was weary.

The museum is not huge but a very nice size. The permanent collections are impressive. I was delighted to see a large canvas by Robert Goodnough, an artist I had met in the 1970s in New York. It was like seeing an old friend when I saw his painting. The photography exhibit was excellent.

The **Sculpture Garden**, a permanent exhibit on five acres is outstanding. The fifty-one sculptures are interspersed throughout the garden. It is a wonderful setting for an impressive experience.

Be sure to check the exhibits and events at the museum and definitely plan to visit.

As I walked back to the trolley stop, I thought the area around the museum seemed nice.

Ogden Museum of Southern Art
925 Camp St.
504-539-9612
www.ogdenmuseum.org

A gem in many ways, this new museum opened to the public in August 2003. The outstanding collections, which range from photography to sculpture to paintings to glass, will be appreciated immediately, but you will enjoy them more and more with each visit. The museum has the proud distinction of having the most comprehensive collection of southern art in the world. Do not miss visiting this impressive, creative, entertaining, and exceptional treasure.

St. Charles Street

St. Charles Street is a mix of beautiful old residences, some shops (see below), and some scruffiness. A streetcar took me up St. Charles to the Convention & Visitors Bureau.

Convention & Visitors Bureau
2020 St. Charles Ave.
800-672-6124
www.neworleanscvb.com

I spent the afternoon with associates from the Convention & Visitors Bureau, and we drove all around. Thank you!

Note: The St. Charles Streetcar is famous and considered a National Historic Landmark. It's an ideal way to see the city and take a self-guided tour, getting on and off as you like. Be sure to get a one- or three-day pass, so you do not have to pay each time you board.

Prima Donna's Closet
1206 St. Charles Ave.
504-525-3327
www.primadonnascloset.com

This shop has excellent items. I found a great pair of new, or newly new, Belgian shoes.

Rubensteins
102 St. Charles Ave.
504-581-6666

Rubensteins has sold fine clothing since 1924.

Magazine Street

Magazine Street is six miles long with a little bit of everything—and I do mean everything. From funky to fabulous, sophisticated to superfluous, be it for two- or four-legged animals, you'll probably find it here. There are items for the petite and the plus, as well as restaurants for all taste buds. It is quite an area. Enjoy, and don't rush. Here are some of the interesting-looking shops I found on Magazine Street. I don't have time to really review them, although I did go into each.

Shoe Nami
3118 Magazine St.
504-895-1717

Earth Savers
5501 Magazine St.
504-899-8555
www.earthsaversonline.com

Scriptura
5423 Magazine St.
504-897-1555
www.scriptura.com

Funky Monkey
3127 Magazine St.
504-899-5587

Slim Goodies Diner
3322 Magazine St.
504-891-3447 (EGGS)

Objective Eye's New Orleans Critique and Observation: New Orleans has so much potential but has let itself go, like a grand dame who hasn't taken care of herself. She has aged, and there is a lot of room for improvements. Run-down conditions have crept in and are gnawing at the core. Perhaps it has been such a gradual process that the natives don't see what has happened. In their mind's eye, it has always been this way. Before it is too late, they must carefully fine-tune. I repeat that perhaps ill winds can blow some good. With the devastations and challenges of the hurricane, perhaps now New Orleans will become updated, maintaining its original credentials.

BATON ROUGE

From New Orleans, the drive to Baton Rouge takes about an hour and a half. It is easy to get onto I-10 and go.

FYI: The name Baton Rouge means "red stick" and was first used by the Indians.

CC's Community Coffee House was my first stop in Baton Rouge.

CC's Community Coffee House
multiple locations; check listings on website
www.communitycoffee.com/ccscommunitycoffeehouse.aspx

I had an appointment with H. Norman Saurage III, chairman of the board, and Matt Saurage, director of business development for **Community Coffees** (www.communitycoffee.com).

Personal Input Suggestion: Always keep your old phonebooks with comments and notes. You never can tell when you might need that old info, as the following evidences.

Years ago when I was on NBC's *The Today Show*, I had the good fortune to introduce and recommend Community Coffees. Little did I know then—although I had been given a verbal invitation of "If you are ever in Baton Rouge . . ."—that I would be accepting the invitation years later and meeting part of this well-known Baton Rouge family. What a delightful time I had! And the coffee is absolutely delicious. The two CC's Coffee Houses that I visited were so nice and female friendly, but then everybody is friendly at Community Coffees.

Here's a little background on the Community Coffee Company. Over eighty-five years ago, H. N. "Cap" Saurage Sr. began serving his special coffee at his small grocery store. The specially brewed coffee became so popular that the store was closed and full time was spent on coffee. Today, it is the most popular brand in Louisiana, Texas, and the Southeast, and its popularity is growing. Community Coffees can be enjoyed not only in your home but in the CC's Coffee Houses. You will also find it served in most of the hotels and restaurants in the area. Community Coffee Company is the largest family-owned retail coffee brand in America. Someone said to me, "CC's coffees were special before specialty coffee became cool."

Observation: Driving to CC's and then on to the Sheraton, I thought Baton Rouge was cleaner, more civilized, and, of course, smaller than New Orleans.

Belle of Baton Rouge (formerly the Sheraton)
103 Frances St.
225-242-2600 or 800-676-4847
www.belleofbatonrouge.com

For me, this was not the usual Sheraton. It is on the river, and the *Belle of Baton Rouge*, a riverboat casino, is at the dock for your gambling convenience. There is direct access from the hotel. A large hotel parking lot is adjacent to the hotel—most convenient.

The newly renovated hotel is large, with three hundred rooms and a very attractive atrium lobby. I now learn that there is a beautiful **Atrium Café**. The check-in was very friendly. My room was large, well appointed, and clean. I was to discover that the mattress, quilt, sheets, and pillows were very good, and I found two terry robes in the closet—just like in the fancy-schmancy hotels!

I checked out the casino, and it was just as expected. The restored carrier USS *Kidd* is docked within walking distance and open for touring seven days a week. It's closed on Thanksgiving and Christmas.

Another thank you to the New Orleans Convention & Visitors Bureau for telling me about this hotel.

Honeymoon Bungalow Collection
3153 Government St.
225-343-4622

Here you'll find antiques, collectibles, and objects of curiosity. This well-displayed collection has all sorts of possible treasures. This is not a fast walk-through. I was short on time but purchased an old cookbook and reluctantly had to leave.

Before leaving, I was told by the owner that they also own Time Warp Boutique.

Time Warp Boutique
3001 Government St.
225-377-8550

This is a big store for all your vintage clothing needs.

The Cabin Restaurant
Hwys. 44 and 22, Burnside
225-473-3007
www.thecabinrestaurant.com

It is easy to get caught up in the Louisiana atmosphere while enjoying Cajun-Creole cooking at this well-known restaurant situated in a former slave home. The building is approximately 140 years old and was part of the Monroe Plantation. The original cypress roof can be seen from the inside—together with a few truly ancient cobwebs. The newspaper—stuck to the walls with a mixture of flour and water—served as insulation, and farming implements hang in many nooks, adding to the ambiance. Age has necessitated several upgrades, and some of the additions are other slave buildings. Needless to say, you are stepping back in time at the Cabin, and there is a lot of history here. The menu selections are as authentic as the decor—you will enjoy both as you sip a beverage from a mason jar. The prices are very reasonable and the atmosphere friendly. Don't miss it! Hours: Monday, 11 a.m. to 3 p.m.; Tuesday, Wednesday, and Sunday: 11 a.m. to 6 p.m.; Friday and Saturday: 11 a.m. to 10 p.m.

Plantations

Visiting a plantation or two or more is an enjoyable must. They will give you insights into living the very gracious, good life.

Houmas House
River Rd., four miles from I-10
225-473-9380
www.houmashouse.com

A jewel! A gem! Upon entering, visitors are given a commemorative hand fan and souvenir beads with a Houmas House medallion—which I immediately put on. There is something about walking around a plantation and fanning yourself. The fan is a great souvenir. On one side is a map of the plantation grounds; on the other side, the language of the fan (I do adore this). The fan says . . .

With handle to lips: Kiss Me.
Carrying in the left hand: I am desirous of acquaintance.
Drawing across the cheek: I love you.
Twirling in right hand: I love another.
Fanning slowly: I am married.
Closing it: I wish to speak with you.

There is more, but this gives you an idea. So civil! Bring back the fan!

This Greek Revival mansion was built in 1812; in 1840 it was attached to the adjacent Latil house. In 1858, John Burnside purchased the property. The twenty thousand acres that made up the plantation grew and processed sugar cane. During the Civil War the Union troops came storming through, but Burnside convinced them that he was an Irishman and a British subject, and the plantation was spared. The plantation remained prosperous until circa 1900, when the lands were sold off and the grand building began to deteriorate. In 1940, Dr. George B. Crozat purchased the house and began restoring it to its 1840 grandeur, adding modern conveniences, since this was to be the doctor's country getaway—from New Orleans.

In 2003, businessman Kevin Kelly realized his dream of owning Houmas House. He continues to re-create the aura, lifestyle, and plantation grandeur of 1840. Touring the house and the magnificent gardens is a grand experience—even if there are too many degrees of Louisiana heat. Use your fan!

There is so much to see and learn at Houmas House. Judy Davis is a great guide who injects life into the tour and your visit. She closes by singing one of the old hymns. Fantastic! Her tour speeches should be taped. The house was featured in the movie *Hush . . . Hush, Sweet Charlotte*, starring Bette Davis. A room is dedicated to her and the movie. A unique feature of Houmas House versus other plantations in the area is its two symmetrical *garçonnières*. What are *garçonnières*, you ask? (Publicizing this may start a fad.) Unique to Louisiana plantations, *garçonnières* housed the adolescent sons of plantation owners. Those at Houmas House are now used as public areas where you can enjoy a cold beverage before touring. They also are perfect chapels for small weddings. A lot of plans for the plantation are on the drawing boards, including an antique shop, a tavern and restaurant, and a Victorian greenhouse botanical garden, which will offer cuttings and samplings from rare and exotic plants on the property.

There is so much to see, admire, and learn at Houmas House. You will definitely enjoy. Admission is approximately $20 per adult. Group rates are available, and the property is wheelchair accessible. Hours: Open daily from 9 a.m. to 5 p.m.

2010 Addendum: I spoke with Kevin Kelly, who, it is obvious from his voice, is a very proud owner. A teahouse has been opened. The surrounding gardens, fountains, ponds, and Japanese bridge are beautiful. The gardens are being touted as among the best in the South. The teahouse, at a twenty-foot elevation, overlooks the plantation. Visit the *Turtle Bar* for your choice of libation and then the award-winning *Latil's Landing Restaurant* (225-473-9380). Reservations are required. Hopefully I will see all of these new additions when on tour. It all sounds fabulous.

Shopping

Bella Bella
3064 Perkins Rd.
225-343-2352

This is an attractive shop for fashionistas. Owner Elise Decoteau now has two other shops It's best to call for directions (252-923-1505 or 225-757-0090).

Imelda's
7865 Jefferson Hwy.
225-923-3737

Owned by Sally Fowler, Imelda's has lots of wonderful shoes— some, of course, pricey. This shop is open every day of the week. Check for hours. I saw on the card that Imelda's has two other stores in Lafayette and Shreveport.

Personal Input to Share

Via Moda
This great little store has shoes, pocketbooks, and small accessories, all sensibly priced. The owner was so bubbly and friendly, and

when she learned I was coming to visit, she made a large bag with *Curves on the Highways* (a previous book of mine) embroidered on the front. Was that not the most original? So very thoughtful! What a super surprise. I admit I found a pink and orange jelly bag on sale that I had to have. Sadly, I called to verify some details and find that the shop has closed, hopefully only temporarily.

Real Life: I share this cute story, which could happen to anyone—especially young mothers. While I was at Via Moda, a young woman ran in. She was obviously dressed up for an event—except for her shoes. It turned out that her child had hidden or misplaced one of the shoes that she was going to wear to a wedding that afternoon. The owner, as well as everyone in the store, pitched in and found her the perfect replacement pair—not too expensive—that she could wear with lots of different kinds of attire. Oh, the trials of wonderful motherhood.

Dining

Coffee Call
3132 College Dr., Ste. F
225-925-9493

This is *the* spot for breakfast. Whoa! Just try to set limits as to how much of a standard Louisiana breakfast—beignets and café au lait—you are going to consume. It's not easy. Coffee Call is a Baton Rouge landmark and gathering place for all Homo sapiens. The Cannatella family opened the business twenty-seven years ago. It's delicious, superclean, and below reasonable in price, with great atmosphere. Can I rave more?

Juban's Creole Restaurant
3739 Perkins Rd.
225-346-8422
www.jubans.com

Acclaimed as one of 1984's best new restaurants by *Esquire*, Juban's, I am glad to emphasize, is owned by two women. Yes! The exceptional menu made choosing what to eat difficult. My selections included

Cajun popcorn: This dish consists of fried crawfish tails served with spicy cocktail sauce. Don't get put off by what Cajun popcorn is. It is delicious.

Filet Juban: The dish of beef tenderloin with maître d'hôtel butter, crabmeat, and béarnaise sauce, was absolutely delicious. I think I split a small salad, and dessert was sweet and decadent.

FYI: One of Juban's signature dishes is Hallelujah Crab, which consists of fried seafood-stuffed soft-shell crab topped with sauce creolaise.

Prices are standard high-end. The atmosphere is upscale casual and definitely friendly. Juban's is located in the **Bocage Shopping Center**, a small but upscale collection of shops, and after dinner I walked around and checked them out.

Paper N Things
7649 Jefferson Hwy.
225-924-7725

What a delightful shop. I purchased some very "me" cards. There were many selections. I discovered, as I spoke with owner Stacey Miremont, that the store does deluxe complimentary gift wrapping. How helpful!

Beausoleil
7731 Jefferson Hwy.
225-926-1172
www.beausoleilrestaurantandbar.com

Also in the Bocage Shopping Center, this delightful place—then called the Silver Spoon—served a delicious, sensibly priced lunch.

The Beausoleil is owned and operated by Michael Boudreaux, Jeff Comaway, Nathan Gresham, and Kenny Juban.

Calandro's Supermarket
4142 Government St.
225-383-7815
12732 Perkins Rd.
225-767-6659
www.calandros.com

In case groceries are needed, I recommend this store, also in the Bocage Shopping Center. It supposedly carries great cheeses, meats, and the like.

The more I saw of Baton Rouge, the more I liked it. I would enjoy returning and discovering more of this Louisiana city. I saw several standard shopping malls. This is a university town, so you are going find a great deal of clothing and items for the college life.

The next day held serendipities of many sorts. I had until 3 p.m., when I would be driving to the next destination. It was Saturday, and I walked around the Main Street Market at Fifth and Main.

Main Street Market
501 Main St.
225-267-5060
www.mainstreetmarketbr.org

The market was in full swing. This is definitely a place to go for everything freshly harvested, preserved, or handmade. The ad card states, "Downtown's Freshest Address." That seemed accurate to me. I would not hesitate to "go to market alone." Everyone was very friendly.

Nottoway Plantation & Resort
31025 Hwy. 405, White Castle
866-668-6929
www.nottoway.com

The drive from Baton Rouge to Nottoway is about one and a half hours. The drive through rural areas puts you in a plantation frame of mind. I found the famed historic Nottoway to be everything that you could ever imagine a plantation to be. It has bed-and-breakfast accommodations. Here are my observations about my Nottoway Plantation experience. I then include what has been added to this most special plantation, which happened to be the largest remaining antebellum mansion in the South with overnight accommodations and restaurant.

As you approach via the long and impressive driveway, this magnificent, enormous, white, Greek Revival mansion looms. One parks in the lot in front and walks into the mansion. A small check-in desk is manned by a competent young man who also helps with my luggage.

All overnight guests, upon arrival, are told the schedule of the complimentary tour and informed that a full plantation breakfast in the **Breakfast Room** will be awaiting them in the morning! Go for this wonderful breakfast. Lunch will not be a consideration.

I recommend a walk around the gardens and up to the levee. The tour of the plantation will be the next morning after breakfast, but all overnight guests can walk through the main house by themselves at night (more on this below).

I was shown to my room, which immediately took me to a place back in time. The four-poster bed, the decor, the ambiance, the carafe of port with sparkling glasses on the table—I wanted to be wearing a full hoop-skirted dress with a corseted waist.

Dinner was scheduled for 7 p.m. in **Randolph Hall**. I had no idea what I was to discover and so thoroughly enjoy. I walked through a small garden to Randolph Hall and was greeted by a hostess. Almost immediately, a chef joined us.

Although chef Johnny "Jambalaya" Percle has retired from Nottoway, he is still involved in his culinary endeavors. I will relate my experience, which was special.

Of course, I let him choose my meal and when I could not decide what to choose chef gave me a sample of each. The Zydeco Salad was so crisp and flavorful that I didn't want to finish it too quickly.

The entrée was a sample of two: a shrimp specialty and trout crisped just right, resulting in one of the best trout dishes I have ever tasted. Dessert was a sampling of several decadent delights. My notes do not seem to include a description of them. I must have been so plied with the outrageous selections that I was too weak to write. With a cup of "guaranteed" decaf coffee, I rate this meal as pretty darn perfect. Thank you!

Randolph Hall is now for meetings and special events. There is the **Mansion Restaurant** on the main level of the plantation. Chef Daniel Thompson is at the helm. There is **Le Café** in the original warming kitchen. Here you can find a collection of decadent delights, creative drinks, and more. Although I have not seen the latest additions, I would not hesitate to say that from all my investigations, everything is only first-rate and done with care and talent.

Two special features:

1. Overnight guest are allowed to go into the big house, walk around, look, and enjoy. I decided to do that, but I confess I was a smidgeon hesitant as I opened the large heavy door and entered the main hall. I felt dwarfed by the largeness of all that surrounded me. What an experience to walk around, alone, in this magnificent, huge plantation. I didn't meet any ghosts, but I think I did sense a spirit or two. I wondered what it would have been like to be a child on this plantation or the mistress of the manor. You can imagine life in a different time and play mind games as you take your private tour.

    The spacious rooms are truly grand, and feeling dwarfed is to be expected. The interior design and furnishings are perfection to the max. The dining room table is set. The bedrooms are readied. The living room is inviting.

2. Four rooms at the plantation can be reserved to spend the night.

Suggestion: Visit Nottoway Plantation on the Internet (www.nottoway .com). Even via the computer screen you will be in awe.

FYI: When the draperies hang full and long to the floor, it is called "puddling" and denotes wealth.

NOTTOWAY HISTORY

Virginian John Hampden Randolph designed and built Nottoway for his wife, Emily Jane, and their (ultimately) ten children. How did he get to Louisiana? His father had been appointed a federal court judge in Mississippi, and the family had moved from Virginia. Randolph married Emily Liddell from a family of wealth. The young couple and children eventually moved to Forest Home, a beautiful plantation. John Randolph decided to change from raising cotton to planting sugar cane. He was extremely successful and decided to build a home befitting his prosperity and station in life. In 1855, he purchased 400 acres and 620 acres of swamp. Part of the property faced the Mississippi, which allowed for watching the steamboats and showboats. Not a penny was spared on the construction of his new home.

The main house has 3 floors, 64 rooms, 6 interior staircases, 165 doors, 200 windows, 15.5-foot ceilings, 11-foot doors, and a total of 53,000 square feet of living space. John Randolph's favorite room was the semicircular ballroom, which was white to show off the natural beauty of women. He put a mirror in the ballroom so that women could see if their hoops or their ankles were showing.

This gives just an idea of what went into this palatial plantation. Many of the original furniture positions are what you see as you visit each room. When the Civil War erupted, John Randolph went with many slaves to Texas and grew cotton to keep solvent.

Emily maintained Nottoway as the surrounding area was ravaged. We learn of the events, struggles, and happenings that the family at Nottoway endured from daughter Cornelia's diary. I reiterate that it was a woman, Emily Jane, who kept and preserved the property. After her husband's death, she sold this magnificent home. It has had several owners since, but today its owner is doing it proud and pleasing the Randolphs. Visit and, even better, stay for a night.

Nottoway has undergone major renovations and now has added a spa to the property. Prices range from about $135 to $275 per night, which includes the carafe of refreshment when you arrive, the guided tour, the prebreakfast coffee and hot muffins delivered to your room, and a full plantation breakfast. I discovered how much I like plantation life, but, alas, back I headed into the modern world.

LAFAYETTE
(POPULATION APPROXIMATELY 110,000)

Note: It was a little difficult to find the various destinations in Lafayette recommended to me as there are restrictions on signage. It was not my imagination that signs were few or very small. Many agree.

It was the Fourth of July. Traffic was not bad to Lafayette. I had been told to go first to the Jean Lafitte Acadian Cultural Center operated by the National Park Service and then on to Vermilionville, where I would visit the replicated exhibits of life in the Attakapas area between 1765 and 1890.

Jean Lafitte Acadian Cultural Center
501 Fisher Rd.
337-232-0789
www.nps.gov/jela

Vermilionville

300 Fisher Rd.
866-992-2968
www.vermilionville.org

I was short on time, but I did make total rounds and quick visits of the above. Both were informative and interesting. Leaving one of the exhibits, I heard live music coming from one of the more modern buildings. Lo and behold, I found a lot of happy people dancing to great music (my type of place!). I don't know if there is a name for the big barn of a building or even the event—maybe it was a Fourth of July celebration—but it certainly was a happy happening.

Bois des Chenes B&B

338 N. Sterling St.
337-233-7816
www.boisdechenes.com

By 5:30 p.m. I had found Bois des Chenes. My immediate first impression was blah, but I was quickly proved so very incorrect. Upon arrival, I was greeted by Coerte Voorhies, who showed me to my accommodations—a cottage away from the main house. He informed me of the property's history and how Bois des Chenes had hosted so many dignitaries, and he said his wife looked forward to meeting me in the morning at breakfast, after which I was scheduled to go on a swamp tour.

The accommodations were most pleasant and comfortable, and being in a separate "abode," the **Carriage House**, added to the many pluses. My room, like the other accommodations, was furnished with antiques of Louisiana French origin. The television was hidden in an armoire, and I noticed a small refrigerator in the room. Nice!

The next morning I walked to the main house, where I met Marjorie Voorhies, a most special hostess, who appeared from the kitchen. We discussed the pending breakfast, which already filled the air with sweet aromas. Breakfast consisted of French toast with Louisiana cane syrup (also served were strawberry and maple syrups) and boudin, which is Acadian sausage (ingredients include pork, rice, and spices). This too can be topped with the cane syrup. There was an apple garnish in the shape of a red rooster and, of course, Louisiana French drip coffee. I enjoyed trying new items, and breakfast was delicious and conversations were scintillating. Marjorie talked about antiquing, and Coerte V. filled in, revealing that he is a semiretired geologist. He was well versed in history, geography, and southern Louisiana's many ethnic cultures. I just learned that he also guides swamp tours.

FYI: "Cajun" is the pronunciation of the word "Acadian" when said in French.

The Atchafalaya Experience
337-261-5150
www.theatchafalayaexperience.com

I discovered that the Atchafalaya Experience swamp tour would be led by Kim Voorhies, son of Marjorie and Coerte. I wasn't quite sure what I was getting into, but I was glad he was the son of, and was himself, retired military. We met at Bois des Chenes, and in the short drive to the boat, I discovered he was extremely knowledgeable about the marshes and swamps, ecosystems, and environment—as well as politics. The Atchafalaya is North America's largest river swamp. Arriving dockside, we put the boat over and headed out. Everything that you have ever seen on a screen or in pictures about a swamp, you will see in real life as you tour. One should definitely take the swamp tour. I was amazed at the debris that is tossed into the swamp. Kim, I discovered, always stops and picks up the trash. I was not to be left sitting on my duff, and I readily joined in. We accumulated so much. I was flabbergasted and took a picture for proof. I will remember this wonderful swamp tour. You too will see for real what has been featured over and over in print and on the Discovery Channel as well as foreign TV channels.

You must call for reservations not only for Bois des Chenes but for the swamp tour.

Prejean's
3480 NE Evangeline Trwy. (I-49), North Lafayette
337-896-3247
www.prejeans.com

This restaurant is definitely casual, definitely friendly, and definitely Cajun. One notation about the restaurant states that it is a Louisiana legend. The place was fairly crowded, and music from a live band filled the air. The manager took me in tow, seated me, and suggested what I should have for dinner. I reiterated what was becoming my stock dining statement: "I would rather taste a little of a lot than have regular portions."

Dinner was good, and the chef tiny-portioned my meal. (I use "tiny" loosely.) Cajun cooking is heavy. The samples I had at Prejean's were no exception. I do not agree with all of the enthusiastic food critiques. The food was good. The friendliness, casualness, and happy atmosphere surpassed my culinary experience, but it could have just been me. Hours: Open for breakfast, lunch, and dinner, 7 a.m. to 10 or 11 p.m.

Thoughts about Lafayette

I enjoyed myself. I have a strong feeling that I would have discovered a whole different Lafayette if I had not been there on the Fourth of July, when so much was closed. What comes to mind about Lafayette is the friendliness, the music, the dancing, and all that I enjoyed at Bois de Chenes.

ARKANSAS

Besides highway signs, there's another way to tell that you are in Arkansas—the roads aren't the best, especially from Memphis to Texarkana. Just be prepared to slow down often. (At least, that is the way I found the road the times I have been driving there.)

The following are some amusing and factual observations as I drove I-40 from the Oklahoma border and into Little Rock. Enjoy!

Alma, Arkansas, proclaims itself the "Spinach Capital of the World," but then, so does Crystal City, Texas. Go figure. Alma boasts an eight-foot-tall statue of Popeye. Popeye-brand spinach comes from Alma.

Pig Trail Scenic Byway (exit 35): I had to look this one up, since "pig" and "scenic" are not words that one normally sees together. It turns out that this scenic route (which I've heard can be spectacular) reminded people of trails created by pigs wandering through the woods. (If you say so!)

Toad Suck Park at Conway: Huh? Was this sign for real? I later had to look this one up too. Apparently, theories about the origin of the name range from an early mispronunciation to the fact that the bargemen on the Arkansas River "sucked on booze/moonshine bottles until they swelled up like toads." That's just a little extraneous info.

LITTLE ROCK

Hotels

Peabody Little Rock

3 Statehouse Plz.
501-906-4000
www.peabodylittlerock.com

Whenever you hear the name Peabody Hotel, you know that you are going to be staying in a most special place augmented with duck quacks. Two other main Peabody hotels are located in Memphis, Tennessee, and Orlando, Florida. The Peabody in Memphis is "wonderfully good" and a delight to visit (see the Tennessee chapter for details). The Peabody Little Rock is a AAA Four Diamond property situated in the expanding and vibrant **River Market District** (more on this below).

A recent $40 million renovation of the hotel's 418 rooms didn't overlook a thing. The main lobby is impressive and always seems abuzz as appropriate piano music plays in the background. The decor is more art deco than traditional, with tall, stately columns sectioning off the large open spaces.

What would a Peabody be without a fountain? What would a Peabody fountain be without ducks? For all its formality, this hotel carries on a tradition begun at the Memphis Peabody, where at precisely 11 a.m., a half dozen or so ducks are escorted by the "duck master" to the lobby fountain, where they are permitted to swim until 5 p.m., when the duck master returns them to their "duck palace." All this is done with great fanfare. The spectacle is free and open to the public, not just hotel guests. (No comments about duck being on the dinner menu, please. It isn't.) The dining and drinking options are several: the **Capriccio Grill Italian Steakhouse**, **Mallard's Bar**, and the **Lobby Bar**.

The owners know how to do things well. The accommodations are attractive, though my room could have used a tiny bit of fine tuning, particularly in the bathroom—not a big deal. Otherwise, the rooms are spacious and comfortable. I do recommend this hotel.

FYI: When the Peabody Little Rock was known as the Excelsior in the 1980s, it was the setting for the first sexual-harassment suit brought against a sitting president some years later, just before the statute of limitations ran out.

Capital Hotel
111 W. Markham St.
501-374-7474
www.thecapitalhotel.com

The historic Capital Hotel in downtown Little Rock originally opened in 1876. This beautiful property has been totally renovated. You feel grand old-world charm the minute you walk in the front door: stately columns, arches framing the balcony, high ceilings, a mosaic floor, a grand double staircase, and stained glass. There are ninety-four rooms at this refined, well-appointed property; my room was nearly perfect, and that was before the most recent renovations. I am sure it is now awesome.

Dining at **Ashley's,** the featured restaurant at the Capital, is an experience that you shouldn't miss. I enjoyed the best *lahvosh* (Armenian cracker bread, now off the menu) as well as other savory delights.

A unique feature of the Capital Hotel is its oversized elevator. One explanation states that it was once meant to transport both horse and rider to the guest's room. One's horse was most valuable. A more plausible explanation is that the elevator was designed to accommodate women in their broad hoop skirts. Regardless, the elevator is large enough to accommodate lots of travel bags with or without the horse or hoop skirt. Be sure to visit.

Shopping

River Market
400 President Clinton Ave.
501-375-2552
www.rivermarket.info

The trendy River Market on the banks of the Arkansas River was once filled with abandoned warehouses and buildings. Restaurants and bars of all varieties have now anchored themselves here, and boutiques and various types of shops sell an eclectic mix of wares. During the summer, there are live concerts to enjoy, and two times a week the area's farmers offer their produce.

MISSOURI

was warned about construction and possible detours into Kansas City, but I was not told that streets would unexpectedly change names! This is particularly challenging for a stranger. I was lost and really did not want to get out of the car in the area where I suddenly found myself.

Here's a personal tidbit too good not to include: I had been in Salina, Kansas, and was almost in Kansas City, Missouri. I was to meet with executive chef Jennifer Maloney at the **Kemper Museum**'s **Café Sebastienne**. I thought my driving instructions to the museum were clear, but I could not find the exit I was to take. I was in an area where I was glad it was daylight. I pulled off the highway and thankfully saw three motorcycle policemen in the parking lot of a fast fooder.

I apologized as I interrupted their conversation to tell them of my plight. They all compared notes to deal with my situation, and after considerable banter, it was decided that the police officer named James was going in the direction I wanted to go. With a smile, he said, "Follow me. We'll get there." What fun to follow a motorcycle policeman! After arriving at the museum, we began to chat. Officer James Evans, Badge 1946, was most interesting, and when I told him about my project, he seemed genuinely interested. I mentioned to him where I would be staying: the **Southmoreland**. "That's right there on that block," he said, pointing in one direction. "But you have to go around that block," he added, pointing to another block. I found you do a lot of that in Kansas City. We exchanged good-byes, and I promised that if I ever came back, particularly for a signing, I would let him know. He said he would bring the entire force. The invitation will soon be on its way.

KANSAS CITY

If you casually ask, "What do you know or envision about Kansas City?" (not specifying Missouri or Kansas), the replies will include "It is way out there" and "Aren't they known for their steaks and barbecue?" Both observations are correct, but there is so much to Kansas City, Missouri, which is correctly nicknamed the "Jewel of the Prairie." I was so surprised by what I discovered when I first visited this "jewel," and with each subsequent visit I am more impressed. Kansas City's attributes are obvious, even to a casual visitor. It is clean, and beauty and friendliness abound. This spirited town is also a jazz mecca.

Driving Diva Factoid: The corporate headquarters of the greeding card company Hallmark is an anchor of the area.

Shopping

Country Club Plaza
4750 Broadway
816-753-0100
www.countryclubplaza.com

This fantastic shopping enclave in the center of town features Spanish architecture, fountains, and attractive landscaping. It has over 150 shops and a myriad of restaurants. Do not be taken aback by the name. It is not a club in the usual sense of the word. People are all there enjoying the area and shopping. There is a lot to see and be tempted by here. An alternative to walking around is taking a horse-drawn carriage ride . . . but then, why not do both? Walk first, then recoup with a carriage ride. Country Club Plaza is one of the most attractive shopping areas I have seen. It is an absolute delight—even if you only window-shop.

Halls Plaza
211 Nichols Rd.
816-274-3222
www.halls.com

This prestigious store is a museum in itself with lapis floors, Baccarat chandeliers, and ebony-embellished, pear-wood furnishings. Luxury is found throughout. Visit this beauty and enjoy—it won't be hard to do. There is a parking facility with direct access to the store. Joyce C. Hall, the founder of Hallmark, obviously believed in "unparalleled access to the exceptional."

Bob Jones Shoes
1914 Grand Blvd.
816-474-4212
www.bobjonesshoes.com

Bob Jones Shoes is a warehouse full of current shoe styles in all price ranges. Be prepared for some "serious essential purchases."

Act II Inc.
1417 W. Forty-seventh St.
816-531-7572
www.actiiinc.com

This consignment shop for designer clothing is upscale and sensibly priced—especially for those things that just happen to be on sale. Act II's mega "Stupid Sale" is held twice a year. This trove of treasures was started by Gloria Everhart more than fifty years ago. Thank you! As is printed on the business card, "Clothier to the best dressed men and women in Kansas City." Another paper reads, "Clothier to the Frugal Woman and Man."

Webster House: Antiques + Designs + Dining
1644 Wyandotte St.
816-221-4713
www.websterhousekc.com

Webster House has an impressive selection of antiques. I don't think you will find any bargains, but you might find something you have always wanted. The designs are first rate.

Rainy Day Books
2706 W. Fifty-third St.
913-384-3126
www.rainydaybooks.com

This cozy, upbeat bookstore's business card reads, "One civilized reader is worth a thousand boneheads." Vivian Jennings is the founder and president of Rainy Day Books, which is the oldest bookstore in the Kansas City area and considered one of the leading independent booksellers in the country. That's quite an accolade! The shop's calendar boasts impressive, very popular author events. I read that Vivian and partner Roger Doeren's philosophy is "Bigger isn't better. Better is better." They believe that books can expand awareness, improve health, make us laugh, touch hearts, and encourage people to live a better life in a better world. Those words are a heavy dogma but something for each author to aim for. Needless to say, Rainy Day Books is definitely a place to check out.

Kaplan's Fabric Store
430 Ward Pkwy.
816-531-4818
www.kaplansfabrics.com

This store has great fabrics at sensible prices. I purchased half a yard of uniquely patterned cloth that would make a great scarf and wonderful souvenir. I checked and am delighted to know that Kaplan's is still there. I suggest you visit and get a few yards.

Crown Center
200 E. Twenty-fifth St.
816-545-2121
www.crowncenter.com

In the center of the city, Crown Center has a contemporary design with three levels of shops, restaurants, theaters, and movies all under the umbrella of the world headquarters of Hallmark. From all I have gleaned, a lot of thought was given to this center.

Restaurants

Plaza III: The Steakhouse
4749 Pennsylvania Ave.
816-753-0000
www.plazaiiisteakhouse.com

So delicious! Fully describing Plaza III and my dining experience would take too many adjectives, and then you would not believe me, thinking that my arm had been twisted for this review. Not so! First of all, if you decide to go, be sure to make a reservation and be hungry when you arrive. Tasting one of this establishment's steaks will let you know what a steak should taste like and why Plaza III is considered one of the top ten steak houses in America. The waitress was most knowledgeable with recommendations. The baked potato was large enough for three, maybe four people. The side of steamed fresh asparagus was also huge, so one order will do. Enjoy! It's not hard to do.

For **Café Sebastienne** at the Kemper Museum and the **Raphael Restaurant**, see below.

Hotels

Raphael Hotel

325 Ward Pkwy.
816-756-3800
www.raphaelkc.com

Privately owned and managed, this property has definite old-world charm. The original owners sold this historic property to the Walker family. The Walkers respect historic properties like the Raphael and are committed to preserving while upgrading the property. I learned from the general manager, Carol Chandler, that a lot has been done, and upgrades are continual, but the historical elements are always retained.

Originally built as an apartment building in 1927, the Raphael was then renovated and opened as a hotel in 1975. When I first stayed on property, the "originals" were evident. The halls were long and narrow, and the moldings impressive. The decor was dark, and the bathroom was not glitzy—but then, nothing was. I certainly didn't mind the chain tub stopper because I knew it worked. The faucet handles were hard to turn, but at least they were clearly marked. The bathroom floor tiles were the tiny handset ones. I like these as they remind me of my bathroom when I was growing up. The monogrammed *R* towels were great and remain. The bed was comfortable, and everything was clean. The Raphael was female friendly, and I felt very safe.

The new owners have spent millions in renovations, and my tiny bathroom tiles, I am sure, are a thing of the past. This charming boutique hotel has given a lot of thought to every detail.

Chaz on the Plaza, located in the Raphael, is *the* place. From all I have gleaned, the menu is delicious, the people delightful, and the ambiance exceptional. The summer Strings on the Green features string ensembles presenting all types of great music. The **Chaz Lounge** has a Happy Hour, which I am sure should not be missed.

There are many special packages. The "Girlfriends Getaway" includes one night in a suite with a spacious parlor, two bedrooms, and two bathrooms. For four girls, the cost is about $456 per night. The getaway includes chick flicks, popcorn, margaritas, M&M's, disposable cameras, a continental breakfast, shopping discounts, valet parking, and a few more things, such as massages and chauffeur services.

Billed as "Kansas City's Elegant 'Little' Hotel," the Raphael is definitely a delightful destination and has been called "One of the World's Best Places to Stay" by *Condé Nast Traveler*. The Raphael will remain a gem—just now a polished updated one.

InterContinental
401 Ward Pkwy.
816-756-1500
www.intercontinental.com

When I was here, it was called the Fairmont, but it was originally named the Alameda Plaza when it opened in 1972. This edifice has been an outstanding commercial property. On my visit, it was not overly cozy, though definitely welcoming. There was appropriate valet parking, and my accommodations were pleasant. During my stay, I noted that "better signage" in halls and throughout the property was needed, and I hear that this has been implemented.

My room was large, clean, and comfortable but bland. There was no clock, but when I informed the staff, one was quickly delivered. The bedspread did not fit the bed well. My room had a delightful porch with a beautiful view, which compensated for a flaw or two. The standard safe, iron, and ironing board were in the closet. The TV was in a lower-than-usual cabinet but seeable, thus bearable. The bathroom was well done but standard. It included such upscale amenities as a magnifying mirror, deluxe towels, and a bathroom phone.

My comments here may be a little outdated since I know the entire hotel was recently upgraded and megamillions were spent. I have been told that it is definitely a sparkling property. The new general manger receives rave reviews.

I was also told that the **Club Lounge** on the **Concierge Floor** remains unchanged. It is extremely well appointed and well run. The host greeted me nicely and introduced himself. Immediately, I knew that breakfast was going to be a nice experience, and as I was to discover, it was also delicious. Silver serving dishes shone brightly. The variety of fruits was excellent, and the orange juice was fresh. There was an attractive display of various dry cereals as well as steaming oatmeal. The coffee was delicious. Tea and other beverages were also available. The bow-front sideboard was attractive, as were all the furnishings. The fresh flowers were beautiful.

Southmoreland on the Plaza: An Urban Inn

116 E. Forty-sixth St.
816-531-7979
www.southmoreland.com

Check-in at Southmoreland consisted of saying, "I am here." Since my room was not ready, I went to revisit this special city. Although the Southmoreland is within walking distance of the Country Club Plaza, I drove to save my energies for walking around the plaza and its environs.

It was a nice revisit. Kansas City had not changed from when I was last there. It was still thriving with friendly people; everything was clean, and the streets remained well organized. Once again, I found my way back to **Act II** (see above), and as luck would have it, the shop's big sale was going full tilt. I also revisited **Halls Plaza** to see that it was still luxuriously glamorous.

Once I was able to check in, I realized that this attractive inn/bed-and-breakfast had thought of everything. Parking is in the back by the beautiful garden. I immediately felt at home with the cordial and upbeat greeting I received. I was told of the options: Wine and cheese is served from 4:30 to 6 p.m. Homemade cookies are served at nighttime. The breakfast format and general history of the Southmoreland was also included in the "Welcome to Southmoreland" information. I was shown to my room, which was most attractive. The twelve guest rooms are individually named. There is a luxury suite in the **Carriage House** behind the main house. The surroundings were most appealing. *Everything* was attractive and well considered.

My small, but "just right" room had a wonderful porch to enjoy. Sherry was available in the room; there was no TV, but one could be had on request. In the drawer, there was a "sound machine" if needed to camouflage unwanted noise.

FYI: A sound machine makes a low humming sound to block out peripheral noises. Some have a mix of sounds, like the rain, the ocean, and the like. The noises of downtown Kansas City are not loud. As a New Yorker, I thought the city was quiet. I enjoyed sitting on the porch in the glider and writing my travel notes.

The bathroom was suitable to the room, but the tub with shower was deep and could have used a safety bar.

I spent a restful, quiet night, and the sound machine remained in the drawer. Before I knew it, I was downstairs on the porch, eating breakfast, and chatting with the other guests.

Mark Reichle and his wife, Nancy, own the Southmoreland. Mark prepares the breakfast, and what an exceptional, gourmet breakfast it is! Available from this most special bed-and-breakfast are homemade pies for special holidays as well as barbecue. Southmoreland on the Plaza is a must-visit, and the prices are most appropriate for the delightful experience you will enjoy.

Museums

There are also many impressive museums:

Kemper Museum of Contemporary Art
4420 Warwick Blvd.
816-753-5784
www.kemperart.org

There is free admission and free parking. The Kemper Museum is small but delightful, and the art is impressive. **Café Sebastienne** (816-561-7740) is one of Kansas City's leading restaurants. Many kudos to executive chef Jennifer Maloney, who provided a delicious lunch in exceptional surroundings. Lunch included four types of bread, cucumber soup with a slight hint of almond, tomato mozzarella tart with basil pesto on arugula with a saffron vinaigrette, and grilled Moroccan lamb sausage (merguez) with saffron, stewed onions, peppers, and couscous. For dessert the chef's signature chocolate budino (*budino* is Italian for "pudding") was delicious. This treat is sometimes described as a "flourless chocolate torte." Describe it anyway you want, it was amazing. The coffee was perfect, and I was told the special flavor was derived from roasted pecans.

Science City at Union Station
30 W. Pershing Rd.
816-460-2000
www.unionstation.org

Nelson-Adkins Museum of Art
4525 Oak St.
816-751-1278
www.nelson-atkins.org

Negro Leagues Baseball Museum
1616 E. Eighteenth St.
816-221-1920
www.nlbm.com

Kansas City Art Institute
4415 Warwick Blvd.
800-522-5224
www.kcai.edu

Driving Diva Factoid: You will discover that I-70 is one of the straightest roads in the United States. There are probably others, but this one is long and straight. The bucolic scenery all around you looks like a Grandma Moses picture, full of flat farmed fields.

Humorous Sighting:

Atlasta Motel
17395 Hwy. 87, Boonville
660-882-5770

This hotel has twenty-five units.

HERMANN

This place is unique, picturesque, inviting, caring, and special. How did I find out about Hermann? A public relations friend in Clayton told me if I was heading east from Kansas City, I should stop in Hermann. Promptly researching, I found the town and discovered that Hermann is Missouri's B&B capital (with forty properties) and home to **Stone Hill Winery**. About three hours from Kansas City and an hour from St. Louis in the Missouri River valley, Hermann was founded by the German Settlement Society of Philadelphia in the early 1800s. Settlers thought they would find farmable land but instead discovered harsh ground. With true German tenacity and ingenuity, they planted grapes and developed vineyards that subsequently became very successful. Unfortunately, fate brought Prohibition, the Depression, and then a war that prompted hostile feelings toward the Germans. In spite of these adversities, Hermann remained an original, which was its saving grace. It is a picture-book community with rolling hills, original buildings, and church steeples accenting the landscape and sky.

Lydia Johnson Inn
204 Market St.
573-486-0110
www.lydiajohnsoninn.com

I spent my first night in Hermann at this inn. I was greeted by Betty Hartbauer. She and her husband, Chuck, are the innkeepers. Immediately I felt at home. My room was on the main floor. For more of the story, see below.

Stone Hill Winery

1110 Stone Hill Hwy.
800-909-9463 (WINE)
www.stonehillwinery.com

Anxious and curious, I headed for my scheduled visit to the winery. I followed the signs up a small hill pass with manicured grapevines and parked in the designated area. Little did I realize what I was going to experience. Fabulous would be an understatement. I was amazed by how many other people were also there. The parking lots were quite full. Without further adieu, here is the history of the winery, itself as special as the wine it produces.

Stone Hill Winery is truly a family operation. Established in 1847, it became the second-largest winery in the United States and, by the end of the nineteenth century, was shipping over 1 million gallons of wine per year. The underground arched cellars were the largest in America. Then, in the 1920s, Prohibition brought the winery to a screeching halt. The vaulted cellars were then used to grow mushrooms!

In 1965, Jim and Betty Held, with their four children in tow, bought Stone Hill and started the long and arduous process of restoring the winery. What a job they have done! Today, they produce more than two hundred thousand plus gallons of award-winning wine on their 182 acres with the help of their state-of-the-art equipment.

Two of the Held children are on board—all hold degrees in enology and viticulture (the sciences of wine making and grape growing.) Also on board is one of the country's best winemakers, Dave Johnson.

In 1979, with the same care they use in producing wines, the Helds restored the winery's former carriage house and horse barn, preserving as much of the original decor and ambiance as they could. They did a great job, and the **Vintage Restaurant** (573-486-3479) serves thousands of delighted guests, who order from a menu that includes many German specialties as well as steaks and fresh seafood. I was fortunate to have dinner here with Jim and Betty Held. I definitely give both the dinner and the unique setting accolades.

Be certain to plan a tour of the winery and see firsthand the arched cellars and production facilities, then, of course, stop in the wine-tasting room. Here you will readily see why the awards to the winery have been ongoing. There is also a very sensibly stocked gift shop.

Driving Diva Factoid: There are two other Stone Hill Winery locations in Missouri, one in New Florence at the junction of I-70 and Hwy. 19 and the other in Branson.

After a wonderful Stonehill evening, I returned to the Lydia Johnson Inn, driving through a totally quiet, peaceful town. I enjoyed a pleasant night in my cozy room. The next morning, since it was just me, I insisted on not breakfasting alone in the dining room but joined Betty in the kitchen. Breakfast was delicious. It was so much fun to talk with Betty as we sat at the kitchen table. I enjoyed her homemade Lydia's Strawberry Custard Muffins and even received a copy of the recipe.

Wine Valley Inn
403 Market St.
573-486-0706
www.wine-valley-inn.com

A bit more "downtown" and also termed a bed-and-breakfast, Wine Valley is definitely more of an inn. It is in Hermann's historic Begermann Building, and when I was there, it was operated by Gloria Birk and Pamela Gillig. They have retired. From the stories I heard, getting the inn to where it is today entailed many challenges. The eight beautiful suites are not fancy, just very nice. Every suite has a kitchenette, dining area, and television. Five come with a Jacuzzi-style tub. My accommodations were delightful, cozy, and creative. My one suggestion would be to have a door on the bathroom. Maybe there is one now. A full, complimentary breakfast is served every morning on the first floor. There is an elevator if needed. Make a reservation and enjoy.

Discover Hermann by walking around and stopping in the shops. What fun and what a friendly group of people! Some of the places I visited included the following, but there are many more, so walk, discover, and enjoy.

Stuff & Nonsense
114 E. Fourth St.
573-486-4444

Back Home Again
307 Schiller St.
573-486-0581

Antiques Unlimited
207 E. First St.
573-486-8860

Seasonal Treasures & Gifts
226 E. First St.
573-486-0803

ST. LOUIS

St. Louis is a true hub city where several major interstates—I-70, I-55, I-44, and I-64—meet. I was surprised to discover how many other major cities in nearby states are truly just a stone's throw from St. Louis. Check your map.

For my first visit to St. Louis, I had the hotel fax me specific directions, something everyone should consider when venturing into a city for the first time. (Their directions were excellent.)

St. Louis Union Station Marriott
1820 Market St.
314-621-5262
www.marriott.com/hotels/travel/stlus-st-louis-union-station-marriott

Built around St. Louis's old rail station, the hotel uses as its lobby the famed **Union Station Grand Hall**. Inside and out, this old train station is magnificent. Built in 1894 and once deemed the largest and most beautiful terminal in the United States, it has been completely restored, from its barrel-vaulted ceiling with Romanesque arches to its stained glass windows and ornate moldings. So much happened at this station that a self-guided walking tour will bring much of this magnificent structure's history alive. (Discover the secret of the **Whispering Arch**.) Also on-site are restaurants, specialty shops, marketplaces, stores, and (unbelievably) a one-acre lake. Although the name has changed since I was first there, the bones and ambiance of this pleasant hotel are still most appealing.

How Things Were and How They Have Changed

Fred Harvey left England in 1850 and came to America at the age of fifteen. He held many jobs, one as postal clerk and agent for the Burlington Railroad. He traveled a great deal and was absolutely disgusted by what was served at restaurants in railroad stations. He hatched and soon implemented a brilliant idea. The Burlington Railroad didn't subscribe to it but told him to contact the Atchison, Topeka & Santa Fe—the fastest growing railroad in the West.

In 1876, Fred Harvey took over the restaurant at the Santa Fe depot in Topeka, and history was made. His name would become synonymous with good food, clean restaurants, and an all-female staff soon called the "Harvey Girls." To become a Harvey Girl, a woman had to have a high moral character, be between the ages of eighteen and twenty, attractive, and intelligent, and had to vow not to marry for a year after employment. A housemother chaperoned the girls and enforced their 10 p.m. curfew. MGM made a movie titled *The Harvey Girls* staring Judy Garland. Fred Harvey, thank you, even though only a few recognize your name and acclaim.

Gateway Arch

Do not leave St. Louis without visiting the Gateway Arch on the St. Louis riverfront. The story of its construction is fascinating. In order to get to the top of the arch, one must ride in a small, four-seat "compartment," an experience not for the claustrophobic. There is also a museum with several displays pertaining to westward expansion.

CLAYTON

I had no idea what I was getting into. I had only read about Clayton in hotel brochures. After map studying, I decided this probably should be a stop. I had been to St. Louis and done the sights, so it was time to "discover" Clayton—a well-kept secret. Clayton is an upscale "suburb" with a business area. The streets are clean, the people are friendly, and during my stay, the weather was summer perfect.

Clayton on the Park
8025 Bonhomme Ave.
314-290-1500

Clayton on the Park was a state-of-the-art luxury hotel and residential property with the logo "Where Style and Comfort Collide." I mention this property because is was outstanding in every way possible. It has been converted into a luxury retirement property. So be it . . .

An added perk to this first visit was the **Jazz Festival** (www .stlouis.com/festivals) in **Shaw Park** in Clayton.

Driving Diva Factoid: As St. Louis grew, Clayton developed. The area that became Clayton was derived from donated farmlands owned by two Virginians: Ralph Clayton and Martin Hanley.

Seven Gables Inn

26 N. Meramec Ave.
314-863-8400
www.sevengablesinn.com

This National Historic Landmark property has much potential. There is a blend of styles with nothing fancy or ostentatious. It is friendly and convenient to downtown Clayton. While staying there, I discovered that a lot of the staff has been there for years, and there is a definite family feeling. There are no elevators, so one must use the steps. They are obviously original but have now been carpeted, making the actual step tread narrow. I found it a bit hazardous; plus, the small design on the carpet can play tricks on the eyes.

There are thirty-two guest rooms, six of them on the main floor, providing easy access if required. My room was large and had the usual amenities. The bathroom was nice, and though the decor colors were dark, all was clean and the bed comfortable.

I tried (several times) to get firsthand updates but received no response. As of these edits, I learn that a lot has been redone, but I have no specifics. The **Molly Darcy's**, a popular Irish Pub, is on the property. I felt comfortable with the parking arrangement. Valet service is available, and the parking area is just across the street.

Shopping Discoveries

The ScholarShop

8211 Clayton Rd.
314-725-3456
www.sfstl.org

Across from the **St. Louis Galleria Mall** (www.saintlouisgalleria .com), this sizeable shop specializes in "new and gently used designer and brand name clothing and accessories for the entire family—all at resale prices!" Proceeds support area students through the **Scholarship Foundation of St. Louis** (www.sfstl.org), "a non-profit organization that provides access to higher education to members of our community without financial resources." I definitely arrived on the right day—just a little late. If I had only known!

Immediately, I knew this was my type of store, but little did I realize how much so. I walked in and was immediately handed a large brown grocery bag. My perplexed expression provoked the response, "Everything you can fit in the bag will be $25!" I smiled and quickly refrained from charging around like a bull in a china shop. Within a blink of an eye, my bag seemed half full. Suddenly someone came over and informed me that if I folded or rolled items tightly, I could fit more in the bag. Grateful for the tip, I was thrilled by how tightly I could suddenly roll items! I was in hog heaven!

Obviously this bag day is not a daily happening. It is also obvious that this is a professionally run shop. I can attest to the fact that it is organized and clean. The staff is most friendly, and I look forward to visiting this treasure shop again . . . even if I have to detour a bit.

Woman's Exchange

9214 Clayton Rd.
314-997-4411
www.stlouiswomansexchange.com

A nonprofit organization created in 1934, the Woman's Exchange today has venues throughout the United States. The goal is to create a market for items made by talented craftspeople. Through the sale of these incredibly beautiful articles, the artists are able to help support themselves in a productive manner.

This beautiful St. Louis Woman's Exchange not only includes exquisite items for sale but has a fantastic tearoom. I had the salad bowl, a lemon square for dessert, and coffee—absolutely delicious. Had "space" permitted, I would have tried the Exchange's signature yellow cake smothered with coconut butter frosting. I was given a taste, and it was outrageous. Since the tearoom is a charity organization, there is no tax. All the personnel were so friendly.

FYI: They also do carryout. It's always good to know where you can get a takeaway meal that is not fast food.

About one hundred miles from Clayton I saw a sign for Nostalgiaville, USA.

Nostalgiaville, USA
Junction of I-70 and U.S. 54, Kingdom City
573-642-7955
www.nostalgiavilleusa.com

Wouldn't you stop? Of course, and so did I. The business card reads:

Nostalgiaville USA
"Where Elvis, Marilyn & the Duke Hang Out"

Judi Dunwoody	Gwynne LaRue	Ron Dunwoody
MAYOR	CITY MANAGER	TOWN FOOL

Barbara Chaill and Helen Willingham
Phillis Dunwoody Sarah Dunwoody
COLLECTORS OF REVENUE

Nostalgiaville USA is a collection of buildings that, from the outside, actually look like props from a movie set. The signs on the stores read "Goody's Candy Store," "Heartbreak Hotel," "G. C. Dunwoody," and "Mercantile." The ad says, "Largest Selection of 50s, 60s, 70s Collectibles & Memorabilia."

Inside you will find Elvis videos, 1950s fashions, photos, and items pertaining to Elvis, Marilyn Monroe, the Three Stooges,

James Dean, *The Dukes of Hazzard*, Barney Fife (of *The Andy Griffith Show*), Betty Boop, and on and on. Looking for saddle shoes? Here they are.

Driving Diva Factoid: The Truck Stops of America are excellent places to stop. I feel safe, and they are generally friendly and clean. They usually carry state pins, which I collect, and miscellaneous car items of every variety can be found at these truck stops.

IOWA

-80 West from Chicago was a little rough when I last I drove it—but perhaps by now the road has been repaired.

DAVENPORT
(POPULATION APPROXIMATELY 98,000)

Between the state line and Des Moines, there are plenty of places to stop for the night, but I favored the Hampton Inn in the sizable city of Davenport. This particular one has moved, but another Hampton Inn is just a very short distance away.

Hampton Inn
5290 Utica Ridge Rd.
563-441-0001
www.hamptoninn.com

I was just there for one night, but as I initially drove about in the late afternoon, I discovered interesting places within walking distance. After checking in and finding my room, I went out to investigate. The people were friendly, and the area was clean and inviting. I did not feel like a stranger. I enjoyed walking around, peeking into shops, then getting a sandwich and taking it back to my room.

FYI: The Mississippi (that big *M* really gets around!) traces Iowa's east border, and Davenport is very close to the river. Riverboat gambling is just a mile away.

WALCOTT

Walcott boasts the world's largest truck stop.

Iowa 80
755 W. Iowa 80 Rd. (I-80, Exit 284)
563-284-6961
www.iowa80truckstop.com

Iowa 80 Truck Stop: Largest in America—this is a must-stop. Aside from big trucks, lots of cars and colorful signs, you are greeted by a sign reading "Chapel Dentist Massage." What a combo! When I stopped, I was not in need of these services, but the concept of the trio prompted me to seek out the marketing director, who told me that the three "offerings" are often required by long-haul truckers. She also provided me with the following Iowa 80 fun facts:

In thirty-six years of being in business, 12.5 million eggs have been served, 1.5 million cups of coffee are served per year, and over 55 million customers have been served. It has been a while since I was here, and I am sure the stats have increased.

The store contains fifty thousand items, and the truck stop sees five thousand customers a day.

You'll also find a three-hundred-seat restaurant with a fifty-foot-long salad bar as well as several fast-food options—and the list of amenities goes on.

From what I hear, you just might want to plan your trip around the **Walcott Truckers Jamboree** held in July. I guarantee your memories will be priceless. You will be able to see the Super Truck Beauty Contest, eat one-and-a-half-inch-thick Iowa pork chops, enjoy live music, view one hundred antique trucks. Who could ask for more?

West on I-80 there are plenty of places to stop for food, gas, and lodging, but **Williamsburg** and **Grinnell** probably have the most to offer, especially Williamsburg, which has a large outlet mall.

I definitely look forward to discovering more about Iowa and perhaps attending the Walcott Truckers Jamboree!

MINNESOTA

The big state of Minnesota is known for its cold weather and such "creations" as eccentric former governor Jesse Ventura, the largest U.S. mall—Mall of America—its football team, the Mayo Clinic, and more. The natives' speech has a very distinctive twang that is really quite enjoyable. No question, Minnesota is a beautiful place and a should-visit, particularly in the summer. Before my visit, I did not realize that the Mississippi River runs through Minnesota. I learned a lot about the Mississippi Valley and watched fascinated as the boats navigated the locks. The more I learn about Minnesota, the more I want to return—in the summer.

WABASHA (POPULATION APPROXIMATELY 3,000)

Wabasha is straight up the Mississippi on U.S. 61 off I-95, past the town of Winona. I drove around Winona to find that it is a small, friendly place with a lot of interesting history.

Wabasha, the oldest city in Minnesota, was founded by a steamboat captain in 1851. Not that far from bustling Rochester, it is seventy miles southeast of Minneapolis and St. Paul. When I arrived in Wabasha, I felt like I had stumbled onto a movie set. The town is spotless. The countryside and the Mississippi River are beautiful. In Wabasha, with its relaxed, wonderful lifestyle, you feel as if you are actually stepping into a different era. It has a mix of interesting shops, and many of the original structures have been maintained or are being restored.

The river seems to be the center of activity, from fishing to bald eagle watching. The *Delta Queen* and other river cruise ships call at Wabasha. The movie *Grumpy Old Men* was written and set here in little Wabasha.

Note: I include the following because it is a unique tidbit, a bit of local history, and unfortunately a sign of our times.

Anderson House
333 Main St.
651-565-2500

When I visited several years ago, my stay at this landmark was an experience and, in ways, a step back in time. This hotel opened in or around 1856, when small Wabasha was a bustling Mississippi River town. In 1909 the Anderson family bought the hotel, and it became the Anderson House. Aside from its hospitality, it was known for its authentic Grandma Anderson cooking and the "cat option." If you wished, you could choose a resident cat from the cat suite as a companion during your stay. Anderson House was indeed unique. A few years ago, when I began this manuscript, I called to check if everything had stayed the same since my visit. "All is status quo," said new owners Teresa and Mike Smith. Unfortunately, in 2009, due to the economy, Anderson House closed. Hopefully, a new owner will be found to carry on its traditions.

Restaurants

Eagles Nest Coffee House
330 Second St. W
651-565-2077

This lovely coffee house is a must-visit spot. When I called to see if it was still there, a nice gentleman answered. We chatted and had a delightful conversation, both bemoaning the Anderson House situation. When he learned of my book, he said, if I visit, perhaps Eagles Nest would do an author's event. Oh, yes!

Slippery's Tavern and Restaurant
10 Church St.
651-565-4748

This wonderful watering hole is the bar seen in the movie *Grumpy Old Men* and has been in existence since the 1970s. This was a fun spot. I don't think there was a sad face in the joint.

FYI: The movies *Grumpy Old Men* and *Grumpier Old Men* were written by Mark Steven Johnson about his father, a native of Wabasha.

Sightseeing

A walk around town is very enjoyable. Just a stone's throw from the Anderson House I discovered an **Antique Center**, Wabasha's **Old Town Shops**, and the Old City Hall.

Old City Hall
257 Main St.
651-565-2585

There is a year-round indoor flea market with a farmer's market, home-baked goodies, and possibly a treasure or two to find.

National Eagle Center
50 Pembroke Ave. S.
651-565-4989
www.nationaleasglecenter.org

Here you can see Harriett, Angel, and Columbia, three injured eagles that cannot be released back into the wild and have become stars. Some girls have real luck after adversity. The center teaches observation and conservation. The staff visits places with the three feathery girls, who are always main attractions at the center or on the road trips.

Wind, Whisper, West
128 Main St.
651-565-2002
www.windwhisperwest.com

This gallery, now dubbed "the Kimono Capital," was not open when I was in Wabasha, but I think it bears mentioning. In this little town, you will find the world's largest collection of Japanese wedding kimonos. No two are the same. Making these kimonos is a fading art. Kimonos can cost from $8,000 to $60,000. If a purchase is not on your agenda, know that a kimono can be rented for three hours for $2,000 to $8,000. Owner Richard Fuller, a retired marine, brought the collection here to his wife's hometown. These beautiful garments (produced in the 1970s and 1980s) are on sale for a fraction of the original price.

LARK Toys
Lark Lane, 63604 170th Ave., Kellogg
507-767-3387
www.larktoys.com

To be accurate, LARK is in the tiny town of Kellogg, a very short drive from Wabasha. Take scenic Highway 61. Lark is right along the highway. Just turn off onto County Road 18 and make a left on Lark Lane. What fun it is to be in this big toy factory, regardless of your age. LARK Toys will do you good, and you will only smile and want to stay and stay and stay. The enterprise was started in 1983 by two talented teachers who in their spare time made toys and sold them at fairs. Taking friends' advice, they started their toy factory, and the rest is history. In 2008 they decided to retire and sold the establishment, but all has remained the same. There is truly something for everyone, be it riding the carousel with its hand-carved animals, playing miniature golf, taking a rest at the **Café**, or indulging in some butter and cream fudge made in the **Fudge Tree** shop, or seeing and petting the miniature llamas—Francis, Eliot, and Irving. You will never see so many toys under one roof again. Trying to choose what to buy is a yeoman's task, but what a fun challenge. It is a great place to do some Christmas shopping, whatever time of year it is.

Visit Wabasha; you will be charmed.

FYI: Mall of Americas is just fifty-five miles from Wabasha. I have been told that it's a shopping mecca.

RED WING (POPULATION APPROXIMATELY 15,561)

Red Wing is but a short distance north. I did not have time to visit, but next time.

Historic Red Wing Pottery
1920 Old West Main St.
651-388-3562
www.redwingpottery.com

This third-generation family business began over 140 years ago.

Red Wing Stoneware Company
4909 Moundview Dr.
651-388-4610 or 800-352-4877
www.redwingstoneware.com

This company has maintained its "American-made" status since 1860.

AUSTIN (POPULATION APPROXIMATELY 25,000)

Everyone knows SPAM, the king of curious and mysterious meats. Well, Austin has devoted an entire museum to it!

SPAM Museum

1 Hormel Pl.

507-437-5100

www.spam.com

Austin is off of I-90 and intersects U.S. Hwy 218. Take Exit 178B for the museum, where you will learn more than you ever thought could be attributed to this unusual but always (for the most part) popular meat concoction. Forty-four thousand cans of SPAM come off the assembly line per hour, and it is cooked in the can! When founder George Hormel decided to retire and take his wife to California, he gave the business to his son Jay, who would become a most (understatement) creative entrepreneur in the world of meats. Aside from SPAM, there three thousand other Hormel products!

Note: One cannot mention Minnesota without giving Garrison Keillor a mention. No one is quite like the man who talks about Lake Wobegon, created *A Prairie Home Companion*, and ad-libs to perfection. I smile just writing his name and reflect on how much I admire and enjoy his shows and music. I am glad to be driving when his program is on, and listening to it two days in a row is just fine.

Rumor has it that GK is retiring. Alas, but his CD's will help.

SOUTH DAKOTA

This beautiful state should be investigated and enjoyed. I-90 across South Dakota is a great road with some extraordinary sights that are natural wonders. At the welcome centers, be sure to pick up brochures on various South Dakota places. I found several excellent ones, especially the "Guide to Antique Shops in South Dakota."

MITCHELL

About a quarter of the way (heading west) into the state, Mitchell is definitely a good place to stop. For one thing, the mayor was a woman when I was there. How wise to have a woman at the helm. While Mitchell has the usual mix of stores, gas stations, and motels, it also features a variety of unusual museums, including the following, among others:

Enchanted World Doll Museum
615 N. Main St.
605-996-9896

Middle Border Museum of American Indian and Pioneer Life
1331 S. Duff St.
605996-2122

Soukup & Thomas International Balloon & Airship Museum
700 Main St.
605-996-5533

Corn Palace
604 N. Main St.
605-995-8427
www.cornpalace.com

This is a one and only. To say it is unique would be an understatement. The original Corn Palace, a huge mosque-like building,
was built in 1892, but the establishment moved two blocks away
in 1914. It moved again in 1921 to its present site. It was originally
built to show and emphasize the early settlers' harvest. The siding of
the building is real corn sawed lengthwise and applied to the sides.
It is definitely uniquely artistic. Each year the corn is stripped off
and a new scene is "painted." The murals on the walls depict South
Dakota lifestyles. The palace is used for many different events. You
can purchase all kinds, and I do mean all kinds, of corn products.
What a good opportunity to pick up that unusual gift. This building
has another name: World's Largest Bird Feeder. Everyone must try
to visit the Corn Palace at least once. You will not be alone as there
are about five hundred thousand visitors a year. Admission is free.

Outside the Corn Palace there are antique shops, as well, of
course, as various tourist traps. Mitchell has a special, albeit a bit
touristy, feel, but I recommend a visit. Just don't forget the winter
weather. Leaving Mitchell, the drive along I-90 is a delight. The
sights are beautiful, and the places to stop are many.

Badlands National Park
I-90, Exit 131 for those travelling west, Exit 110 at Wall for those traveling east
605-433-5361
www.nps.gov/badl

It has taken 30 million years to produce the Badlands with its multicolored buttes and rough stone spires. All 240,000 acres are impressive.

There are three main units in the Badlands. I drove the **North Unit**, which is a loop road with many scenic overlooks. The interpretive signs at the pull-outs are excellent and informative. I could easily ramble on about the Badlands, with their red and brown hues, massive formations, and winds, but it is all in the eyes of the beholder. Don't miss seeing this American wonder. It is another magnificent treasure. Stop at the **Ben Reifel Visitors Center** (605-433-5361) five miles into the park. You have time to plan your visit; geologists state that with the two-inch-per-year erosion rate, it will take five hundred thousand years for the Badlands to disappear.

WALL

Wall Drug
510 Main St.
605-279-2175
www.walldrug.com

Wall Drug is located at the junction of I-90 and Route 240. Don't worry, you won't miss it as many billboards will remind you of this gathering spot. Originally just a small town in South Dakota with a drug store, a Catholic church, and fewer than five hundred very poor residents, Wall was transformed in or around 1931 when Dorothy and Ted Hustead bought the drug store. I think it was Dorothy who, after a rough start, came up with the idea of offering free ice water to travelers crossing the hot prairie. A burgeoning business was born. Now there are long blocks of tourist temptations in the numerous old-fashioned stores. Many consider Wall Drug a national institution, and it still offers free water. More than twenty thousand tourists stop at Wall on a typical summer day! Hours: 6:30 a.m. to 8 p.m., seven days a week, year-round, except New Year's Day, Easter, Thanksgiving, and Christmas. I have learned that since I was at Wall, so much has been done: the mining and panning display has been enlarged, the shooting gallery has been doubled, there are two singing raccoons, the original pharmacy has been moved and enlarged, and the art collection is most impressive.

Driving Diva Observation: See what happens when you have a product that is in demand, the price is right (ice was free in Wall), the promotion is sensible, and the place is convenient.

A stone's throw from Wall Drug is the **Buffalo Gap National Grassland Visitors Center**. Its slogan is "Anyone can love the mountains, but it takes soul to love the prairie."

DEADWOOD (POPULATION LESS THAN 2,000)

Readily accessible from I-90, Deadwood is a real cowboy, stagecoach, and gambling town, albeit with modern facilities, set in the **Black Hills** (actually they're dark green). The entire city of Deadwood was named a National Historic Landmark; therefore, its original character and flavors have been maintained. I think you will find it hard not to like Deadwood. Do not think the town is without modern amenities. It has all the necessities, but the old-timey aspects add to its wonderful aura.

History: In 1875 John B. Pearson found gold in a narrow canyon in the Black Hills, where, without question, the gold rush was on. Thousands of greedy and hopeful prospectors filled the area with competitive, rowdy tempers frequently flaring up. Deadwood proper was established in 1876. By 1877, the wild community was becoming more orderly and organized.

In 1891, thanks to the railroad, Deadwood started to prosper, but wild shoot-'em-ups were still happening. Wild Bill Hickok and

Calamity Jane were often in town. It was in Deadwood that Wild Bill, while playing poker, was shot in the back of the head by Jack McCall. Wild Bill was holding a hand of aces and eights, now known as the "dead man's hand." And then there was the mysterious murder on a Sunday in 1876 of the Rev. Henry W. Smith (the first Methodist minister to come to the Black Hills). Needless to say, many of this ilk are buried in the **Mount Moriah Cemetery** on the fringe of the city, including Wild Bill Hickok and Calamity Jane.

Gambling and prostitution were common in this South Dakota town. Even during Prohibition a lot of these activities went on behind closed doors. Prostitution remained a business until 1950, when the state shut down many of the brothels. It wasn't until 1980 that the last brothel, Pam's Purple Door, was closed.

In the 1980s local businessmen lobbied to legalize gambling to help increase tourism and preserve the historic buildings of Deadwood, many of which are Victorian in style.

Each evening (except Sunday), there is a reenactment of the capture of Jack McCall on historic **Main Street**. All the spectators follow the actors to **Old Town Hall** for McCall's trial. This is a must-do! A visit to this historic landmark city is indeed unique and an experience to be savored.

Note: During the first two weeks of August, this area is visited by about five hundred thousand "hog riders"—motorcyclists attending the *Sturgis Rally* (www.sturgis.com). It is quite an event at which everything is going on and then some.

Silverado Franklin (formerly the Franklin Hotel)
709 Main St.
605-578-3670
www.silveradofranklin.com

This hotel creaks with history. From the minute I ascended the front steps and walked across the front porch, I was delighted to be on the property, although I wish I had dressed for the scene. When

I was there, its big porch with rocking chairs was inviting. They are now gone. The original, meticulously laid tile floor in the main lobby was covered with slot machines the last time I was there. Now I learn the machines are all across the street, and the tile floor is covered with a rug. Since my visit, the Silverado has purchased the property, the gambling has become more prominent, and although there are still shades of "back when," new formats are definitely evident. One of the hotel's motto is "Stay and Play." Good luck.

The wide, prominent staircase in the lobby leads to the **Emerald Room** on the second floor, where, back when, the ladies would meet. Remember that separate rooms for ladies and gentlemen were the norm. There is the famous fainting couch in case a lady felt a "spell" coming on. Do try it, but don't faint.

The Franklin is now under the ownership of Silverado Gaming. One cannot talk about this hotel without mentioning Mr. Bill Walsh, the man who kept this historic gem going for so many years before the ownership changed.

The rooms at the Franklin were named after stars who had stayed there. I had plastic flowers in my suite, as well as a sink in the living room, leading me to surmise that these accommodations had obviously at one time been an apartment. I felt secure there, and everything was clean and comfortable. I did enjoy the real western style. The upgrades are ongoing, and a spa has gone in where the florist and barber shop used to be.

Although the hotel dining room has closed, it claims to be the oldest dining room in South Dakota. I found everyone very friendly. Many famous people have stayed at this special hotel. Don't hesitate to add your name to the roster.

Midnight Star

677 Main St.
800-999-6482
www.themidnightstar.com

On historic Main Street is a building called the Midnight Star. Here you will find the award-winning **Jakes** (605-578-3656) restaurant, where dining is a fabulous experience. Of course, you will also find the gambling and imbibing at **Diamond Lil's** (605-578-3550). All this is owned by South Dakota native Kevin Costner. The decorations and displayed memorabilia are items from his celebrated career. This is a fabulous restaurant, and reservations are a must.

Driving Diva's Favorite Deadwood Signs:
No Dancing on the Table with Spurs On
No Sniveling
Don't Worry, You'll Never Get Out of This World Alive

Driving Diva Discovery: Heading from Deadwood to *Rapid City* (population approximately 60,000), I discovered a *Maurice's* (www .maurices.com). This savvy store has very savvy clothes for the savvy female. Sensibly priced, Maurice's now has more than seven hundred stores in forty-four states. I so enjoy finding a Maurice's as I travel.

MOUNT RUSHMORE

An hour or so outside Deadwood is Rapid City. About twenty miles farther along, you will find Mount Rushmore.

Mount Rushmore National Memorial
13000 Hwy. 244, Bldg. 81, Keystone
605-574-2515
www.mtrushmorenationalmemorial.com

This carved-granite tribute to Presidents George Washington, Thomas Jefferson, Abraham Lincoln, and Theodore Roosevelt, created by Lincoln Borglum, is definitely something to see and admire. Be sure to visit the **Lincoln Borglum Museum**. In the exhibition area, learn just how massive this rock carving is and how it was made without sophisticated tools. It is so huge that a man can stand inside Lincoln's ear. Be prepared for a lot of walking that is not on flat ground.

South Dakota may not be on the top of the commercial vacation planner's roster, but put it on yours. I look forward to returning.

NEBRASKA

OMAHA

-80 takes you across Nebraska, and Omaha is the first major Nebraska city heading west.

A delightful surprise, Omaha is a pocketful of treasures. Each time I have only visited for a night or two, but I have driven around the city and found everything rather impressive. The streets are clean, the areas well marked, and the people most friendly. There is a lot to discover in Omaha. It seems that the town fathers consider carefully how to add to the city. Glitz is not obvious—thank goodness!

Magnolia Omaha Hotel
1615 Howard St.
402-342-2222
www.magnoliahotelomaha.com

This attractive hotel in the historic downtown area is easy to find with directions. It is a place where women can feel secure and all guests can feel welcomed. The self-parking, a stone's throw from the hotel, is convenient and safe. The property's 146 well-designed guest rooms are a very comfortable size and have all the necessary amenities. The furnishings in the public areas, as well as in the rooms, are attractive, with emphasis on mahogany furniture, oriental rugs, and sparkling crystal chandeliers. The small, separate areas in the main areas are pleasant and inviting. The hotel is well run. Several upgrades have taken place since my visit. Everything is well placed, and the dining room is now named **Hitz on Howard** (402-231-6091). Remember this property if you are going to Omaha. *Forbes* named Omaha "The Best Bang for the Buck City."

The Magnolia Omaha is within walking distance of the **Old Market District** (www.oldmarket.com), a wonderful twelve-square-block area that I highly recommend. Cobblestone streets and nineteenth-century buildings are now filled with boutiques, bookstores, restaurants, and whatever is trendy. Allow lots of time, and be sure to enjoy one of the restaurants. Also near the hotel is the **Orpheum Theater** (www.omahaperformingarts.org/orpheum). Perhaps you'll catch a Broadway show, an opera, or symphony during your visit. There is a lot going on in Omaha and near this hotel. Be sure to check for places and events.

Interesting: There must be something in the Nebraska water or air as a lot of very well-known people are from this state: Marlon Brando, Fred Astaire, Warren Buffett, Johnny Carson, Dick Cavett, Dorothy McGuire, Darryl F. Zanuck, and the list goes on.

KANSAS

As corny as this may sound, I confess that, as I drove along I-70 into Kansas, I started singing, "I'm as corny as Kansas in August . . ."

There is little question that Kansas is, well, very flat, but the countryside is beautiful. I even had a Norman Rockwell moment when I came upon a robust farmer in faded denim overalls atop a rusty red tractor, an umbrella protecting his skin from the summer sun.

Topeka is a little like the Emerald City of Oz, with its impressive skyline surrounded by huge farmed fields. When I was driving by, I did not have time to discover the downtown (although I was invited), but the fields were a brilliant green. A sign read, "One Kansas Farmer Feeds 128 People Plus You."

Down the road in **Alma** you'll find Grandma Hoerner's.

Grandma Hoerner's Shop and Factory

31862 Thompson Rd.
785-765-2300
www.grandmahoerners.com

On a country road where horses have left their calling cards, Grandma Hoerner's is in a bright red building. As you enter, the distinctive smell of apples fills the air. Here is a repository of apple products of all varieties. When I visited, a very attractive woman with the most unbelievable flaming red hair, movie star's torso, appropriate summer dress, and high heels appeared on the scene. (I mention the high heels because I didn't expect to see anyone wearing such attractive shoes at a "factory." As a shoe aficionado, I had to make note.) It turns out she was the wife of Grandma Hoerner's grandson, Duane McCoy, who now runs the business.

Duane's mother, Evangeline, daughter of Grandma Mable Hoerner, gave her mother's recipe to her son Duane. It was general knowledge that everyone liked Grandma's applesauce, made with the firmest apples and natural fresh seasonings cooked slowly in spring water. Duane remembered the delicious applesauce, and when his mother gave him the recipe, he checked to see if there was anything on the market similar to his grandmother's chunky concoction. He found nothing comparable, and so, the production of Grandma Hoerner's old-fashioned applesauce began in 1987 and led to the development of all sorts of high-quality organic sauces, jams, toppings, dry mixes, and condiments. Obviously a thriving business in the middle of what many would call nowhere, Grandma Hoerner's products are available online if "nowhere" isn't on your travel itinerary.

LAWRENCE
(POPULATION APPROXIMATELY 65,000)

At first this seemed like a relatively small city until I started to drive around and learned how much is actually in Lawrence, home to the University of Kansas. One of the main thoroughfares is **Massachusetts Avenue**, where I came upon several interesting shops.

Saffees Gallery of Fashions
911 Massachusetts Ave.
785-843-6375

What a delightful shop, with attractive apparel and very friendly people. I learned that Saffees is a family-owned business, and there are four Saffees in Missouri, the "mother store" (as they call it) being in Jefferson City. Although I didn't buy anything, they seemed happy that I stopped by.

At Saffees I was told about another shop, which turned out to be another great discovery:

Lasting Impressions Consignment Store
711 W. Twenty-third St.
785-749-5122

This shop has lots of well-displayed and -priced merchandize.

Back on I-70—the temperature was 97 degrees with strong winds—I came across a bad accident in which a large tractor trailer had flipped. Its back was off in a field, and the red cab was turned over. You can't help but wonder how, on such a big, wide-open road, this could have happened. Perhaps the driver fell asleep, or maybe it was the wind. Not a pleasant sight!

SALINA

This is a small, "real" American city, with clean streets and large houses, "considered the crossroads of America" since it's where I-35 and I-70 meet. One of my competitors has stated that "there is nothing there" in Salina. Hogwash!

Endiron Estate B&B
100 S. College Ave.
785-452-9300
www.endiron.com

The creative name derives from the fact that this big, wonderful house is at the *end* of *Iron* Street. I was delighted to see the setting sun give the big, neocolonial-style structure with its quarry-face limestone (native to Kansas) a glow—a limestone glow. I would spend the night here, and I was more than curious.

I was greeted by a young, petite woman, Debra Redman, who was obviously no stranger to exercise. We began chatting as if we had known each other for more than just a few minutes. She then showed me around her B&B, with the admonition "I still have a lot to do" on the place. What I saw, however, was fantastic: inlaid floors, including a center hall with a large, inlaid starburst design in the center; leaded windows; oak moldings; and Prairie Movement designs throughout the big old house, actually a former bible college. As I checked for updates, I discovered that Debra Redman has done a lot because the city of Salina and the Heritage Commission presented her with an award in recognition of her preservation and work on the Endiron Estate. I look forward to congratulating her in person and seeing all that she has done to Salina's only B&B.

Debra's neighbor, David Petty, owned *the* store in town.

Martha and David
108 S. Santa Fe Ave.
785-827-9990

Debra insisted on calling David to have him reopen the store just for little old me (it was after hours). He happily obliged. I felt like a rock star, having such attention. His fantastic establishment is actually several stores in one, with fashions on one side and gourmet items on the other. I enjoyed purchasing several items. This savvy, creative businessman expanded the store, but I now learn that he recently retired. The new owners have changed and renamed the store.

Across the street is an old-fashioned toy store.

Toy Parade
119 S. Santa Fe Ave.
785-823-2231
www.thetoyparade.net

I just learned about a "must-do" in Salina and here it is. Note that I have yet to visit.

The Cozy Inn

108 N. Seventh St.

785-825-2699

www.cozyburger.com

In eighty-eight years, neither the product (hamburgers) nor the grill they are cooked on has changed. This tiny "inn" has six seats along an old counter that is covered with Cozy Inn articles. The inside smells of cooking hamburger, and if this is not what you want, then, as they say, use the walk-up window. The hamburgers are served one way only: with onions. They cost less than $1, and you can buy them "by the sack." The only other items sold are potato chips, soda, coffee, hot chocolate, and Cozy Inn souvenirs.

Confession: I am craving a sack of Cozy Inn hamburgers now!

Driving Diva Factoid: In March 2005, Salina made history when Steve Fossett set out to become the first person to fly solo around the world without stopping to refuel. After sixty-seven hours, he landed back in Salina on March 3, setting the world record. There to greet him with a champagne shower was Virgin Airline's Sir Richard Branson. Sadly, Fossett disappeared while on a recreational flight over the Nevada desert in September 2007. No trace of the plane has ever been found.

What was that comment about Salina? There is a lot in this town!

HAYS (POPULATION 200)

The drive along the interstate in Kansas is functional, and I enjoyed it. When I arrived in Hays, I thought, Hampton Inn, where are you? I have a reservation, so you must exist. Eventually I found it, no thanks to the poor signage.

Hampton Inn
4002 General Hays Rd.
785-621-4444
www.hamptoninn.com

Hays is home to Fort Hays State University. The median household income is about $25,000 a year, and median rent is $175.

Driving Diva Alert: When I checked in to the Hampton Inn the temperature was 97 degrees. The next morning it was 61 degrees! Be wary of sudden temperature changes on our Great Plains.

Driving Diva Anecdote: I was approached by a friendly and gregarious young boy of about twelve as I got out of the car at the Hampton Inn. He was traveling with his family to a church conference. As he followed his father toward their room he said, "Call me if you need anything." When he saw me at breakfast the following morning, he asked if he could sit with me. This provided wonderful entertainment for the whole dining area as he proceeded to tell me a joke. How about that? It's not often you get a breakfast date at the Hampton Inn. Fun!

Back on I-70, all still looked like a Grandma Moses picture—flat, bucolic farmed fields.

GOODLAND
(POPULATION APPROXIMATELY 8,000)

Sitting in the northwest corner of Kansas at the Colorado state line, Goodland is known as the Pheasant Capital of the World. It is also popular for hunting prairie dogs, coyote, wild turkey, antelope, and deer.

The side of a big grain bin reads, "Happiness Is a Crock of Beans."
Enjoy Kansas.

OKLAHOMA

Before my first trip to Oklahoma, I pictured its horizons as peppered with oil rigs and lots of cowboys all around—a "vision" augmented by an Oklahoman college classmate. She and her mother's Manhattan shopping sprees attired each in ultra designers' garb. I pictured a lot of Oklahoma women (particularly wives and daughters of the big ranchers and oil barons) of the same milieu. This assumption was definitely wrong. I knew where the state is located and the words to the songs Oscar Hammerstein and Richard Rodgers wrote about the state. How wonderful it was to discover the real Oklahoma,

OKLAHOMA CITY
(POPULATION APPROXIMATELY 3 MILLION)

Oklahoma City was my first introduction to the state. On that visit, I was an absolute novice at this travel-writing procedure. The chamber of commerce proved a tremendous help in ensuring that I saw a lot of the city in the short time I had scheduled to "discover." I was escorted around the city, which was unpretentious but with definite upscale aspects. It was clean and seemed rather laid-back, though by no means lazy. Definitely impressed, I was totally enjoying my tour when we turned a corner, pulled up to the curb, and parked. We were at the once-innocent spot that became suddenly infamous on April 19, 1995. I faced a chain-link fence covered with notes, tiny stuffed animals, pictures, flowers, and many other items. I quietly lost it. I broke down. Deep breaths didn't help. This was the spot where the **Alfred P. Murrah Federal Building** once stood. I felt the tragedy and heartache undeniably as the faces, eyes, and expressions looked back at me from the photos. I will never forget that provincial yet impressive, impromptu memorial. Vivid and heart wrenching are my vivid mental images of the bombing disaster and the absolute class and style of the governor, firemen, policemen, and all who lost loved ones. It was impressive and exemplary. Visiting the state, I was to learn how much more there is to O-K-L-A-H-O-M-A.

Now a new park, with its signature memorial chairs, is on the site, and a museum has been built.

Oklahoma City National Memorial & Museum

620 N. Harvey Ave.
405-235-3313
www.oklahomacitynationalmemorial.org

From what I have read about the museum, the storyline is in ten parts from "chaos" to "hope." I feel this must be indicative of the people of Oklahoma. I urge all to visit the site. While heart wrenching, the site and story will help all to put life into perspective. We must never forget this tragic event, but we must also realize that today, tomorrow, or sometime is unknown.

We come here to remember
Those who were killed, Those who survived and Those changed Forever.
May all who leave here know the impact of violence
May this memorial offer comfort, strength, peace, hope and serenity.

– – – – –

Oklahoma means "land of the red people" in the Choctaw language. Bordered by six states—Texas, Kansas, New Mexico, Colorado, Missouri, and Arkansas—it is equidistant from Los Angeles and New York. When studying the map and planning my route, I discovered that I-40, I-35, and I-44 all take you to Oklahoma City.

National Cowboy & Western Heritage Museum

1700 NE Sixty-third St.

405-478-2250

www.nationalcowboymuseum.org

This museum is most impressive. Plan on a long visit as its two hundred thousand square feet are inspiring. The museum, located on **Persimmon Hill**, opened in 1965. The galleries are fantastic. The fourteen-thousand-square-foot replica of Prosperity Junction, a 1900s western cattle town, is exact, and it shows both how far we have come and how spoiled we are in the 2000s.

Oklahoma City Museum of Art

415 Couch Dr.

405-236-3100

www.okcmoa.com

I recently discovered that the largest permanent collection of Dale Chihuly glass art is here.

In 2003, by absolute chance, I found myself spending the night in Oklahoma City, but not exactly downtown. How I ended up at the Oklahoma City Biltmore is an interesting sidebar that illustrates the admonition "Be prepared!"

Biltmore Hotel Oklahoma

401 S. Meridian Ave.

405-947-7681

www.biltmoreokc.com

How it happened: I called information (old-fashioned as it sounds) for a Biltmore Hotel that I thought might be of interest to include in the book. I was given a Biltmore number and called it, only to find out that it was in Oklahoma! (Not the state I had in mind!) By chance I was speaking with the general manager, William Davis. Because of our shared last name, we become phone pals. He said, "You really should visit our property." That's the short version of the serendipity.

Chain of events: Mr. Davis sent me a brochure: "Biltmore Hotel: Oklahoma's Largest Hotel Conference Center." It looked safe, and Mr. Davis was convincing. I schedule a stop. I was also to learn (via the Internet) that the amenities were numerous, the hotel was absolutely pet friendly, and many said that, with its rustic elegance, the hotel was the "best kept secret." I was on my way.

I drove north from Dallas on I-35 to Oklahoma City. After the flatlands of the Dallas area, the scenery begins to get more hilly. It is an easy drive, and at around 1 p.m., I was in Oklahoma.

FYI: In my notes of personal minutiae, I see that arriving in Oklahoma I had traveled 8,097.6 miles so far on that particular odyssey. After all these traveled miles, my car needed some grooming. I didn't know what my namesake might think of my messy car, so I stopped at a rest stop.

Oklahoma Discoveries and Observations: Back on the interstate, I passed *Braum's Ice Cream* (www.braums.com). There were lots of cars, and it was only 3:12 p.m. Hmmm. Again, I should have stopped, but I didn't. I have since researched Braum's, and what a story.

This family business was started in Emporia, Kansas. It was a small butter- and milk-processing plant that then added ice-cream processing. The wholesale part of the business was sold, and the family began specializing in ice cream. It was not long before the company had retail ice cream stores in Oklahoma—with processing still in Kansas. The next move was to bring everything to

Oklahoma, and now there are over forty thousand acres—that's sixty-two square miles of purportedly some of the very best farm and ranch land in America.

In addition to the ice creams and dairy products sold in the retail stores, a bakery produces bakery items for the stores. There are 280 Braum's Ice Cream and Diary Stores in Oklahoma, Kansas, Texas, Missouri, and Arkansas. Braum's is the only major ice-cream maker in the country that milks its own cows—ten thousand of them! It is the largest milking herd and milking parlor of its kind in the world. The cows are milked three times a day, twenty-four hours a day, seven days a week. I am in awe!

Needless to say, the next time I see a Braum's Retail Shop, I am stopping, diet or no diet. I passed the **Oklahoma Horseshoeing School**, and then a sign announced that I was in **Norman**. I remember a beau (we were both in our late teens) who was flying in the navy and stationed there, writing me from this place that sounded so far away from my New York City life.

At 4:15 p.m., I arrived in the area and began looking for the Biltmore Hotel Oklahoma. Not realizing I had passed it, I continued down the road to discover more in the immediate area. I found some aviation history and lots of motels.

Will Rodgers World Airport
7100 Terminal Dr.
405-316-3262
www.flyokc.com

Ninety-nines Museum of Women Pilots
4300 Amelia Earhart Rd.
405-685-9990
www.museumofwomenpilots.com

Backtracking, I found the Biltmore, and I immediately knew it was nice and friendly, cowboy casual and clean. The brochure is a little more airbrushed than what my eyes saw—but that was alright.

Checking in was easy, with no rigmarole. My room was plain and simple but comfortable. I had been invited for a drink at around 5 p.m. with Mr. Davis and his friends, who, I was to learn, were "the regulars." I decided to see a bit more of the area before joining "the boys." I drove around and decided to stop at Sheplers, "The World's Largest Western Stores."

Sheplers
812 S. Meridian
405-947-6831
www.sheplers.com

Well, slap my jeans, straighten my bandana, and secure my hat—this is one big store! There is western apparel in every size, shape, and color. I learned that there are twenty retail locations in eight states, and the catalogue business is big. Their guarantee is, "You have our handshake on it." Right on, guys.

Then, it was time to meet the boys, whom I found in one of their favorite positions—seated at the bar, beverage of choice in hand, and fun on their lips. I joined the group, and we talked about "them and me." Linda, the major hotel assistant, was also in the group, so I wasn't the only woman. What fun those boys were, and it was obvious what fun they had. Each one sounded—from talk—very successful. They seemed to have their afternoon ritual down pat. Some left relatively soon, and others stayed. I left in the middle, went back to my room, and organized for the next day.

I was told that, oh my! the next day the Hall of Fame Cowboys would be arriving. No way! I said to myself, and I wouldn't be there! The next morning, I said good by to Linda and Mr. Davis, and I was sincere when I said, "Thank you so much and maybe another visit in the future."

If you are in the Oklahoma City area, spend a night at the Biltmore. There is a lot to discover in the area.

I-40 was easy to find and proved a good road. I passed lots of green fields and farms. After about an hour of driving, I drove by

Okemah. Something about this place smiled at me as I passed. I know that sounds crazy. Maybe the thousands of miles of driving were affecting me. This area is definitely Indian land, and from my vantage, I discerned that it was probably very good hunting land.

FYI: Two thousand miles later, while transcribing my scribbled notes, I decide to look up Okemah. Meaning "things up high," Okemah is named for a Kickapoo Indian chief and is expected to look up and live up to his name. The town, incorporated in 1903, is the home of Woody Guthrie.

Continuing down the interstate, I saw the enormous, twelve-hundred-acre **Lake Eufaula** (www.lakeeufaula.com), one of Oklahoma's top fishing lakes. Why not stop and do a little fishing—if you have a fishing rod? String and a hook sometimes suffice—if you just want to see what you might catch.

The interstate is good but be prepared for long stretches without services.

Two Places I Saw:

Sallisaw: From the highway you can see this is a big area with lots of shops, industry, schools, and so forth. One ad read, "Sedation Dentists: Sallisaw, Oklahoma." That is a first for me.

Sequoyah: There is a big truck stop diner.

TEXAS

Driving Diva Tip: Texas is a big state and has long stretches of highway with few services. Be sure to fill the gas tank (and your stomach) whenever possible. You don't want to be stranded or driving on an empty stomach, which can make one very drowsy.

SMALL-TOWN STOPS

-40 is good. The drive from Santa Fe, New Mexico, to **Dallas**, Texas, heading east and then south, can be done in a day, but it's a long haul. In **Amarillo**, you get on U.S. 287 from I-40, a good road that takes you through some delightful and interesting towns.

Clarendon (population approximately 2,067) offers the visitor or resident a **1929 Landmark Subs & Sodas, Coyote Den Books**, and the **It'll Do Motel**.

Hedley (population approximately 391) has tempting fruit stands. Don't miss the big signs for peaches.

Memphis (population approximately 2,465) has antique shops and a tearoom.

Childress (population approximately 6,664) is the area's point for shipping and supplies for the neighboring grain and cattle ranches. Proudly displayed as you drive through town is a sign that reads, "Hometown of Roy Cooper, Eight Times World Champion Calf Roper." Other sights include the **Restwell Motel** (perfect name!), an **All Handmade Quilts** store, a **Dollar General Store**, **Morgan's Catfish Diner** (at least I think that was the name), and a sign for the **Heritage Museum**. In its heyday, this must have been quite a town.

Iowa Park (population approximately 6,000) looked at first, I thought, like cattle ranch; then my bleary eyes (it was 7 p.m.) focused on the cattle. I did a double take and laughed out loud. The cattle were camels.

Driving Diva Factoid: The signage into Dallas could definitely be more defined. Be alert.

DALLAS (POPULATION OVER 1 MILLION)

Dallas's more than 384 square miles have grown since the city's beginning in 1839. In the 1980s *Fortune* magazine named Dallas the number one business center in the land. Driving might be a bit of a challenge for the visitor. Heading south from **Wichita Falls**, as I neared Dallas, repeat, I definitely found the signage confusing, and more would have been helpful. Several interstates and U.S. highways take you into Dallas. I am certain a few small roads, and possibly some dirt roads, also lead into the Big D.

I am usually in Dallas in the summertime and, needless to say, have found it hot, quiet, and in some ways relaxed. This is probably due to the heat, but there is always purpose, determination, upscale demeanor, and fun in Dallas. Of course, glamour and glitz are omnipresent, and aside from the occasional street person, which is a universal concern, I have found most aspects of Dallas extremely nice, though it does help to have deep pockets. This big city has a lot of small-town ambiance, and it is hard not to have a good time here.

The downtown area is enjoying a revival after undergoing a bit of a slump. I adore this part of Dallas. Here you will find the **Adolphus Hotel, Neiman Marcus**, the **Dallas Art District** (www .thedallasartsdistrict.org), the **Historic West End District** (www .dallaswestend.org), and lots more. Don't forget about all the museums, galleries, and malls. The downtown museum dedicated to the 1963 Kennedy assassination is located in the **Texas School Book Depository**, where Lee Harvey Oswald fired the fatal shots. As with most spots that have changed history, this building definitely sends chills through the body.

Sixth Floor Museum at Dealey Plaza

411 Elm St.
214-747-6660
www.jfk.org

Hotels

Adolphus Hotel

1321 Commerce St.
214-742-8200 or 800-221-9083
www.hoteladolphus.com

This grand, luxurious, and historic hotel in downtown Dallas is one of the finest hotels. It has old-world charm with class and style. It is a treasure. If—I repeat if—a hotel could be perfect, the Adolphus would certainly rank among such a rarefied group.

The Adolphus's history starts in 1912. Woodrow Wilson was president. The Boston Red Sox won the World Series. The fourth down was added to U.S. football, and a touchdown was valued at six points. Picasso was the talk of the art world, and the Titanic sank.

The youngest of twenty-one children, Adolphus Busch (born 1839), at the age of twenty-one married, Lilly Anheuser of St.

Louis. This marriage merged two names that would become indelible in the world of beers. Adolphus became a successful St. Louis businessman and was convinced by representatives of the Dallas Chamber of Commerce to build a first-rate hotel. This would be the first expansion of the Anheuser-Busch empire outside St. Louis. There are many stories as to why this St. Louis businessman decided to build in Dallas. Some are political; some just say that he wanted to thank the people of Dallas for supporting his beer. Regardless, it was a coup for Dallas.

Driving Diva Factoid: Architectural turrets crown the building; some say they look like beer steins. You look and see.

As you arrive at the Adolphus, you always receive a most welcoming greeting. The main desk is well attended with efficient, friendly, and knowledgeable staff. The hallways are well defined, and finding your room after the initial introduction by the bellman is easy.

The rooms are comfortable and very attractive. Of course, a property the size of the Adolphus offers many types of accommodation to choose from. You will not be disappointed.

The main floor is truly a museum of sorts. Art surrounds you on every wall, and the beautiful furniture is magnificent. The large, early Flemish tapestries are impressive. The Steinway piano is played, and sitting in this beautiful setting, it is not hard to enjoy and to reflect on life in a bygone era.

Important: Obtain an art guide booklet, and tour the magnificent downstairs areas.

Consider enjoying Saturday afternoon tea in the lobby. A tradition at the Adolphus, it truly adds to the old-world ambiance. Tea at the

Adolphus is an event. To quote one of the hotel's announcements, which says it so well, "The perfect place to experience the decadent traditions of this classical afternoon respite." The Adolphus offers an assorted choice of teas that complement three courses.

First course: At least five types of miniature sandwiches
Second course: Assorted miniature pastries
Third course: Assorted chocolate truffles

Piano music permeates the air as you sip your tea, enjoy a scone or two, and relax in this exquisite setting. The cost is approximately $38 per person plus tax and gratuity. Tea schedules change with the holidays, so call to check the agenda.

Perfection and beauty are synonymous with the exquisite, award-winning **French Room**. From the hand-blown crystal chandeliers to the marble flooring to the period furnishings to the shining silverware, everything is beautiful. The menu is exceptional. James Donahue is the maître d', and Marcos Segovia is the chef de cuisine. The French Room is first-rate and upscale in every way. Reservations are a must, and I was told they are often made from season to season as many guests make the French Room dining experience a tradition. To dine in the French Room is outstanding. Jackets are required for the men, and ties are optional. (I think the latter should be rescinded.) Thank goodness denim and sneakers are prohibited. The French Room is closed Sunday and Monday.

The **Bistro**, open for breakfast and lunch, provides a special, casual ambiance that is done properly. It is beautiful, well appointed, and luxurious. You cannot help but enjoy.

The **Rodeo Bar and Grill** is so western and so Dallas, serving hamburgers, Tex-Mex favorites, barbecue, and all those good types of fare with all the trimmings. It's open for lunch and dinner seven days a week.

The Adolphus Hotel's executive chef is Marcus Strietzel. Speak with the concierge and find out about the Adolphus's complimentary limo service for short rides.

At any grand hotel that has maintained its prominence, credit must be given to its long-lasting staff. For over twenty years, David Davis has guided the public relations and marketing in a most exemplary fashion. He should be cloned. Kevin Henry has been resident manager for twenty-nine years, and James Donahue has been maître d' at the French Room for twenty-five years.

There is little doubt in my mind that you will be marking off the days till you will return to the Adolphus. It is special.

The Joule

1530 Main St.
214-748-1300
www.thejouledallas.com

"Unique," "luxurious," and "exceptional" are just a few of the adjectives one could apply to this new downtown hotel. To me, one of the special aspects of this property is that it encompasses the 1920's Dallas National Bank building and has an adjoining ten-story tower of 129 guest rooms and suites. To use or reuse the old in the new, I applaud. The pièce de résistance at the Joule is the cantilevered pool on the tenth floor that juts eight feet over the sidewalk! At night, this pool displays a light show from the 132 fiber-optic lights in the pool. Adam D. Tihany's talents and creativity are seen throughout the hotel, and Charlie Palmer's delicious gastronomical creations are enjoyed by all at his restaurant.

This property, from every syllable I have heard, is sumptuous, chic, totally enjoyable, and probably awesome. I look forward to seeing the Joule, whose name refers to a unit of energy.

Observation: I know downtown Dallas, and I think that the Joule will spur the renaissance into overdrive.

Rosewood Crescent Hotel (formerly Hotel Crescent Court)

400 Crescent Ct.
214-871-3200
www.crescentcourt.com

Rosewood Crescent Hotel is a stately and large building with an impressive courtyard. It is definitely luxurious, big, and nice, but not extremely warm and fuzzy—but then, I don't think Buckingham Palace is either. The attendants are well trained, and many await your arrival. Be sure to call for directions as it can be a bit confusing finding the hotel.

Driving Diva Tip: At grand hotels, it is normal for two or three attendants to be at your side with beaming smiles to carry your bags from the car to the room. They may even park the car. Don't be afraid to tip all the smiling faces. I believe that tips should be given to all who perform a service, be it one or seven, but not those who smile and just tag along.

Check-in was efficient. Everyone who greeted me was helpful and courteous. The lobby is large and definitely Texas-grand in decor. The lobby has marble floors, high vaulted ceilings, big columns, floor-to-ceiling windows, and limestone walls. There are impressive furnishings too.

In the lobby is **Beau's**—obviously a place to see and possibly be seen. It is a most attractive cocktail lounge.

There are several dining choices. I am told that **Nobu** (214-252-7000) is one of the most innovative, new-style Japanese restaurants in America. There is the **Crescent Gourmet**, a convenient deli and coffeehouse—my type of place. In the morning, for breakfast and also lunch, the **Conservatory** overlooks the courtyard. A **Starbuck's** is also on property.

This impressive property has 191 guest rooms. The bedding during my stay had a high linen thread count of 480, and the bath linens were 100 percent cotton. The living room area with a bar and TV was attractive, but the placement of the TV/entertainment center was off. In my room it was not comfortable to watch the TV, as the screen was at a strange angle to the bed.

The housekeeping staff wear smoke-gray uniforms and look upscale-professional. This attire should be copied in other upscale properties.

The **Spa at the Crescent** (214-871-3232) is exceptional with excellent service. There are over seventy-five unusual treatments. The massage rooms were comfortable and not too small. In the pedicure area, curtains can be drawn for privacy. The attendants were well trained and friendly. One of the waiting areas had a variety of teas and fresh fruit in the refrigerator to enjoy. You could also enjoy a smoothie with lavender cookies.

There is a large outdoor pool with lounging facilities on the second floor. It was well done, although when I was there, there were city noises in the background, but they were not too objectionable.

The Rosewood Crescent Hotel is an upscale experience, where security is to the max, and the property is delightful—just what you would expect and more from Rosewood Hotels and Resorts.

One of my favorite on-property places was **Lady Primrose's Shopping English Countryside** (decorative arts galore) and **Lady Primrose's Thatched Cottage Pantry**. The owners have retired, which is good for them and bad for us. Lady Primrose bath products are still used at the hotel and can be purchased at the **Spa Boutique**.

Magnolia Hotel

1401 Commerce St.
214-915-6500
www.magnoliahoteldallas.com

Located in downtown Dallas, this hotel is situated in the former Pegasus Building, which served as the headquarters for the Magnolia Oil Corporation. On top of the building, the flying red horse logo has returned as a beacon for all. When built, it was the tallest building in downtown Dallas. The Magnolia Hotel is convenient to downtown with all of its attractions and, of course, **Neiman Marcus**. The hotel is modern in decor, although many of the original features have been kept. The beautiful marble floor in the lobby, the art deco staircase, the ornate woods, and the high ceilings are each impressive in their own right. Together, they make for a grand presentation.

Check-in was pleasant and the staff most obliging. The two hundred rooms are nice and attractive—no glitz, which was all right by me. The rooms have everything the traveler might need. Some of the suites have full kitchens, which is particularly convenient for longer stays. (Who wants to eat out every night?) The rates are sensible. There is onsite parking and a complimentary breakfast. Each evening there is complimentary wine, beer, and soft drinks from 5:30 p.m. to 6:30 p.m., and then there is the cookie buffet from 8 p.m. to 10 p.m. This very nice property has a lot of perks, and there have been renovations and upgrades. I definitely recommend Magnolia Hotel, which also has sister properties in Houston, Denver, and Omaha.

Warwick Melrose Hotel

3015 Oak Lawn Ave.
214-521-5151
www.melrosehoteldallas.com

This charming boutique hotel, built in 1924, is only slightly out of the downtown area. I adored this property at first sight. My staying there was a fluke, but I am delighted I did. I was in the middle of a cross-country odyssey, when my agenda changed. I was to arrive in Dallas and needed a place to stay, and the Melrose was suggested. To obtain a spur-of-the-moment reservation in one of the 184 rooms was a wonderful experience.

The Melrose is off the main drag and rather clandestine, yet friendly and gracious. Can I say more? On-site parking is convenient. I was informed that the hotel has a complimentary car service to downtown.

Check-in was perfect. I was taken to my room, and immediately I felt at home. All the modern amenities that you could wish for in a room were in place, including a few that caused me to reflect on younger days growing up in a city apartment with high ceilings, layered moldings, push-button light switches, inlaid floors, and glass doorknobs.

The **Library Bar** (214-224-3152, www.landmarkrestodallas.com), an "in" meeting place, has been voted the best piano and martini bar in Dallas. It serves one hundred different varieties of martinis. There is also live entertainment.

The award-winning **Landmark Restaurant** (214-224-3152, www .landmarkrestodallas.com) is comfortable for all and serves American fare with many European touches. A Sunday champagne brunch is a nice way to start the week. Stay at the Warwick Melrose and experience this gem of a property.

Mansion on Turtle Creek

2821 Turtle Creek Blvd.
214-559-2100
www.mansiononturtlecreek.com

I always enjoy this wonderful property. Originally a private home, this stately, award-winning hotel is one of distinction and decorum. The restoration of the Sheppard King Mansion, which sits on just over four acres, has been extremely well done.

Upon entering the property, you delight in the feeling of a private home of ultra dimensions. The original owner, Mr. King, was a son of a Confederate Civil War veteran who had many successful enterprises. Unfortunately, in 1935 the Kings lost their fortune. The property had several owners, then Caroline Rose Hunt and the Rosewood Property Company purchased the King mansion in 1979. What a wise move! The property was enhanced in the 1980s by a 142-room hotel tower.

Elegant, superb, sophisticated: the Mansion is supreme. The spacious rooms are beautifully decorated in quiet, upscale appointments and colors. The small patio off of some of the rooms is delightful. You will never feel on your own at the Mansion (unless that is your wish) as the staff is always available to help.

Originally the dining room of the King Mansion, the **Bar** is a great place! The hunting-themed art and the ambiance make it a favorite of mine. The bar is a good place to people watch, imagining what might be his or her claim to fame as you sip on one of the

Bar's cocktail revivals, such as the Jack Ras, Blue Moon, Monkey Gland, Corpse Reviver, and more!

The **Mansion Restaurant** (214-443-4747) is situated in the mansion's former living room. For more than twenty years, this was Chef Dean Fearing's domain, where his southwestern cuisine was applauded. He has since opened his dream restaurant. Now at the helm of the Restaurant since 2009 is Bruno Davaillon, who brings outstanding credentials and creative acumen to the Mansion. As he was raised on a farm in the Loire valley in France, his penchant for fresh ingredients and simple but exceptional fare is most understandable. He has won many accolades. The Mansion's signature tortilla soup and lobster tacos remain. I have always enjoyed dining at the Mansion, savoring every morsel and the beautiful surroundings.

Driving Diva Factoid: When I first visited the Mansion, the dress code was old-world, and I immediately gave the establishment a big, bright platinum star. A sign of the times (unfortunately), my star has dulled. Now, the Bar permits jeans. In the Restaurant, the dress code is casual elegant or business casual. I don't think jackets and ties are required. So sad!

Hotel ZaZa

2332 Leonard St.
214-468-8399
www.hotelzaza.com

This property, whose colorful reputation preceded my arrival, was definitely worth a visit, even though I couldn't spend the night. It is eclectic, funky, boutiquey, colorful, bohemian, and sensual. You feel as if you are in another country. Get the picture?

I was shown a few rooms. Very attractive, they look like upscale display rooms, and each is themed—for instance, there are the Texas Suite, Medusa Suite, Erotica Suite, Zen Suite, and Shag-a-delic Suite.

In the years since I visited, a lot of touch-ups and tweaks have been done, but from all I have gleaned, the ZaZa's unique combinations in decor and ambiance have not been lost—only enhanced and improved.

Amelia's Place

1108 S. Akard St., No. 13
214-421-7427

Told to check out this place out, I asked a friend (Ms. Carolyn C.), who is a Dallas resident, about it, and she said, "I'll take you there. It will speak for itself."

What I read on the Internet didn't intimidate me: a so-called bed-and-breakfast in an old factory building owned by Louisiana native, Amelia C. Jenkins. She receives huge raves for her huge breakfasts. I also read that there are six guest rooms decorated in their own style, each named for a woman who has made a contribution to Dallas. It still didn't sound too bad. As of this writing, I find that the rooms have been rearranged.

My friend and I arrived on **Young Street**, and I was glad I was not alone. It looked a little sketchy. We entered through a curious door, reminiscent of a speakeasy, and walked up the stairs to be greeted by the bohemian-eclectic and friendly Amelia. Looking around, we were informed that the other guests had just left and that they had had quite a stay. I would not question the latter for a split second. I felt like I was in a fraternity house after a big weekend. We walked around, thanked Amelia, and left.

You are on your own for this one.

Shopping

The Dallas woman knows how to dress and, of course, how to shop.

Neiman Marcus

1618 Main St.
214-741-6911
www.neimanmarcus.com

The original Neiman Marcus is located just two blocks from the Adolphus. Of course, the downtown Neiman Marcus was the fashion center for years. Mr. Marcus knew what was wanted and presented ultra as well as regular fashions to his adoring public.

I find there's something special about the original Neiman Marcus, all of these stores offer an experience to enjoy. Temptation too! In the original Neiman Marcus, the **Zodiac Restaurant** (214-573-5800) is on the sixth level. I adore this restaurant and would not miss having lunch here when in Dallas. It reminds me of an upscale department store tearoom, the kind that was prevalent in department stores in the 1950s. When my mother took me to one, I would wear a dress, Mary Jane patent leather shoes, and a big bow in my hair. There would often be a casual fashion show. Those department store tearooms were wonderful, but they too are a thing of the past. Thank goodness at least the Zodiac remains. The soups are a great starter, but unless it will be your meal, only get a cup. Whether you order a salad or a sandwich, you will not be disappointed. I cannot resist the signature oversized popovers that are placed on the table along with freshly made strawberry butter. Oh my! The Zodiac is a delight, and as they say, "You can feast in fashion."

Just going from floor to floor in Neiman Marcus is a delight and an experience. Look carefully. There is so much to see, consider, and enjoy.

Clothes Circuit

6105 Sherry Ln., Preston Center
214-696-8634
www.clothescircuit.com

With the motto "Decidedly Upscale Resale," this serious consignment shop is well run and organized. Its founder and owner, Irene Mylan, arrived in Dallas in 1983 with her law professor husband and two young daughters. Her mother had introduced her to "upscale resale fashions" in California when she and her sisters were young. Here in Dallas, every day hundreds of hand-selected items are strategically placed to tempt and delight—and these aren't just any items! These are designer and top-of-the-line. This fun place is full of treasures.

Buffalo Exchange: New & Recycled Fashions
3424 Greenville
214-826-7544
www.buffaloexchange.com

Also a serious resale store, the Buffalo Exchange was started in Tucson, Arizona, by Kerstin and Spencer Block in 1974. Kerstin's love of fashion and the scavenger challenges of finding great bargains led to the creation of a company that now has twenty-eight stores, three franchises in twelve states, and over $43 million a year in sales. Indeed, this is a serious enterprise! Buffalo Exchange has a history and an interesting purpose. Check the website; perhaps there is a store in your area. Lucky!

Note: Check the phone book or the Internet if you are an avid consignment shopper. In cities where the women preen and pride themselves in wonderful adornments, you will find treasures at these resale haunts.

FYI: Gaylord Texan is in *Grapevine*, between Dallas and *Ft. Worth*.

Gaylord Texan Hotel & Convention Center
1501 Gaylord Tr.
817-778-1000
www.gaylordhotels.com/gaylord-texan

I would not include it except I have this info from the most reliable source. It is a special, almost over-the-top resort, and the food was absolutely exceptional.

Leaving Dallas always gives me a little twinge. I really like the Big D.

DRIVING DIVA'S CHANCE FINDINGS

Sidenote: One might wonder how I have discovered some of the places included in this book. Some certainly weren't planned and proved bona fide discoveries. The following is an excellent example. It is a unique find that proved a true and enjoyable serendipity.

I have driven from Dallas to Santa Fe via several different routes. This time, desiring a new route, I studied the map and tried to discern what of interest might be along the way. My study didn't present a lot. How I found **Turkey**, Texas, I am truly not sure. Turkey, as tiny as its name is on the map, popped out at me. It was on the way to Santa Fe—sort of. I looked up Turkey on the Internet, saw that it was indeed there, and thought, Why not go for it! I started to plan and learn and wonder.

Driving Diva's Note: The Turkey, Texas, experience was special and good. I share, and I hope you enjoy and perhaps visit this special place.

TURKEY
(POPULATION APPROXIMATELY 553)

Named for the wild turkeys that lived along the creek, this was a railroad town from where many cattle, grains, and cotton were shipped. I also found out that **Palo Duro Canyon State Park** (www .palodurocanyon.com), **Caprock Canyons State Park**, and the **Grand**

Canyon of Texas are all near Turkey. See **Texas Parks & Wildlife** (www.tpwd.state.tx.us). There is a lot to learn about this little place called Turkey.

The King of Western Swing, Bob Wills, was raised on a farm just north of town, and there is now a **Bob Wills Museum** (www .bobwills.com). A monument to the star is at the western end of **Main Street**. Thousands attend a large annual event held the last Sunday in April. Turkey is considered the Western Swing Capital of the World. There is a hotel: the **Turkey Hotel**.

I called and spoke with the then owner, Mona Boles, a most articulate and enthusiastic woman. Deciding that I must see this discovery in person, I reserved a room. Rates ranged from $50 to $80 (then). You can also rent the entire hotel for $1,200 per night. I thought, Can this be? I didn't need a confirmation number and was told that they looked forward to my arrival. I continued to wonder what was I getting into but consoled myself by saying, "They did have a telephone. They spoke English. They were on the Internet and were found at K-5 on the Texas map in the Rand McNally Atlas."

Investigating the Internet information a little bit more, I selected "What's Nearby?" "Nearby Restaurants," "Nearby Accommodations," "Nearby Museums," "Nearby Attractions." The reply in each case was, "We are unable to locate any . . ."

I was now filled with curiosity and a bit of determination to see this place at K-5 on the map. A friend, Angela M., had met me in Dallas and would be with me for the next week or so. I had sent her a printout of the travel agenda. Dallas was one thing, but I knew she was not too sure about Turkey. What had her friend gotten her into? She confessed, however, that she too was sort of curious about my discovery.

Beginning the discovery: As we left Dallas, the interstate was busy into **Denton** (population about 66,000), and then traffic thinned out. Once we passed Wichita Falls (population about 96,000), the road was fairly empty.

At **Vernon** (population about 12,000), a KFC loomed, and lunch was obtained. Now we were on **Hwy 287**. The next town was **Qua-**

nah (population about 3,000). Populations were definitely dwindling. We stopped on Highway 287 at Past & Present: Antiques & Collectibles.

Past & Present
1800 E. Eleventh St.
940-663-6300

Then we drove on to **Childress** (population about 5,000). Still on U.S. 287, we stopped at the Wild Plum.

Wild Plum West: Unique Home Furnishings & Accessories
1101 Ave. F NW
940-937-6565

Along the way there were other nice-looking shops for those who decide to stop.

In this new area, which can be considered remote, it is a good idea to double-check every so often to be certain you are on the right road. Yes, off of Highway 287, you take "Road Highway 86" to Turkey. Oh! And it is a long road! It's a good road but has few services and few houses. "You is out there a-lone." This is not a night road for visitors . . . maybe for the locals.

A small sign announced Turkey, Texas. It was around 3:30 p.m. People? I don't think I saw a soul. Main Street could be renamed "Only Street." Still, there were buildings—standing and with all the windowpanes intact. Turkey Hotel, where are you? If someone had said I was on an old John Wayne or Clint Eastwood movie set, I would not have disputed it.

Turkey Hotel
Third and Alexander
806-423-1151

In 1927 this hotel was constructed for $85,000. That is a lot of 1927 dollars! From 1931 to 1988, it was owned by the same family. Around the time of the Depression, it sold for $10,000. Now owned by Turkey resident Cody Bell and listed in the state and national historic registries, this hotel has remained in continuous operation.

Walking up to the hotel, you can easily envision where the horses were tied up years ago. After stepping onto the creaky porch and through the front door, I was amazed to see mannequins dressed in western-style clothing. My friend and I smiled at each other, a bit bewildered about what I had gotten us into. In the next room, we saw the front desk. We tapped the bell as instructed, and after the third ring, an attractive woman appeared smiling. It was then owner Mona Boles. "Oh, I am so glad you are here," she said.

We were not really convinced that we should stay, so I said that we had made such good time (which was very true) getting to Turkey, perhaps we should go on as we had lots of miles still to drive.

Mona's expression turned to sadness as she said, "Oh, I turned on the air conditioner for you this morning." I started to say that I would be glad to pay for a night, but something sealed my lips. We chatted, Mona shared a few local details, and I said that we were going to venture into town and explore before we settled in. My friend and I returned to the car to decide on our plan. We voted that Mona was too nice. We couldn't let her down. I truly wanted to see our accommodations and everything about the Turkey Hotel.

We spent the rest of the afternoon driving on long, straight roads where we saw only an occasional pickup truck, a stray cow, and lots of dust. We made it to Caprock Canyon, a pretty place to visit and home to the remaining original free-roaming bison herd belonging to Col. C. Goodnight.

We sensibly turned around and returned to the hotel before dark. A stop at the **Turkey Gas Station and Store** was an experience. My friend, a gourmet chef and former hotel owner, decided to go into the store to find our dinner fixings—maybe just some heavy munchies to go with our traveling vino. I waited in the car, and a few minutes later, laughing from head to toe, she walked out of the store holding a small bag and a stalk of bent-over yellow celery.

"I don't think it will poison us," my chef friend said. "We'll have a good drink for sure." We headed back to the hotel.

Mona was waiting. We followed her to our room. Along the stairs and in the hallway of the second floor were more mannequins dressed in period clothing. Our room was decorated with memorabilia. I washed my face and hands, and as we headed back downstairs, I admit, I peeked behind a few unlocked doors in the hallway. I saw more creatively decorated rooms. Mona had been joined by her granddaughter. Mona looked so young. The two "girls" showed us out to the very pleasant back garden. We brought a glass of wine downstairs as well as our "groceries." It was really very nice, sitting in the garden, debating about our hors d'oeuvres, and reflecting on our day. I was glad to have stayed, and the next event underscored this feeling. The birds were chirping; the air was cooling. Mona and her granddaughter came out, and we all shared stories. They went into the house and suddenly return with a big tray. Mona had prepared dinner for us! They were so happy to share and, oh! did I feel like a jerk for my previous thoughts. Eat your hearts out, fancy-schmancy hotels. This is real, genuine hospitality. It was wonderful. We all talked for quite a while, and Mona revealed that she, her husband, and their children had lived not far from Turkey. Her husband had had, I think, a radio station. One of her daughters was a country-western singer. Her granddaughter was finishing school. Before we went upstairs, Mona told us about the breakfast selections. "I'll just have some juice—fruit if it's available, a piece of toast or muffin, and some coffee. I really don't eat much in the morning—especially when traveling." My friend decided to have a bit more.

Up to our room we went. The evening shower was cooling, and the bed was comfortable. I was glad the air-conditioning had been turned on. As I looked around the room at the memorabilia, I wished it all could talk. My eyes quickly shut, and without a toss or turn, I awoke as morning was dawning.

Chatting at breakfast was most pleasant as we learned more about the area. This place would be a fantastic major corporate retreat and hunting camp. "I like that idea" said Mona.

It was time to leave. We all hugged. It had been a treat and an experience to be in Turkey, Texas, at the Turkey Hotel.

Update: As stated, Cody Bell now owns the Turkey Hotel. The mannequins and decorative tidbits have gone. A lot has been done to the hotel, as I discovered when I spoke with René Valdez. He and his wife, Marsha, manage the hotel and are glad to be back in Turkey rather than Houston.

Driving out of Turkey, one sees very attractive wrought iron signs on the sides of the road, some with turkeys, birds, and trees, stating, "Turkey, Texas, Home of Bob Wills." Another showed seven male figures playing musical instruments with the same statement. I also discovered that Turkey has a 1950s-style drive-in movie theater open in the summer.

Leaving Turkey on Route 86: Turn off onto I-70 North; then take Highway 287 North through Clarendon to Amarillo. Eventually you connect back up with I-40. Yes! Back on an interstate and into the hubbub of progress!

Observation: It is not hard to appreciate tiny towns and to acknowledge their way of life. We all have the same basic life functions; the residents of these towns watch the same TV shows you do and like many of the same things. They are, in ways, inspirational, and you can learn a lot, even if the population numbers fewer than five hundred. You may not want the life of denizen of a tiny town, and those denizens probably do not want yours—but both can give and share so much.

AMARILLO (POPULATION OVER 150,000)

Heading west, Amarillo is the last major Texas town before you cross the border into New Mexico. See the New Mexico chapter for places in New Mexico near the Texas border.

TO HOUSTON ON I-10

The road was as expected. There are several places of real interest on the **Gulf of Mexico**, such as **Galveston**, but I did not have time on this trip to stop. Next time.

HOUSTON

Houston, this country's fourth-largest city, is nice, and I was impressed. Driving toward the city, the skyline was arresting. I found Houston to be a big city with a small-town ambiance of camaraderie. In some of the residential areas, Texas wealth was not in question.

Hotel Icon
220 Main St.
713-224-4266
www.hotelicon.com

I drove into the garage, and two attendants approached the car. One said, "Greetings, Ms. Davis." Caught off guard and slightly snowed by the greeting, I returned their smiles. The attendants looked at my stuffed car, and I could read their thoughts on their faces. They were obviously relieved when I said I would only need two bags. I asked if my car could be parked close by, and they pointed to a spot a stone's throw away. Perfect.

I walked into the hotel and was immediately impressed. The fact that it was once a big Texas bank can easily be perceived, especially when you are at the desk checking in and notice the big bank safe in front of you. The lobby, with its huge columns dividing the massive space, is about two stories tall. The decor is dark, but with the frosted-glass chandeliers illuminating the space, all works well. The updated original elevators still have the tracking panel on the main floor. I love nostalgia!

My room was spacious, with dark decor and a fantastic view of the main thoroughfare of Houston. I was pleasantly surprised by how clean and wide the streets are.

Important Note: There is a metro rail in the middle of the main street. I learned when I took it that you buy your ticket from the machine for the designated period that you want it to be valid (more on the metro rail below).

My room had an attractive mirrored niche for a bar and a coffeemaker. The most noticeable points needing attention I found in the large bathroom. The sides of the tub are very high. Directions for the French shower/sprayer are needed; I could not get it to work. The glassed-in shower was as large as a studio apartment. Very nice! The shower's bathing gel, shampoo, and conditioner are in pump bottles attached to the wall. Also very nice! The amenities for the bath were on the vanity by the sink—a little far away when one is soaking. But there was no horseshoe toilet seat, thank goodness. There was only one small hook—a bull's head on the bath wall—and I did not find a long mirror anywhere. There was no telephone in the bathroom, so remember to take the cordless from the bedroom if necessary.

In the closet I found the usual two robes, two pairs of slippers, umbrella, safe, iron, ironing board, laundry bag, and, this is a first, a Federal Express envelope with label. This is minor, but the lights on each side of the bed were too high and the switches a little hard to find. The mattress was very comfortable and the sheets excellent. The staff was most helpful in telling me about the property.

Dining: There is the **Voice Restaurant** and **Voice Bar/Lounge.** Voice (formerly called the Bank), a beautiful, sophisticated restaurant, is located in the lobby. The dinner I enjoyed was memorable and delicious. As you indulge, look around the spacious area and imagine what this bustling bank was like in its heyday.

The Hotel Icon is convenient to many of Houston's downtown attractions. It would be hard not to enjoy a stay at this acclaimed hotel or just an evening of delicious dining.

There is a **fitness and day spa** (832-667-4466), which I did not have time to enjoy.

The Alden (formerly the Sam Hotel)

1117 Prairie St.
832-200-8800
www.aldenhotels.com

The Alden (meaning "old friend") is a luxury hotel in downtown Houston's business district. Upon entering, you are surrounded by upscale, modern, sleek decor and ambiance. Since it is one of the oldest hotels in the city (built in 1924), many claim that a ghost from the 1920s is present. (I love those ghosts.) There are ninety-seven luxurious guest rooms and nine suites.

Upon my arrival, the staff made me feel as if they have known me for years. The check-in took place at a large oval desk where I sat down to do the necessary check-in particulars. I felt that I was in someone's office or library. Given my key card, I noticed that the hotel's telephone number and address were written on it. So smart!

It would be hard not to be impressed by the lobby's wall-size light installation titled "Invitation" by David Lander. The light colors fade and return in different forms and hues throughout the day, evening, and night. One would have to sit in the lobby for three days to watch the entire sequence.

The signage was good. I found my way to the room, a junior suite, easily. The living room area was pleasant with sofa, coffee table, and entertainment center. When I returned to my room after dinner, I found chocolate-covered strawberries and a bottle of wine on the coffee table. Thank you!

The bedroom was comfortable and not too big. Of course, the bedding was Egyptian cotton with a three hundred thread count. The bathroom was modern with slick, gray granite countertops, a large tub, and a superlarge glass-enclosed shower. All the amenities are in order.

*17 (832-200-8888)—yes, just "*17"—is the restaurant at the Alden. I was to learn that the name derives from years past when Houston was a destination for seventeen railroads. How original to name the restaurant "*17"! It wasn't until I was perusing the menu and saw all the delicious seafood choices that I remembered Houston is on the sea. Whether you are having the gulf shrimp curry or the sea scallops with granny smith apples, you will enjoy it to the max. I found the meal's accompaniments to be in the right proportions.

Although I had little room left for dessert, I did get a sample plate, and each taste was delicious.

The lounge at the Alden, the **Sam Bar** is a perfect, unpretentious spot to unwind or wind up.

The Alden is not a hotel of a cookie-cutter format; it has its own descriptive umbrella.

Museum of Fine Arts Houston
1001 Bissonnet St.
713-639-7300
www.mfah.org

The metro rail took me by several different areas and turned into a sightseeing event in itself. Arriving at the museum, I was immediately impressed. It is hard to camouflage excellence. I read that it is "the largest art museum [in America] south of Chicago, west of Washington, DC, and east of Los Angeles." I discovered that I could not see it all on my visit, as it has three hundred thousand square feet of display space. I did see the photography exhibit of Diane Arbus's excellent and moving work. It is accurate, real-life, superb photography. Perhaps as a New Yorker, I could relate as so many of her photographs are taken in Manhattan.

Also at the museum was an interesting and very well-displayed Murano glass exhibit. There was so much to see, but during this visit, just walking in the various galleries would have to suffice. Without a doubt, the Museum of Fine Arts Houston is impressive.

Note: If you are anywhere near a Diane Arbus exhibit, be sure to see it. Or get one of her books.

Rienzi

1406 Kirby Dr.
713-639-7800
www.mfah.org/visit/rienzi/Rienzi-Education

Part of the Museum of Fine Arts Houston, this former private home houses a most important collection of European decorative arts. Aside from seeing one of the world's finest collections of Worchester porcelain, you will tour the rooms where the Rienzi family actually lived. The house is magnificent but very livable. The more you look, the more you see and feel the warmth of a real family home.

Great Finds

Harwin Street

Harwin Street is located two blocks off **Hilcroft Street**, two miles west of Highway 59. Time and comfortable shoes are a must! You are going to see so many things you want to need, but do not go crazy buying, even though you feel you've found a bargain—and there are bargains. The area is not fancy, but you'll find a wealth of faux designer fashions, perfumes, and such. There is a shop for everything from watches, to eyeglasses, to lingerie, to whatever you thought you needed. Don't be shy. Practice your haggling skills, and put them to use. Don't go dressed up. Wear something very casual and nothing froufrou. Have fun, but be sensible and thrifty.

Charming Charlie's
6959 Harwin St.
713-579-1911

This is a place to visit.

Westheimer Street in the Montrose Area

There are so many funky, eclectic, wonderful places of all varieties in this area. To list them would be a task. To visit them is a treat.

The Galleria
5085 Westheimer
713-622-0663
www.galleriahouston.com

With about 350 stores, the Galleria is the fifth-largest mall in the country. Houston is full of high-end stores in the various shopping areas, which is to be expected in high-end Houston.

Driving Diva Tip: To view some Texas-style Houston homes, drive slowly through *Heights*, *River Oats*, and *River Road*.

I saw a lot of antique shops on **Woodhead Street** that looked less like shops than impressive homes. I wouldn't anticipate any bargains, but it would certainly be fun to look around.

I was recently told that I missed scoping out the Guild Shop, whose sales benefit various charities.

Guild Shop
2009 Dunlavy St.
713-528-5095
www.theguildshop.org

How could I miss this? What a must-do! Don't you miss it.

ArtCar Museum

140 Heights Blvd.

713-861-5526

www.artcarmuseum.com

Also known as the Garage Mahal, this funky automobile museum opened in 1998. What a fun escape from the norm. Just walk around. Thought: Should I make my next cross-country odyssey in an art car?

Twice New Consignment Boutique

2005-D W. Gray, River Oaks Retail Center

713-523-2212

www.twicenew.com

This shop has a good selection, but I thought the prices were rather high.

Restaurants

Empire Café

1732 Westheimer Rd.

713-528-5282

www.empirecafe.com

This is an absolute must! We are not talking fancy-schmancy, just delicious, sensibly priced, and nice. Although it looks like a sit-down restaurant, it isn't. There is a procedure: You line up (you will not be alone, but the line moves fast), place your order at the counter, and then go and sit down. Your order is then brought to you. I found it very difficult to make up my mind about what to order and ended up choosing the tomato basil soup and chicken salad. I also had a taste of the carrot cake and lemon poppy seed cake. You will not be disappointed. The coffees are delicious, and you might want to try the Italian sodas.

Every Monday is half-price cake night. You can sample pine-apple carrot cake, Toll House cookie crunch cake, or whatever is special on the cake menu that day.

Rainbow Lodge

2011 Ella Blvd.

713-861-8666

www.rainbow-lodge.com

I did not know a thing about the Rainbow Lodge, but I found it to be a fantastic place. Deemed one of the most romantic restaurants, it has also received many awards. I discovered that the proprietor, a woman named Donnette Hansen (yes!), has owned the Rainbow Lodge for thirty years. My dinner date was a friend whom I had not seen for years. He now lives in Houston and knows the best places.

The lodge's history is interesting. The **Tied Fly Bar** is unique and definitely something to see. The carvings, which resemble a busy trout stream, were installed in seven pieces and are over twenty feet long. The menu was exceptional and varied, with selections ranging from the normal to the not so normal. For example, you can order the signature buffalo rib eye, a wild game mixed grill, roasted elk, or pine nut–crusted rainbow trout, and the selections go on. Of course, availability of some of these exotic choices will depend on the season. The Rainbow Lodge is definitely a must-see. It is a place where the food is as exceptional as the decor.

Crostini

3411 Shepherd

713-524-8558

What a nice, friendly restaurant. Although I had already eaten dinner, I sat at the bar talking with new friends introduced to me by my dinner date. They were kind enough to offer a taste or two from some of Crostini's Italian dishes. All were very good with southwestern flavorings. Judging from the menu, selections are many and the prices sensible.

HUNTSVILLE

I had left Houston and was heading for Dallas with no specific plans for the next couple of hours when suddenly I saw a sign for the Huntsville Visitors Bureau and a huge statue of Sam Houston.

Huntsville Visitors Bureau
7600 Hwy. 75 South
936-291-9726
www.huntsvilletexas.com

As I was to learn at the welcome center, there is a lot to Huntsville, and not just the usual attractions. Huntsville, home to the Texas Department of Criminal Justice, has a historic downtown walking tour and a prison driving tour. Seven prisons are located in the county. On the driving tour, you will see the Texas Prison Museum, area prisons, and the prison cemetery.

Texas Prison Museum
491 Hwy. 75 North
936-295-2155
www.txprisonmuseum.org

Huntsville also has the Sam Houston University and the HEARTS (Helping Every American Remember through Serving) Veterans Museum.

HEARTS Veterans Museum
463 Hwy. 75 North
936-295-5959
www.heartsmuseum.com

The great outdoors should not be overlooked with the state park and the **Blue Lagoon**, where artesian springs feed into an old rock quarry. You can even scuba dive. Before you leave, be sure to visit King's Candies and Ice Cream.

King's Candies and Ice Cream
1112 Eleventh St.
936-291-6988

At this old-fashioned ice-cream parlor and candy factory, you can get sandwiches, soups, and salads, as well as old-fashioned fountain delights. Oh yes! My kind of place.

EL PASO

Driving Diva Sharing: The real reason I came to El Paso (besides that it was on the way) was that my friend, Nancy P., who was traveling with me for part of this odyssey, had not been to the city since her husband was stationed there during the war. More importantly, she told me that their first daughter had been born there. I knew it would mean a lot to her to see the area and the hospital. And it did.

Camino Real Hotel
101 S. El Paso St.
915-534-3024
www.caminoreal.com

Located in downtown El Paso, this hotel definitely has a Mexican feel. It was not hard to find, but check-in was only okay. I was expected, and my name was in the computer, but we just didn't get a warm welcome. How could anyone not be happy and friendly in such an attractive property?

I was to be in El Paso only until noon the next day, so I decided to take a walk around the area. It was hot, the shops were closing for the day, and I did not really feel that comfortable.

In 1912, the Camino Real Hotel was an elegant gem in the center of El Paso—and it is still a gem. The lobby is attractive with the focal point being a very impressive Tiffany glass dome. The chandeliers are beautiful, as are the stained glass windows. I could quickly discern that a lot of planning and pennies went into the building of this property. The hotel seemed slightly incongruous to the area—like a diamond in the rough.

It has 359 large rooms and suites. The accommodations were nice and clean, and the general decor was attractive. The **Dome** dining room and bar was relaxed and beautiful. Jason, the server, was excellent, not only in his service but also in relating the history of the area and hotel. This type of hotel personnel is extremely valuable. The light fare (by choice) was delicious. The bread basket contained a mix of hot, home-baked rolls, one of which was a biscuit with a walnut crust. Butter and jalapeno cream cheese were served with the bread basket. You could easily make a meal of the breads. For breakfast, you could choose from a large Mexican buffet or order American fare.

Upon leaving, I realized that this hotel represents a definite meeting of the old and new worlds and of America and Mexico. The area east of downtown was under development, and there are at least two large malls. There is a lot to discover.

Driving Diva Mileage: I-10 East is a good interstate, but the drive to *San Antonio* is long and straight. In fact, it is over five hundred miles, with long stretches without a thing. Keep an eye on the gas gauge.

If you are hungry on the way to San Antonio, stop at Camp House BBQ in **Ft. Stockton** (population approximately 8,500).

Camp House BBQ
1216 N. Hwy. 285
432-336-9791

It was very good and not too greasy. I definitely recommend it.

The Ft. Stockton press states that it is "the Friendliest Town in Texas." I discovered the following: The **Texas Main Street**

Program helps revitalize historic downtowns, and it is one of the most successful in the nation. I read that Ft. Stockton has one thousand motel rooms, pecan orchards, a museum, **Ste. Genevieve Wines** (432-365-2417), an eighteen-hole golf course, a B&B, and RV sites. Interesting.

SAN ANTONIO

Arriving in San Antonio, I immediately felt joy and friendship. I think you will feel it too.

FYI: The street to remember as a landmark is *Broadway*.

Hotels

Menger Hotel
204 Alamo Plaza
210-223-4361
www.mengerhotel.com

It was not difficult to find the downtown area where the historic Menger is located, right across from the **Alamo** (www.thealamo .org). The advertisement reads, "On the Riverwalk." I pictured it on the banks of a river. More on this very wrong assumption later! There are lots of traditions and history at the Menger, as well as several culinary features, one being the mango ice cream, which has been on the menu for over a hundred years. The **Colonial Room** (the main dining room) was previously known for its wild game and exotic dishes, such as wild turkey stuffed with chestnuts, soft-shell turtle soup made from turtles caught in the San Antonio River, dried buffalo tongue, and potted antelope. Does this mean intoxicated antelope? Just joshing. These exotic choices are no more, but the more regular choices are excellent.

The oldest hotel in San Antonio, the Menger proves to be a history lesson of sorts for all who are on property. Check-in was friendly and efficient. It is a delightful historic hotel, and although I could see that fine tuning was needed, I knew I would have a most pleasant stay. Major domo Ernesto Malacara, who has been with the hotel for over twenty-eight years, proved to be an interesting and friendly guide, as well as a wealth of information about the hotel and the area. The Menger is convenient to many attractions.

Driving Diva Confession: It was early evening and time to discover the *Riverwalk* and areas around the Menger. There were lots of people and police in the area, so I felt safe. Remember that the ad says, "The Menger on the Riverwalk"? Well, I expected to see a river close by. I walked, and I looked and looked. No river. Finally, sheepishly, I asked a policeman, "Where is the river?" He replied with a smile, "You have to go downstairs," and pointed to steps descending from the street. I smiled perplexedly, as I thought, Down the steps to the River? Descend I did, and, indeed, there you find another world. The "river" was perhaps more accurately described as an underground canal. Truthfully though, it is a river, or part of one, that surfaces on the grounds of the University of the Incarnate World. All along the river there are shops, restaurants, people, noise, lights, music, and gaiety. You won't have a problem finding things to do but rather just deciding what you want to do. It is fun.

Menger history: In 1840 many German immigrants came to Texas. Two of them were Will Menger and Mary Baumschleuter, who married soon after arriving in Texas. Will Menger built his first beer brewery shortly afterward, and Will's beer became very popular. Since so many people were enjoying too much of it, he decided a hotel was needed for the sleepy partiers. In 1857, Menger contracted for the construction of a hotel. In 1871, Menger died, and his good German wife continued to run the hotel for the next ten years. The Menger continues today and has become a true and significant San Antonio historic landmark.

The **Menger Bar** is a replica of the House of Lords Pub in London. It was in this bar that Teddy Roosevelt recruited some of his Rough Riders, or volunteers for the cavalry who fought during the Spanish-American War. The bar was carefully dismantled during Prohibition and finally reassembled in its present location.

Obtain the complimentary brochure for a self-guided tour. It is well done and explains the many attributes of the hotel, as well as its decorative arts.

This oldest continually operated hotel west of the Mississippi has ghosts. Ernesto Malacara, director of public relations, will relate stories from his experiences. These are not just about bumps in the night and flying objects but sightings of people without full bodies. Unfortunately, I did not experience any apparitions, but the stories are fascinating. Here's my favorite: Captain R. King, founder of the King Ranch, appears entering his room, the King Suite. He does not enter through the present door but through the wall where the door was when he had his suite. Many guests and employees have seen Captain King.

The Menger's accommodations were pleasant but needed updating, which I hear, as of this writing, have been done. The hallways are long and of medium width. The walls are thick, as in all older construction; therefore sounds are muffled, and quiet prevails. The Menger is a place to stay or visit for sure.

Hotel Havana San Antonio Riverwalk

1015 Navarro St.
210-222-2008
www.havanasanantonio.com

Located at the northern end of the Riverwalk, this twenty-eight room (nonsmoking) property is upscale, whimsical, and bohemian, with absolutely beautiful antique decor. It was built in 1914, and there were many ups and downs in the beginning. In 1992, Theresa Greer, realizing its undeniable potentials, purchased the property and made it the unquestionable glowing gem that it is today. All is well appointed, eclectic, tasteful, modern, and unique. It is also romantic. The hotel is a state and national historic landmark and has received numerous well-deserved travel accolades.

After a tour of the Havana's rooms and hallways, the next stop on the property was the patio overlooking the Riverwalk. Here, at **OCHO Lounge**, one can dine or just imbibe. Breakfast, lunch and dinner are served as well as a late night fare. There are several different sitting areas, my favorite being where one can watch the river action and gaiety. In 2005 they received the Best New Restaurant award and in 2011 they were voted one of the fifty best small hotels in the world I can truly say that I did not spy a thing that was not perfection.

Shopping and Sightseeing

Market Square
514 W. Commerce St.
210-207-8600
www.marketsquaresa.com

Here, in this bustling area, is **El Mercado** (www.marketsquaresa .com), comprising thirty-two shops modeled after an authentic Mexican market. What a collection of items of all varieties. Don't hesitate to bargain. There are also about eighty shops in this area called the **Farmers Market Plaza**. The smiling faces, the strains of mariachi music that fill the air, and the bright colors indeed create an exciting atmosphere at Market Square.

St. John's Company Store
7959 Broadway, Ste. 406
210-829-5366
www.stjohnknits.com

St. John's is about twelve minutes from downtown, and although I did not have time to shop all the boutique stores in the area, I did manage to stop here. This attractive store has friendly personnel, the manager being Debra Fox. The sophisticated designs are pricey, but not quite as pricey as those at other shops. There is something special about a St. John's knit.

Dining

Mi Terra

218 Produce Row
210-225-1262
www.mitierracafe.com

Mi Terra is said to be "a little loco and a lot of fun." I agree, and what a way to start the day! For some reason I knew that anything I ordered would probably be enough food for several days. My guess proved correct.

Mi Terra provides a delicious mix of aromas, large spaces, gaiety, bright colors, and twinkling Christmas lights of all sizes hanging from the ceiling and everywhere! Mexican music plays in the background. You enter near the bakery area, where you can purchase, or just feast your eyes on, the Texas-sized cookies, pralines, biscuits, and more. Nothing is *pocieto* (Spanish for "small")! The prices are very sensible. You cannot be anything but happy and very full at Mi Terra.

Established in 1940 by Pete and Cruz Llanes Cortez, Mi Terra has been open twenty-four hours a day serving breakfast, lunch, and dinner ever since its opening day. The Cortezes started this small business and proudly named it Mi Terra (meaning "my country"). Pete Cortez would often say, "I am an American by choice not by chance." Their children and grandchildren are seeing that the traditions are maintained. Many of the employees are considered family—some having worked there for over twenty-five years.

The breakfast specialties are:

Huevos rancheros $8.25
Chorizo con huevo $7.25
Chilaquiles $9.25
Steak and eggs $9.50

In my notes on Mi Tierra, I found this good quote: "It is better to die on your feet than to live on your knees."

The Alamo
300 Alamo Plaza
210-225-1391
www.thealamo.org

Of course, you cannot miss visiting the Alamo, which is just a few steps from the Menger. At this famous Texas spot in 1836, 189 brave and determined soldiers defended the old mission for thirteen days from 4,000 Mexican troops led by Gen. Antonio López de Santa Anna. The Alamo fell on March 6, 1836. Standing on the actual ground of a history-changing event is unforgettable.

A stone's throw from the Menger and the Alamo is the **post office**. What an impressive building! It is also a court house.

San Antonio is a thriving, happy gem. A wonderful place.

AUSTIN

Driskill Hotel
604 Brazos St.
512-474-5911
www.driskillhotel.com

The Driskill Hotel is a formidable edifice, with evident elegance and opulence. It was built by Jesse Driskill, who came from Missouri and later became a Texas cattle baron. Driskill wanted to build "one of the finest hotels in the whole country." In 1886 he did just that, and so the traditions began. In the 1880s, the Driskill family lost their fortune and sold the hotel. But Driskill is not forgotten. His life-size portrait hangs in the lobby today.

In December 1995, Great American Life Insurance purchased the hotel, announcing plans to spend $30 million to restore it totally. What a restoration was done! Of course, there was an impressive building to start with, but the foresight of the restoration teams can only be admired.

I wasn't hesitant to turn my car over to the pleasant and helpful front-door staff. The lobby is definitely august and dignified. The stained glass in the center of the ceiling reflects on the glossy marble floor, as do the chandeliers. The large floor-to-ceiling pillars define the lobby. The colors are primarily beige and maroon, and large potted palms with graceful bending branches add softness to the area.

The hotel has twelve floors and 188 rooms. When I got off the elevator to go to my room, I felt like I was in a private library with a bookcase lining every wall. As I walked down the hall, I realized the hallways are art galleries.

The room accommodations were nice, but as I was to discover, some attention to details and changes needed to be made. I have recently been informed that the rooms have been updated without losing their historical integrity.

I report on my experience. The room was rather Victorian with dark colors. Lace curtains with heavy damask draperies were on the windows. The quilt was of a very heavy variety with too many decorative throw pillows. The lamps were finely decorated but not good for reading. There was an oversized pullout sofa, which was really too big for the area. The air conditioner vent was right over the bed—not good. The closet was too small, and you couldn't open the door fully to use the mirror. The bathroom definitely needed tuning. I did not mind the fact that it was not large. It was a nice size. The magnifying mirror could have had a light. The glass shower door did not fit well. Water escaped onto the floor. There were few places to hang a towel. And there was a horseshoe toilet seat.

The hangers were of the moveable variety (thank you!), so I could hang up a dress and then hang it in the bathroom for a little bit of steaming. There was no coffeemaker in the room, and as I was to find out, the Driskill has no concierge or club floor.

I have just learned (but not seen) that there has been a lot of fine tuning at the property. Maybe some of my comments were learned via osmosis and have been considered.

I visited the acclaimed **Driskill Grill** (512-391-7162), which has a beautiful setting indeed. I ate in the **1886 Café and Bakery**, which is open for breakfast, lunch and dinner and on Friday and Saturday until midnight. The café is most pleasant and attractive, and the prices were sensible.

Sightseeing

Texas Capitol Visitors Center
112 E. Eleventh St.
512-305-8400
www.tspb.state.tx.us/SPB/capitol/texcap.htm

The capitol building is an impressive pink granite structure with a brilliant gold dome that sits high and prominently on the Austin skyline.

University of Texas at Austin
1 University Station
512-475-7348
www.utexas.edu

The University of Texas at Austin has fifty thousand students. Tours of both the capitol and the university are available.

Lake Austin is near downtown and offers bike and hiking trails, as well as paths for jogging and walking. A short walk from the Driskill you find the eclectic downtown area. I would not hesitate to walk alone in the area in the daytime, but late at night is a slightly different story.

Art, music, history, and pleasant lifestyles all contribute to Austin. The more I read about this area, the more I realize how much this Texas town has to offer.

Driving Diva Serendipity: Approximately fifty miles north of Austin on I-35 North, I saw a sign for Salado, Texas, and the steering wheel pulled. Yes!

SALADO

As reports state, Salado is a historic—definitely touristy—town famous for its shopping and its bed-and-breakfast inns. It is a shopper's destination with (as I was informed) one hundred shopping venues. It is definitely not a mall. There is a little bit of everything, including art, gifts, antiques, clothing, jewelry, handcrafts, and more. What an absolutely charming place. Visit even if you have to detour.

I first toured Salado from my car, driving up and then down the main street. "What a treasure!" I proclaimed. I decided to park in front of a long, two-story building that contained a shop called Heirlooms.

Heirlooms
26 Rock Creek Dr.
254-947-0336

A long, wooden porch was inviting, and the many treasures and friendly atmosphere once inside could not be denied.

You will find galleries of well-known Texas artists. The collection of dolls with attention to details is impressive. The blue and white porcelain is a collector's delight. If nostalgia is your penchant, then you spend most of your time in the rooms full of touring hats, dresses, and the like.

I did not have time to see everything, but I did visit the following stores:

Texan by Design
3 Old Town
254-947-4479

Springhouse
120 Royal St.
254-947-0747
www.springhousesalado.com

Old Town Salado Store
15 Old Town
254-947-9000

Angelic Herbs & Inspirations
3 N. Main St.
254-947-1909
www.saladoangelicherbs.com

Chic, innovative, fun, and enjoyable would easily apply to the shops in Salado.

McCains Café & Bakery
(formerly Uncommon Grounds Café)
417 N. Main St.
254-947-3354

An excellent choice! I learned from Lucas R. Martin that the food is better than ever. It is homemade food with Texas hospitality.

Salado has about twenty dining options and about an equal number of bed-and-breakfasts. *Salado* is a Native American word meaning "spring-fed creek." It was the stopping place for stagecoaches and cattle drives. I was informed that you can still see the ruts in the bottom of the creek from the wagon wheels. Two Texas governors and authors have come from this little town of approximately twenty-three hundred people. Sam Houston, Gen. George Custer, and bandit Sam Bass thought of Salado as their away home. This is a must-visit-again.

NEW MEXICO

New Mexico is an interesting state. I-40 (which goes practically all the way across the United States) and I-25 (running north-south) are the main highways. Heading in any direction, you will experience long stretches without services, and then you will find an area full of many stores, but don't gamble (except at the casinos)! Keep your gas tank half full and always have plenty of water.

Driving Diva Mileage: Driving from very big Texas, I thought I would never see the New Mexico border welcome sign. On this particular part of the trip, I had traveled about three thousand miles, and it felt like twenty-five hundred had been spent just getting through Texas.

Silver Moon Restaurant
3701 Will Rodgers Dr., Santa Rosa
505-472-3162

Driving along I-40, I had not been in New Mexico for long when this small building caught my eye. It is a roadside delight of delicious foods and friendly hospitality with the goal of maintaining an original established tradition. The chicken quesadillas were fresh and just right. The price is absolutely sensible. The woman who managed the restaurant told me they had been there a long time and that the restaurant was actually on historic **Route 66** (www.historic66.com). It turns out that part of I-40 follows that older road. The Silver Moon Restaurant, to me, was a multistar restaurant that you will enjoy. Don't pass it by.

Driving Diva Factoid: Santa Rosa (population approximately 2,500) is a city of natural lakes and other attractions like Route 66 Auto Museum.

Route 66 Auto Museum
2866 Will Rogers Ave.
575-472-1966
www.route66automuseum.com

In 1930, Route 66 "arrived" in town, and it became a traveler's oasis. In 1935, Club Café opened with its soon-to-be-famous smiling Fatman logo, which many still remember. The café closed in 1991. The famous train scene in the 1940 movie *Grapes of Wrath*, in which Tom Joad, played by Henry Fonda, watches the train steam over the Pecos River, was filmed here. There are interesting tidbits to every tiny town.

CLINES CORNER

Right off I-40 as you head out of Santa Rosa toward *Santa Fe*, this is a great stop for gas, food, restrooms, hats, Mexican jewelry, a selection of clothing, shoes, trinkets, jellies, and souvenirs. Check your map.

For a shortcut to Santa Fe, take Highway 285, a very good road.

SANTA FE
(POPULATION APPROXIMATELY 65,000)

Santa Fe is growing rapidly, but its historic downtown remains its main hub. It is called the "City Different" with attributes of exceptional merit. The Santa Fe streets are a little confusing, but don't get frustrated. So what if you go around the block twice. Charming in many different ways, Santa Fe mixes the old world with the tourist world but never overlooks its Native American roots.

I recommend you obtain a map for a self-guided walking tour. It will prove very interesting. You can see more on foot in Santa Fe than in many other cities; the museums, art galleries, and shops are all within walking distance. Wear comfortable shoes and weather-appropriate clothing and be in a positive haggling mode for street shopping.

The Plaza and the Historic District

The Plaza, with its inviting park, is the center of the downtown historic area. Across from the street, at the **Palace of the Governors** (www.palaceofthegovernors.org), many local Native Americans arrive each morning to sell their wares. You will find that shopping in Santa Fe is world-class, but as when shopping anywhere, be savvy, alert, and aware.

When in Santa Fe, I feel a certain artsy emotion. I enjoy the city with its diverse cultures, artistic mixes, and upscale places. During the summer, there are a lot of visitors. I cannot stress enough that the buyer should beware. Does it really compute that so many "handmade" items could all look exactly the same?

You'll find a lot of Zuni art and wares; one should probably learn about Zuni art before buying. This goes for buying any kind of art anywhere.

Driving Diva Factoid: You will see an immense number of fetishes—objects believed to have magic powers. Usually in the shape of a carved animal, they can be single items or strung in a collection on a necklace. Check the construction carefully.

Hotels

Inn of the Anasazi

113 Washington Ave.
505-988-3030
www.innoftheanasazi.com

The staff that greeted me was very attentive, both in parking my car and at the front desk. This is a very charming upscale property with only fifty-seven guest rooms. The traditional southwestern architecture and decor are extremely attractive; the service is professional. The rooms are little works of art and very romantic, with a four-poster bed, a gas-lit kiva fireplace, and appropriate art.

The inn is environmentally attuned, acknowledging that our resources are precious and must be conserved. High-tech water-filtration and conservation equipment have been installed. The Inn of the Anasazi, just a few steps from the Plaza, is indeed well situated.

The **Anasazi Restaurant & Bar** is attractive. During previous visits, I found the food tasty, but this time it was not up to par. However, the service was very good. That can happen sometimes. I have been told that Chef Oliver Ridgeway is now at the helm in the kitchen and that the restaurant will not disappoint. I definitely recommend visiting this charming establishment.

Driving Diva Factoid: Anasazi is Navajo for "ancient ones."

Las Palomas

460 W. San Francisco St.
877-982-5560
www.laspalomas.com

This small, delightful hotel (I have heard it called a bed-and-breakfast too) is owned and run by noted opera tenor Neil Rosenshine, whose enthusiasm for life, his family, and his Las Palomas is immediately evident when you meet him. Neil has retired from the stage and is now teaching in Santa Fe, New York City, and Europe.

Las Palomas is nestled into a small street called West San Francisco, which is actually just a few blocks from the Plaza and other sights in Santa Fe. It is easy to find. Parking is in the courtyard—so convenient. Immediately, as I walked up onto the porch, I noticed how friendly and hospitable everyone was.

After checking in, I was shown to my room. Each room seemed like a little casita constructed from adobe bricks. My casita had a small porch. The room was large and had sitting and kitchen areas. A complimentary continental breakfast is offered and can be enjoyed in your casita or in the reception area. Breakfast was definitely very delicious!

Though not ultrafancy, Las Palomas is a delightful and comfortable oasis for the traveler. The pluses far outweigh any minuses, although I would recommend more lighting in the room. (This may have changed or was perhaps just a tiny oversight when I was there.) I look forward to going back to Las Palomas. It is relaxing, convenient, and totally charming.

Recently, Las Palomas was able to acquire the two adjoining B&Bs—how fortunate! Also, a few blocks away, **Zona Rosa Suites** (429 San Francisco St.) is under the umbrella of Las Palomas/Neil Rosenshine. These are large accommodations of varying sizes with kitchens and full amenities, ideal for families visiting the area for a length of time or perhaps for the Opera season.

Inn and Spa at Loretto

211 Old Santa Fe Trail
800-727-5531
www.innatloretto.com

The Inn and Spa at Loretto in downtown Santa Fe is comfortable and convenient, with all the perks and amenities you could expect from a AAA Four Diamond property. In the couple of years since I was there, Condé Nast has ranked the inn number eighty-one in the United State and the spa number thirteen. Over $8 million has been spent—and spent well. I look forward to seeing the new inn and spa in person.

From the outside, the hotel looks as though it's constructed of adobe building blocks placed at different angles on top of each other. At night, the entire edifice looks magical, as lights brighten and accent surfaces here and there. The main floor is large, with many hallways, shops, and such.

Luminaria (505-984-7915), the delightful restaurant on property, is open for breakfast, lunch, dinner, and Sunday brunch. Each meal I have enjoyed at this restaurant has been good or delicious. The patio, surrounded with flowers and sculpture, is open during the summer months.

I look forward to visiting the Spa at Loretto (505-984-7997) so I can experience the "Sacred Stone" and "Native Desert Sage" massages.

Loretto Chapel

This small but magnificent chapel has a twenty-two-foot-high staircase with no center support. The construction has baffled everyone, and the builder remains unknown. As the story goes, the chapel's construction was completed, but accessing the choir loft had never been addressed and a choir loft was essential. The nuns prayed for an answer and made a novena (a nine-day period of prayer) to St. Joseph, the patron saint of carpenters. On the final day of prayers, a man looking for work arrived on a donkey with a toolbox. He immediately began work and, when he was finished, vanished, never even asking for payment. Despite repeated efforts, he never was found, and some believe it was Saint Joseph himself. Constructed with wooden pegs, the staircase has thirty-three steps and makes two complete 360-degree turns. Sit a while in the chapel. It is beautiful—a must-see!

Bishop's Lodge

Bishop's Lodge Rd.
505-983-6377
www.bishopslodge.com

This is a ranch resort for the entire family, and it is only five minutes from downtown Santa Fe. Accommodations are attractive, the hospitality friendly, and the food delicious. The resort offers a complimentary year-round shuttle to town and, in the winter, transportation to the nearby ski area.

Bishop's Lodge is a cross between a sports complex, a wellness center, a retreat, and, if desired, an escape from life's usual agendas. There are the trails for hiking and horseback riding, ranges for skeet and trap shooting, tennis, swimming, and other activities for children and adults. The latest addition, the **Villas**, can be rented for a real home away from home.

The **Las Fuentes Restaurant & Bar** has many menu options and sits in a beautiful setting. The Bishops Lodge, though just a short distance from bustling Santa Fe, allows you feel as if you are miles away.

La Posada de Santa Fe Resort and Spa

330 E. Palace Ave.
505-986-0000
www.laposada.rockresorts.com

Easy to find by car and a short walk from downtown, this property is truly an oasis. Once inside, you feel as if you are miles away from anywhere.

As of this writing, La Posada has a few very nice rituals, all gratis:

Monday: Margarita Monday (don't forget the aspirin)
Tuesday: Tropical exotic drinks by the pool
Wednesday: Wine tasting
Thursday: Cheese tasting
Friday: Chef's reception in the kitchen

Also, on Tuesday and Friday, s'mores are served by the fireplace. What pleasant ways to meet other guests! Check the rituals and plan accordingly!

The public rooms are very attractive and inviting. You feel more like you are in a private home than in a hotel. There are 159 rooms nestled into the property—a number that I would not have guessed because they are truly nestled. The rooms are attractive and well appointed. Earth tones ranging from light to dark accented the turquoise and bright orange in the decor. The art is displayed nicely, and the amenities are many. Some of the rooms have kiva fireplaces and a patio or porch. The romantic setting is unquestionably a delight for all.

Driving Diva Factoid: The original building was built by Abraham Staab in 1882 for his wife and soon-to-be-large family. It was constructed in the French Second Empire style and decorated with the finest European furnishings. Staab and his wife, Julia, entertained here. There are many stories—some of which underscore the truth that wealth does not eliminate sadness—but be that as it may, legend has it that Julia adored her home so much that she rarely left it. Some claim she is still very much on the property. Julia passed away in 1896 and Abraham in 1913. In the 1930s, the Nasons owned the property and turned it into a hotel called La Posada (Spanish for "inn" or "resting place").

Fuego is La Posada's AAA Four Diamond Award–winning restaurant. It is very attractive. I didn't feel as if I was in a commercial eatery. It is southwestern cozy. Fuego serves breakfast, lunch, dinner, and a Rancher's Brunch on Sundays. One can also dine on the Garden Patio, **Viga**, but at the end of the day, a nightcap should be had in the **Staab House**, said to be "Santa Fe's Most Romantic Bar."

The **Rock Resort Spa** is a full-service spa and "an oasis for the senses." Perhaps it is the oasis atmosphere that gives it a special feeling. It is very professional, and the facial, massage, and adobe mud wrap were excellent. Reservation are suggested. La Posada is continually upgrading, and major renovations were completed in 2009.

La Fonda

100 E. San Francisco St.
505-982-5511
www.lafondasantafe.com

This historic property was built in 1922. In 1925, the Atchinson, Topeka, & Santa Fe Railroad acquired it and leased it to the legendary Fred Harvey, who established the Harvey House hotels throughout the United States. In 1968, La Fonda came under local ownership, and its presence in downtown Santa Fe remains. The original adobe hotel was known to be "at the end of the Santa Fe trail," which happens to be in the Plaza. Its pueblo-style architecture, thick visible beams, and New Mexican decor take you away from the real world. La Fonda is not only a focal point in itself but a hub of activity with its restaurants, shops, and attractions.

There are 167 well-decorated rooms and suites. The hand-painted furniture is most attractive, and of course the southwestern architecture, furnishings, and artistic appointments all blend to provide a special ambiance. The rooms are spacious.

La Plazuela (505-995-2334) is a large, colorful restaurant, which I think was originally a courtyard and later enclosed. I found the meals good, except for one. It is a festive spot. Breakfast, lunch, and dinner are served daily, and because of its popularity, reservations are recommended.

La Fiesta Lounge is a casual spot with a light menu and a New Mexican buffet at lunchtime. At night, there is live entertainment and dancing. The sunset views are beautiful from the fifth-floor **Bell Tower Bar**. It is open seasonally. Go and enjoy a drink as you drink in the view. (Oh my!)

When I learned that the general manager, the head of public relations and marketing, and some of the staff have been part of

La Fonda for over ten years (some even longer), I was impressed. I think that is a most positive representation for the property.

Restaurants

Plaza Café
54 Lincoln Ave.
505-982-1664
www.thefamousplazacafe.com

This fifty-year-old landmark is deliciously fun. It feels more like an oversized diner with its booths, tables, and long counter. The latter I found to be an ideal place to eat and chat. Everyone is friendly and seems to have a joyous demeanor. The food is good, the staff has never met a stranger, and the prices are right. If you don't enjoy being at the Plaza Café, then there is something wrong with you. I look forward—again and again—to dining here.

Gabriel's Restaurant
4 Banana Ln., Hwy. 285
505-455-7000
www.restauranteur.com/gabriels

A short drive from downtown Santa Fe on Old Taos Highway is Gabriel's, home of some of the best ribs I've eaten. The guacamole and Caesar salad are prepared at your table, and the margaritas are made with premium tequila. The atmosphere is very casual, and the food is very excellent. If you're by yourself, you can sit at the bar for dinner and engage in friendly banter with your neighbors. This is a popular place, so reservations are important.

Café Pasqual's
121 Don Gasper
505-983-9340
www.pasquals.com

A well-known and popular place located just a block from the Plaza, Café Pasqual's is small, seating about fifty people. I was there for breakfast. I arrived early (as suggested) because Pasqual's fills up fast. The reviews are of the best variety. I think I should go back again because I would not rate it quite so highly. The decor and ambiance were great, but breakfast was only okay. Go to this landmark and decide for yourself.

Dinner for Two

106 N. Guadalupe St.
505-820-2075
www.dinnerfortwonm.com

This is just a few minutes from Las Palomas. I did go in to snoop, and what a charming and attractive family-owned restaurant. From all I saw, Chef Andrew Barnes prepares fabulous meals. Lunch is deliciously normal, while dinner he calls "eclectic continental." Looking at the menu, I noticed that all entrees are served with soup, homemade bread, and salad. Prices were reasonable. Judging from the ambiance and menu, I do not think you will be disappointed dining here.

Other Attractions

Kaune Neighborhood Market

511 Old Santa Fe Trail
505-982-2629
www.kaunes.com

This excellent grocery store also has a real butcher's shop! The latter you will probably not use, but to find a real butcher's shop is unique. I enjoyed a fresh sandwich and soup. It was just right for a tired bod and taking a meal to go. Kosher foods are also available. Kaune is pronounced "connie." Kaune should be cloned.

Georgia O'Keeffe Museum

217 Johnson St.
505-946-1000
www.okeeffemuseum.org

Georgia O'Keeffe's art is unique, and although it may not appeal to you, you should definitely go and see it. Her work makes up an impressive collection. O'Keeffe's paintings of flowers, as if seen very close up, have become almost a trademark, but there is so much more to this artist.

Born in Wisconsin on November 15, 1887, one of seven children, she never faltered in her artistic ambitions. It was when Alfred Stieglitz, the internationally known photographer, saw her work that Georgia O'Keeffe started to gain prominence.

Stieglitz was her mentor and later became her husband. They lived in New York, taking summer trips to New Mexico. Reading even a brief bio of this unique woman will give you more insight into her art. Until his death in 1946, Stieglitz untiringly promoted his wife's work. Upon his death Georgia O'Keeffe moved to her beloved New Mexico, living at her **Ghost Ranch** (www.ghostranch .org) and then in Abiquiu. She continued to work almost until her death at the age of ninety-eight.

Consignment Shops

Barkin Boutique

1107 Pen Rd.
505-986-0699

Take the phone number with you as it is a little hard to find, but it's worth the effort once you find it (at least it was when I was there). Not far from the Plaza, it is just a little out of the way for strangers to find.

Act 2: Vintage to Modern Clothing and Collectibles

839-A Paseo De Peralta
505-983-8585

This is around the block from La Posada. The owners are very friendly and offer a large selection. Their logo is "Affordable Retail Therapy."

Double Take
320 Aztec St.
505-989-8886

This includes **Double Take at the Ranch, Double Take Vintage, Double Take Santa Fe Pottery, Double Take Baby Store, Double Take Encore 505** (upscale apparel), and **Double Take Santa Fe Pottery**. All of these wonderful stores are combined in one great gathering place.

What a find! It is like a department store. You will do a "double take" when you walk into this fabulous emporium. There are so many items of quality: western, vintage, boutique, ultra upscale, collectibles, kitsch of all kinds, furniture ranging from funky to retro to fine. Then there is the maternity and baby shop and anything else you might want. I like shoes. Here I bought the most unbelievable red satin high-heel sling pumps. The heels are covered with small rhinestones. They are fantastic. They make a statement, and I adore wearing them. Okay, so I don't walk a lot in them and dance only every so often—but boy are they noticed and admired. Awesome!

Whenever I arrive in Santa Fe, I do not dawdle in getting to this Double Take's Encore 505. What a wonderful collection of fabulous chic finds. I refer to it as the Neiman Marcus of consignment shops. My trademark is upscale scarves, and at Encore 505 I always find an excellent selection. The owner is a stylish savvy woman who knows her merchandize, maintains high standards, and prices items to sell. It is very hard not to find something you probably never knew you wanted and decide to purchase.

With all Double Take's divisions, it takes time to discover its treasures. Plan accordingly. Definitely!

Jackalope
2820 Cerrillos Rd.
505-471-8539
www.jackalope.com

If you are in the mood for knickknacks of every variety, as well as wonderful, colorful, unusual oversized items you wish you could take home, then this is the place to visit. Regardless, of your purpose, a visit to this unique shop is a must. There are thousands of items and then some from literally all over the world. Large, small, practical, not so practical, unusual, and ordinary—you will probably find it here at Jackalope. The store is outside of downtown, so you will have to drive, but it is easy to find.

NORTH TO TAOS

The highway is almost a straight shot, although there are several ways to head north: 285 to 84 to 68. Check you map.

You will go through **Espanola** and **Chimayo** and pass a lot of fast fooders, some gas stations, and a few other places to stop. I wish I had had time to stop in Chimayo as I hear that Rancho de Chimayo, a hacienda and a restaurant, is perfect and charming.

Rancho de Chimayo
Ten miles past Espanola on Hwy. 76
505-351-2222
www.ranchodechimayo.com

El Santuario de Chimayo Shrine (www.archdiocesesantafe.org) is an attraction due to its sacred dirt, which, when applied, has healed most miraculously.

Embudo Station
1101 Drive St., Hwy. 68, Embudo
505-852-4707
embudostation.com

Between Santa Fe and Taos on Highway 68, Embudo Station is open from April through October for lunch and dinner. I give this restaurant the subtitle "A Culinary Treasure of Delights." The tables are staggered on different levels along the banks of the Rio

Grande. Music is live, but since you are just a stone's throw from the highway, I could also hear the passing vehicles.

The menu was full of hard choices. I learned that the smoked meats and fish here are some of the best, and the barbecue is delicious. I am not a beer connoisseur, but from what I tasted and from all reports, Embudo Station's brewed beers are some of the best. I learned that Embudo Station may have changed ownership. I hope it was a sale and not a demise!

TAOS

Taos is one of those towns that takes time to get to know. Initially, I found it rather unorganized and not upscale. Now that I have learned more about Taos, I want to go back and explore. I hear that bed-and-breakfast Casa de las Chimeneas (House of Chimneys), is excellent.

Casa de las Chimeneas
405 Cordoba Rd.
505-575-4777

Casa has been awarded the prestigious AAA Four Diamond Award. Applause to its owner and innkeeper, Susan Vernon. Also, it should be noted that despite the hot desert summers, there is skiing close by at Taos Ski Valley.

Taos Ski Valley
PO Box 90
866-968-7386 or 800-776-1111
www.skitaos.org

This is an arty area. I was lucky to be introduced to one of the leading local artists, Walt Gonske. I visited his studio and learned that he had studied in New York, where he was a successful illustrator. He has lived in Taos since the 1970s, and from the look of his vibrant works, you can tell he definitely relates to the area.

El Monte Sagrado
317 Kit Carson Rd.
575-758-3502
www.elmontesagrado.com

Named El Monte Sagrado, meaning "the sacred mountain," because of its view of Taos Mountain, which is sacred to the people of Taos Pueblo, this $50 million resort is the baby of Virginian Tom Worrell, who spared little in the format and imagining of this oasis. This quiet place incorporates state-of-the-art ecological preservations. Now this unique property is under the aegis of Richard Kessler and is in the Kessler Collection.

The property might take a little getting used to as it is not your usual escape. It is beautifully different, almost exotic. Learning about the powers of the amethyst and tourmaline stones, the land, the space, the waters, and the plants added an entirely new perspective and indulgence to my visit at El Monte Sagrado.

Major expansions have taken place. When I was there, there were thirty-six elegantly appointed suites situated around the sacred circle in the middle of the property; now there are eighty-four. The Morocco Suite was my residence for two days. It was spacious, beautifully appointed, cozy, and romantic. I loved the sofa in front of the fireplace. (I wish it would have fit on top of my car!)

The lighting is a bit dim, and the bedside lights are a little hard to turn off. When I was there, the bathrooms were large, and the towels were humongous; in fact, they were almost too big. One of the most pleasant experiences was getting into my own private hot tub outside the room. I could have spent the night in the hot tub, but unshriveling would have been a morning challenge, I am certain.

Dining: My dining at **De La Tierra** (575-737-9855) was prior to Kessler's acquisition. Some of the items I tasted were excellent, and others were not quite so. But then, that can be true at every restaurant. It all depends on the day you are there and the staff. I am certain with the new executive chef and membership in the Kessler Collection, dining is an epicurean delight. The dining room itself is most attractive. The high ceiling, cozy clusters of seating arrangements, soft lighting, and huge, colorful paintings on the high, flat wall surfaces create a special aura and experience.

One must enjoy at least one spa treatment in the unusual and exotic setting of the **Living Spa at El Monte Sagrado**. In my travels, I have experienced a lot of varied treatments, but the "most unique" award goes to what I experienced here: sound and vibrational therapy. "This two-hour session integrates the subtle energy work of Polarity and Cranial Sacral with Acutonics, which is a system that uses tuning forks to balance the head and body with sound vibrations. The goal of this treatment is to interface the physical body . . . with the energetic body, meridians, chakras, and diverse energetic circuits of the body." Did I feel balanced? Heaven knows. I felt just fine, but then I also felt fine when I arrived. It was an experience!

My total experience at El Monte Sagrado was stellar. You must experience this very exceptional place. I love this quote from their brochure: "Take only memories, leave nothing but footprints" (Chief Seattle). I think that is wonderful.

FYI: El Monte Sagrado is now part of Marriott's Autograph Collection, although the property is still independently owned. Those belonging to the Marriott's Club will earn points.

I left Taos on Highway 64 for **Ojo Caliente**. I did not have time to stop, but the Millicent Rogers Museum is along the way.

Millicent Rogers Museum
1504 Millicent Rogers Rd.
575-758-2462
www.millicentrogers.com

Driving Diva Factoid: Millicent Rogers was the granddaughter of the founder of Standard Oil. She was a true beauty and fashion icon.

From all I have read, she lived life to the fullest. Her attraction to the Taos area was immediate. Not only was she a collector, but she designed some noteworthy jewelry. Her youngest son, the late Paul Peralta-Ramos, left many collections to the Millicent Rogers Museum.

Highway 64 is a good road but rather desolate. I went over the **Rio Grande Gorge Bridge**, which is worth a quick stop and a fast picture.

Further along, you discover the Earthship World Headquarters.

Earthship World Headquarters

2 Earthship Way
575-751-0462
earthship.net

Here passive solar houses are made out of recycled materials, including automobile tires. The water used is from the rain, and the power is from the sun. The subdivision sits on 633 acres, and there are approximately forty-six homes. It is designed for 130. There is a visitor's center, a video tour, and an option to rent an Earthship home for just a night or two.

FYI: The "tour" consists of your paying $5, then sitting on a bench to watch a video

Driving Diva Reminder: There's not much around. Remember gas and water.

Ojo Caliente

50 Los Banos Dr.
505-583-2233
www.ojocalientespa.com

About an hour and a half from downtown Santa Fe, this unique oasis of mineral springs is so special that only seeing is believing. It is one of the oldest health resorts in North America and the only one in the world with its combination of four geothermal mineral waters. It is a peaceful and majestic place to visit.

There are seven springs with four different types of mineral water here. The minerals are arsenic, iron, soda, and lithia. The one hundred thousand gallons of geothermal mineral water steam to the surface daily and afford each participant an unusual experience not quickly forgotten. To me they are exceptionally wonderful. You can obtain therapeutic massages and special body and facial treatments here.

I read somewhere, and think it is worth sharing, that drinking any of the waters while bathing helps to eliminate excessive acids and other impurities, creating more vitality and energy.

I have visited Ojo several times. On my first visit, the lodgings are modest, clean, and comfortable. My room had two beds, a TV without a remote, a small porch, a tiny kitchen area, and a bathroom with only a toilet and sink. Remember, you have been soaking all day, and your skin feels so wonderful. You do not need a shower. That was back then. On my second visit, some fixing up had been done, and now I read that a lot has been done. From the pictures on their site, indeed the circa 1930 buildings and aura have changed. Regardless, I know that Ojo Caliente remains a wonderful oasis in every way possible. The fact that it was named one of the "Top 10 Best Hot Springs in the World" says something. Go and enjoy.

Also available to rent are the **Adobe, Hill, and Mauro houses**, each with several bedrooms, complete kitchens, bathrooms, and such.

Personal Testimonial: During this last odyssey, I slashed the top of my arm. It was a deep cut positioned so that I would inadvertently bump it periodically. After my initial soak at Ojo, I applied the indigenous Ojo mud and let it cake on my arm. I baked in the sun for a while, and when the spirit moved me, I got into the spring and cleaned off. I could not believe that the cut on my arm had closed dramatically. By mid-evening, it was truly almost healed!

The **spa** provides massage therapy and body treatments of various descriptions. Yoga classes are exceptional, and the "Stretch and Soak" routine is a must. One can enjoy a wonderful wrap between 8:30 a.m. to 8 p.m. for about $12. I choose the evening. It is recommended that you have a good soak in the geothermal waters to increase your body temperature before being wrapped. You lie on a table in a dimly lit room. An attendant wraps you in a sheet, mummy-like, and you just lie there for about thirty minutes. The purpose is to withdraw impurities from your body. It's a must-do unless you are claustrophobic.

Alert: Consumption of alcohol when using the facilities may impair judgment.

Ojo Caliente's **Artesian Restaurant** is casual dining at its best. The southwestern cuisine is creative. Lighter fare and vegetarian delights are also on the menu. It is truly a friendly place, and the staff obviously enjoy working at Ojo.

There are also mountain bike and horseback trails to enjoy.

Driving Diva Factoid: On the property is the only round barn in New Mexico, and it is said to be the only remaining adobe round barn in the United States. It is a short walk from the main springs. Renovations are ongoing. This unique building will be available for yoga retreats, seminars, and special events.

Rancho de San Juan

U.S. Hwy. 285 between Espanola and Ojo Caliente, 3.5 miles north of the junction of Hwys. 84 and 285
505-783-6818
www.ranchodesanjuan.com

Thirty-five miles from Santa Fe and fifteen minutes from Ojo Caliente, you will find the award-winning Rancho de San Juan. This beautiful desert oasis offers guests gorgeous suites, individual casitas, exceptional dining, and more. Here, in the middle of 225 desert acres, you will find upscale touches everywhere. Starched table linens, polished silver, sparkling crystal, and beautiful dinnerware all enhance the gourmet dining. The Frette linens, the fresh flowers, and all the attention to detail made the accommodations superb.

Fashionable and friendly, Rancho de San Juan, though described in the brochure as a "country inn and restaurant," is anything but. Its owners, David Heath and John Johnson, are perfectionists and professionals. John also has the title of chef, to which I add "outstanding." One does not have to stay at this oasis to dine there.

At this desert haven, you will find the **Sandstone Shrine**, which took artist Ra Paulette two years to complete. Commissioned by the owners, this unique work is in a sandstone butte on the side of **Black Mesa**. Cathedral windows look out onto the Ojo Caliente River valley and toward the **Jemez Mountains**. Strategically placed mirrors and inlays of stones within the interior create a most unique place of meditation. This shrine has been the scene of weddings, small concerts, and special events.

There is much to do in the area, including white-water rafting, swimming, hiking, skiing, and fishing.

Lodge and Ranch at Chama

16253 Hwy. 84 S.
575-756-2133
www.lodgeatchama.com

This is possibly one of the most upscale hunting and fishing lodges I've ever visited. If hunting and fishing are on your agenda, and your pockets are fairly deep, then this is the place to go! It is a trophy. Reservations are a must.

I-25 NORTH TO COLORADO

I did not take the most direct route as I went back to Santa Fe and then onto I-25 North. I will take part of the blame, but for sure, the signage could be better. I was not too perturbed as this long route took me to Las Vegas, New Mexico, which proved a unique serendipity.

LAS VEGAS
(POPULATION APPROXIMATELY 15,000)

Las Vegas, New Mexico, was named over seventy years before that *other* Las Vegas. Driving into town, I immediately felt a special charm and quality. It is not glitzy or bustling, but it oozes something most pleasant.

Entering this New Mexico town, you go over the railroad tracks and straight onto Douglas Avenue, the center of town. It was quite busy. There was a parking place in front of an antique store whose windows were chockablock full (just my type of diversion!). Unfortunately, I just learned that it has closed. Oh my! What a challenge to get rid of all those items. Built in 1898, the Castaneda on Railroad Avenue was one of Fred Harvey's famous Harvey House hotels. Although now closed, it was one of the originals.

El Fidel Hotel
500 Douglas Ave.
505-425-6761
www.hotelelfidel.com

Plaza Hotel
230 Plaza
505-425-3591
www.plazahotel-nm.com

Built in 1882, the Plaza was dubbed "the Belle of the South-west." In 1899 Teddy Roosevelt had a reunion of his Rough Riders at the hotel. Although Victorian in style, it has twenty-first-century amenities since its restoration in 1982. There is also the **Landmark Grill** at the Plaza and a resident ghost, Byron T. Mills.

FYI: More than nine hundred buildings in Las Vegas, New Mexico, are listed on the National Register of Historic Homes. In August, the *People's Fair* takes place, and the crafts sold are all original and hand-made. I am certain this event is fun for all. There is also a fiesta on the Fourth of July and a motorcycle rally at the end of July.

Charlie's Bakery & Cafe
715 Douglas Ave.
505-426-1921

This is the meeting, greeting, and eating place of Las Vegas. Proprietors Charlie and Elizabeth Sandoval offer absolutely delicious fare and friendly service. The delicious quesadillas were made with homemade tortillas. For dessert I chose a fresh homemade donut that had just come out of the fryer. Charlie's is a must if you are ever near Las Vegas, New Mexico. Even if you have to make a detour, just go; you will enjoy.

Driving Diva Surprise Factoid: In 1846, S. W. Kearney delivered a speech in the plaza claiming New Mexico for the United States. In 1880, when the railroad arrived, Las Vegas boomed. The *Duncan Opera House*, a Carnegie library, a Harvey House hotel, an electric street railway, and so much more were built. Many notorious characters were in Las Vegas: Doc Holliday, his girlfriend Big Nose Kate, Billy the Kid, Jesse James, Wyatt Earp, Mysterious Dave Mather, Hoodoo Brown, the Durango Kid, and more! Historian Ralph E. Twitchell said, "Without exception there was no town which harbored a more disreputable gang of desperados and outlaws than Las Vegas, New Mex."

Fast Forward: Movies filmed in Las Vegas include *Easy Rider*, *Convoy*, *Speechless*, *Red Dawn*, *No Country for Old Men*, *Vampires*, and *All the Pretty Horses*. Today, Las Vegas, New Mexico, is starting to boom again. Visit soon. Maybe I'll see you there.

Driving Diva Reminder: On I-25 North, there are long stretches with nada around. Gas up often. A gas station on this road had a large collection of old cars and funky memorabilia. I cannot find details in my notes. (That doesn't happen too often.) I hope you find it. It is fun.

COLORADO

T his is an outdoorsy state with rustic beauty and cosmopolitan ambiance. Sports abound. Everything is tweaked with touches of the spunky, brazen boldness of the old Wild West and today's savvy.

Two major interstates lead to Colorado: I-70 and I-25. The following are discoveries I made on different interstates.

I-70 West from Kansas: If you are going to Denver, Boulder, Vail, Glenwood Springs, or Grand Junction, you stay on I-70. If you are going to Colorado Springs, from I-70 you take Highway 24 and drive south.

TO COLORADO SPRINGS

I-70 Meets Highway 24

Limon

There are quite a few places in Limon, and it is a good place to stretch, get gas, and so forth. I did not see the sign for Highway 24 right away, but shortly there it was. Watch carefully.

FYI: Here is a preview of what I saw and now share with you. Though not bustling, Route 24 is a good road and not boring.

Rusty Spur Bunk and Barn

583 S. Forty Rd., Woodland Park

719-687-4260

www.rustyspurbunkandbarn.com

I think that probably quite a few rusty spurs jingled here. There were mobile homes and a sign for correctional facilities. The area doesn't look very upscale, but there is a Denny's, a MacDonald's, an Arby's, and such. The road is flanked by large farmed fields.

I am not sure I would recommend this road at night to a novice road warrioress. There are not many services, people, or places to stop.

Mathason

Going through Mathason, I saw an antique store too tempting not to visit. There were tables full of all sorts of items in the front by the road. This is the type of place where you would not want to have to do the inventory! Unfortunately, it seems to have closed.

Continuing West on Highway 24

As you drive on, you pass Simla (population 500) and **Ramah** (population 100), with a tiny sign for a post office. I had seen several small post offices at this point. There are still lots of big farmed fields—or maybe they are now ranches. 44 miles to Colorado Springs.

Sights

Big beautiful house. Lots of bails of hay or similar.

A Day's Inn is under construction.

Texaco Station.
Sign: BULLS FOR SALE.
Airport. Frontier Charter Academy.

Bulldog Drive-in
Open Seven Days a Week.

Piper & Son's Insurance

Ace Hardware

Toy Museum

Cadillac Jack's Antique Store
1001 Fifth St., Calhan
719-347-2000
www.cadillacjacksantiques.com

Labeled "Colorado's Most Unique Antique Store," Cadillac Jacks is supposedly rated number one. My steering wheel was pulling, but I did not stop! Mistake! Now that I have researched the shop, oh my! I'm hoping to visit this emporium soon.

Suggestion: Bring a gift list. I think Cadillac Jack's might be a one-stop shopping venture.

Gradually, mountains start to loom on the horizon. They are ominous, awesome, and impressive.

COLORADO SPRINGS

Driving into Colorado Springs, you realize that you are approaching a very special area. Not only are all the standard stores, fast fooders, and emporiums here, but you have a feeling that there is more to the area. Colorado Springs covers a large and beautiful area. There is much to see and do in this special place. The following is only a smattering but represents some of the best—and in some instances the most unusual—of my discoveries. There are hotels and resorts of all sizes and calibers, with wonderful ambiances. Here are a few of the most special.

The Broadmoor
1 Lake Ave.
719-577-5775
www.broadmoor.com

Not one but all aspects of the Broadmoor are exceptional. It is easy to see why this property has, for thirty-one years, held the AAA Five Diamond Award. It is almost as awesome as the mountains in the background.

History: It all began with the unbelievable vision, as well as the luck and timing, of Philadelphia entrepreneur Spencer Penrose. Others had discovered this special area, but Penrose was the force. In 1897 another entrepreneur, Prussian count James Pourtales, had formed the Broadmoor Land and Investment Company and purchased twenty-four hundred acres. He decided to build the Broadmoor Casino as well as a small hotel. Fortunately or unfortunately, depending which side you are on, Pourtales had off-and-on financial problems. In 1916, Spencer Penrose purchased the forty-acre Broadmoor Casino and Hotel together with the adjoining four hundred acres. Contracting the New York architectural firm of Warren and Wetmore, Penrose wished to build the most beautiful resort not just in Colorado but in the world. And so it started and has continued. One must read all about this exceptional place, but for this review, I will pick up the story with my discoveries and experiences at this most special property.

Regardless of how you arrive in Colorado Springs, to get to the Broadmoor, you will be in an automobile. You follow **Circle Drive** until it becomes **Lake Avenue,** and in approximately two miles, you will be face-to-face with this magnificent property.

The Broadmoor is a place you dream of going to and save pennies (more accurately dollar bills) to visit. You will not be disappointed.

Upon your arrival, under the porte cochere, the attendants who greet you are pleasant and professional. Then, as you enter you start to oooh and ahhh. A broad smile covers your face because you realize how lucky you are to be there.

Check-in is friendly and efficient. Wherever on the property you are staying, the well-trained bellman will take you to your accommodations. Despite the size, it is not difficult finding your way around.

From where you enter on the ground level, you can take the escalator to the mezzanine level. There you will find an unobstructed view of the mountains and **Cheyenne Lake**, which is absolutely awesome. The public rooms are furnished in a grand manner. In the corner of one grand room are the knowledgeable, efficient, and most pleasant concierges. Wherever you are on property, you are surrounded by mountain splendor.

Accommodations: Finding your accommodations is not a problem. If you do get lost, there are phones on each floor by the elevator to call for directions.

Many touches simply add up to good planning. The small table in the hall by your door is so convenient.

The rooms are spacious and beautiful. The appointments are correct, and the attention to detail is impressive. The bedroom designs have been created exclusively for the Broadmoor. The beds are possibly some of the most comfortable in the world, judging from my experiences as well as comments I heard from other guests. If rated, it would be off the charts! Comfortable, crisp, and luxurious is an understatement. Something about these Egyptian cotton sheets changes your bedtime demeanor and your night's sleep to dreamy. The bathroom is spacious, with a trendy louvered window that looks into the bedroom. I didn't see one room that was not excellent in every way.

Dining: Each of the eleven restaurants is a gastronomically magnificent culinary delight. Here are some suggestions:

Breakfast: You are on your own. Coffee on the porch is idyllic, as you watch the mountains become more vivid and the lake sparkle in the morning light. The free-ranging ducks are excellent companions as they walk by and check you out. These ducks are permanent Broadmoor residents. Lucky ducks!

Lunch: The **Pool Café** (719-577-5733) is casual, comfortable, and delicious.

Cocktails: A slow "imbibe" at the **Hotel Bar** is delicious. The atmosphere is just right.

Dinner: The **Penrose Room** (719-577-5773) is simply the ultimate. Here you will enjoy French cuisine accompanied by live dinner music, and between courses a turn on the dance floor is suggested.

If less formality is preferred, then consider **Charles Court** (719-577-5774), the **Tavern** (719-577-5772), and the **Lake Terrace Dining Room** (719-577-5771). Each is only excellent.

Shopping: Shopping is challenging. There are fifteen shops. What to buy? What *not* to buy? There is so much, and it's so hard to choose. Maybe just looking is the answer. Have fun!

Sports: The three immaculate golf courses are reserved for Broadmoor guests and club members. The courses play their way through the most beautiful scenery, with the Colorado Rockies as a backdrop and the brilliant sky overhead. You can also choose from among tennis, swimming, hiking, fishing, and horseback riding.

Spa: Choosing the pièce de resistance at this famed property is difficult, but I give an accolade to the **Spa at the Broadmoor** (719-577-5770). Spas are so "in," but from all that I have visited, this beautiful, ninety-thousand-square-foot spa, opened in 1994, is hard to surpass. In 2004 extensive additions were made. It has fifty-five treatment rooms and over one hundred services for men and women. There are now two $100,000 Silver TAG Serenity Showers with nineteen computerized showerheads for varying strengths. A list of all that is available at the Broadmoor Spa would leave one wondering, Can this really be? It can and is. You may not leave the spa looking like a spa model, but you will feel like one, and the experience will be exceptional. Not only is this spa beautiful in design, but it is managed so professionally and warmly. It is nearly perfect, which is rare, and the prices are sensible.

This 744-room, three-thousand-acre property has continually received the AAA Five Diamond and Forbes (formerly Mobil) Five Star awards. The Broadmoor won the Five Star award for the forty-sixth consecutive year in 2005. In 2006 it was awarded the AAA Five Diamond for the thirty-first year. It has also received the *Wine Spectator* and DiRoNA awards.

A property is nothing without its staff. Here the staff on all levels is superb. I compliment Alison Scott, communications director, for the job she does and the way in which she achieves her goals. She deals with all types (the media, celebrities, guests at special events, and more) and handles even the challenging ones masterfully. I have seen her in action, and she somehow makes everyone feel special. What a talent!

FYI: Alison's son is Jeremy Abbot, the Olympic skater.

This most special of mountain properties is almost a city within itself. The Broadmoor is synonymous with exceptional, one-of-a-kind magnificence. Enjoy, even if it is only for a walk through, afternoon tea, a drink, or a meal. You will definitely come away with more than you arrived with—even if it is just the knowledge of this exceptional place.

Old Colorado City

This real gold rush town was founded in 1859, and by 1862 it was on the decline.

Old Town Guesthouse
115 S. Twenty-sixth St.
719-632-9194
www.oldtown-guesthouse.com

Upon entering you realize that this is a serious, upscale, friendly B&B. Built in 1997, it fits well into historic Old Colorado City, which seems to survive more in legend than in actuality.

There are new innkeepers since I was there, Shirley and Don Wicks. The property is more than the usual bed-and-breakfast. There is even an elevator, which is a luxury and not the norm for B&Bs. Each guest room is named for a flower: Victorian Rose, Indian Paintbrush, Old Town Cactus, to name a few. Depending on the selected room, there are fireplaces, hot tubs, private porches, and steam showers. There is a game room with a pool table as well as an exercise room. Guests' safety and total comfort is not in question. The attention to privacy is impressive.

My room was well appointed and cozy, with a small private porch. I enjoyed viewing the area, realizing that I was on the site of, or near to, the 1892 city hall, fire station, and jail, as well as the saloons, gambling parlors, and brothels. I doubt if the word "dull" could ever have been applied Old Colorado City.

Breakfast was a delicious feast. You can be private or gregarious. Old Town Guesthouse is but minutes from so many of the fabulous attractions. A visit will be a delightful experience. Enjoy! Reservations are a must!

MANITOU SPRINGS
(POPULATION APPROXIMATELY 5,000)

Manitou Springs (pronounced "man-it-two") is four miles west of Colorado Springs and sixty-five miles south of Denver. It is absolutely charming, quaint, artsy, and historic, with an elevation of 6,320 feet. Plan to spend some time in Manitou Springs.

During a previous trip to the area, I had enjoyed a delicious lunch with friends on the big porch at the Cliff House as well as a brief tour of the property. It immediately went on my "come back" list. That is just what I did, and I stayed at this attractive property. Put it on your list.

Cliff House at Pikes Peak

306 Cañon Ave.

719-685-3000

www.thecliffhouse.com

The facade is Queen Anne Victorian, and the theme is continued inside on the ground floor. Originally a twenty-room boarding-house, after a $10 million renovation and continual upgrades, the fifty-five-room Cliff House is current and attractive. The celebrity-themed suites are distinctive. This is a cozy, wonderful property.

I stayed in the Clark Gable Suite on the fifth floor—or more ac-curately the fourth and a half floor. You take the elevator to the fourth floor and walk a very few steps up to the door of the suite. I have stayed in many unique rooms, but this suite, with the bath-tub in the bedroom sitting area—totally open—is near the top of the unique list. I have been told that the open bathtub is popular. Whatever they say . . .

Gable was indeed handsome. There are several large pictures of this debonair, immaculately attired gentleman. They don't make them like him anymore! One of his pictures is hanging in a sort of unusual spot. His beautiful eyes are on you in your most personal and private moments. Yes, the toilet seat is heated, as is the towel bar, but the washbasin was not well positioned. The air-conditioning was a bit loud, but that was probably only temporary. The attention to detail is evident. The amenities were nice. A tiny amount of fine tuning would help. Even Gable was fine-tuned for his movie roles. Everyone at this property is friendly, efficient, and top-drawer. The dining room is attractive, but being a person who thrives on color, I thought this room needed a little perking up—even just a few fresh, bright flowers on the tables would help.

Dinner was fine, and the complimentary breakfast buffet was good. The newspaper is delivered to your room when requested.

The Cliff House is well situated if you want to discover and explore the area—and there is a lot to do in Manitou Springs. You cannot help but enjoy the area and this property. Even if you just sit on the big porch and watch the scenery, you will be glad you did.

It is said that the Cliff House is expanding. The hotel has received several prestigious awards. All the fine tuning and awards, I believe, are due to the dedicated general manager Paul York. Congratulations!

Two miscellaneous must-dos in the area are the Pikes Peak Cog Railway and the Flying W Ranch.

Pikes Peak Cog Railway
515 Ruxton Ave.
719-685-5401
www.cograilway.com

What a way to spend three hours and ten minutes! The name Cog Railway refers to the "cog wheel" gear that allows the train to climb far steeper gradients than standard railroads.

I have taken this trip twice and would do it again. It is not only an interesting experience, but you see something different every time you look. It is extremely well run.

Reservations are a must. Adult tickets cost $34; children ride for $18.50 (in 2011). Plan ahead.

Everyone has a seat on the train (therefore reservations are mandatory). The pleasant and informative attendants narrate the thirteen-mile trip as you head up Pikes Peak.

The temperature drops thirty degrees between where you board and the top of Pikes Peak. Take a sweater. Also use the facilities before you get on the train as there are no bathrooms on the railroad, and there is no stopping.

Pikes Peak was named after explorer Zebulon Pike. There is a tremendous amount of interesting history about the famous peak and the development of the cog railroad. Initial credit goes to Zalmon Simmons, inventor and founder of Simmons Mattress Company, for promoting the development of the cog railroad. Spencer Penrose, local entrepreneur and builder of the Broadmoor Hotel, eventually purchased the Cog Railway.

Heading up the mountain, you see vistas of extreme expanses, wild animals, trees, wildflowers, and so much more—all composing a magnificent panorama.

The hostess was pleasant and most informative. She related some of the questions she has been asked,

"At what altitude does a deer change into an elk?"
"What is the distance between mile markers?"

She also reminded us that Katharine Lee Bates, who wrote the lyrics to "America the Beautiful," was inspired by the vistas of Pikes Peak and that Pikes Peak is not the highest mountain in Colorado; that distinction belongs to **Mount Elbert**.

Due to the altitude, it is not unusual to feel woozy. When you get to the top, walk around. There are lots of souvenir shops, food establishments, bathrooms, and magnificent views. A do-not-miss are the homemade, fresh, warm donuts! So good! They seem to settle woozy tummies.

It is fun to make a call from the top of Pikes Peak.

From what I understand, Colorado Springs believes it encompasses Manitou Springs, but Manitou Springs considers itself a separate entity.

Back in Manitou Springs, **Tejon Street** is full of shops of all varieties.

Van Briggle Pottery
1024 S. Tejon St.
719-633-7729
www.vanbriggle.com

Started more than a century ago, Van Briggle is one of the oldest active great potteries in the United States. It was founded by Artus Van Briggle, who came to Colorado Springs after years of studying in America and Europe. He and his talented wife, Anne, began making this fine pottery, which was an immediate success. The designs were art nouveau with satin matte glazes. Today their wares are seen in prominent museums in the United States and abroad.

Unfortunately, Artus succumbed at age thirty-five to tuberculosis, but Anne continued their work, establishing a superb legacy that endures today.

While in the Manitou Springs area, be sure to see some of the unique neighborhoods. There are shops of all varieties. **Colorado Avenue** is a good focal point and landmark to use in the area.

FYI: In the immediate vicinity, there are seven mineral springs that are open to the public free of charge.

Flying W Ranch
3330 Chuckwagon Rd.
719-598-4000 or 800-232-3599 (FLYW)
www.flyingw.com

"Winter, Summer, Spring or Fall, Flying W Ranch has it all" . . . and they aren't fooling! The Flying W is neither fancy nor glamorous nor boring. It is authentic, fun, and a must-do.

I leave you to read the history of this unique ranch on the Internet. Suffice it to say, the Flying W is a working ranch that has specialized in food and entertainment since the 1950s. It is privately owned and operated by Russ Wolfe. His late wife, Marian, who is dearly missed, was an active participant from the beginning. Now several of their children also help manage this one-of-a-kind enterprise.

What will you enjoy if you buy a ticket (in 2011, $22 for adults, $12 for children ages six to twelve, and $5 for children age three to five)? For starters, it will be a most unique evening. You park and walk through the gates into an authentically restored western town filled with many authentic items from the 1800s and early 1900s. Many of the shops have items to sell. The **Blacksmith** and **Christmas** shops, the **Dry Goods Store**, and the **Little Church** are there to visit. Be sure to visit **Marian's Cooking Library**. You can copy recipes on the free copy machine and then try them at home. Tours of the Flying W run from 5 p.m. to 7:15 p.m.

There is outside seating for fourteen hundred people. You are not crowded. If, as they say, "Mother Nature is not kind," there is inside seating for fourteen hundred. I have spent a Flying W evening both outside and in. Not to worry. Regardless of where you are, I repeat, you are not crowded, and you will have a good time with lots of smiles and laughs.

Here's a synopsis of the evening's format: You will arrive early and tour. The dinner bell will sound, and you will (surprisingly) quickly find your seat at one of the long, outdoors chuckwagon picnic tables. Each table has a number. When your table's number is called, you go through the chow line. The menu includes your choice of beef or chicken, foil-wrapped baked potatoes, Flying W beans, chunky applesauce, old-fashioned spice cake, coffee, and lemonade.

By now, if you are at all friendly, you will have spoken with a variety of people. It's so interesting. After dinner, the tables are quickly cleaned, and the show begins. The world-famous **Flying W Wranglers** entertain and put on a real western show. It's a little hokey but very genuine and fun. It is a show you will enjoy from start to finish. You will wish it lasted longer, and you will probably by a CD so you can sing along as you recall this most unique evening.

From Boulder or Colorado Springs, Denver is but a short drive.

DENVER

Situated at the foot of the Rocky Mountains, this delightful Mile High City, aka the Unsinkable Molly Brown City, is attractive, vibrant, and ever improving. It is also a sporty city, with seven professional sports teams, ninety golf courses, and 650 miles of paved bike trails. It also brews more beer than any other city.

I like to stay downtown and recommend the following hotels, listed in alphabetical order: the Brown Palace, the Magnolia, and the Oxford. There are other noteworthy hotels, but with these three, I speak from experience.

Brown Palace Hotel
321 Seventeenth St.
303-297-3111
www.brownpalace.com

The Brown Palace is grand, stately, and impressive, displaying both Victorian and Italian Renaissance architectural styles. As you stand in the lobby and look upward to the impressive six tiers of cast-iron balconies, the stained glass ceiling showers the lobby with colors. Two of the cast-iron panels were installed upside down. Can you spot them? Instead of the ladies dancing on their feet, they are standing on their heads.

It has been a few years since I stayed at the Brown. My accommodations were attractive. The bathroom was all right. A bit of attention was needed, but nothing was objectionable. I recently learned that indeed there has been attention to the rooms, so "good" has probably just become "better and better."

There is a lot to see in this historic property. Be sure to take a guided tour or get a copy of "A Walking Tour of the Brown Palace Hotel" and discover what the walls reveal. Many presidents have stayed at the Brown, and there are lots of tales to tell. President Dwight D. Eisenhower was practicing his golf swing in his room and made a dent in the fireplace. It is still there in what is now called the Eisenhower Suite.

A unique aspect of the Brown that I like is that its water is drawn from its own artesian well deep below the hotel's foundation. It requires no added purifiers. This water is also used in the spa.

The **Spa at the Brown** (303-312-8940) is new since my last visit, but I report some of the general facts. The $3 million spa is fifty-two hundred square feet encompassing two floors. The Brown water is used at the spa. I have read that this is the only place in the United States where Auriege skin care is available. Supposedly these products from the Auriege River have special antiaging elements. All the usual spa treatments are available.

There are several places to dine at the Brown: The **Palace Arms** is continually rated as one of the best Denver restaurants, where fine dining is the norm. The **Churchill** is a cigar bar and restaurant where some of the finest cigars can be purchased and enjoyed. The bar is open every day, with hours varying. Lunch and dinner are served. The **Ship Tavern** is a casual restaurant, which serves its own mircobrewed beer on tap plus a large selection of bottled beers. Casual dining here can include prime rib, seafood, Maine lobster sandwiches, Buffalo burgers, and such. Watching a sporting event on the plasma TV is a given. **Ellyngton's** is for upscale breakfast, lunch, and dinner or a lavish Sunday Dom Perignon Brunch. The **Atrium Lobby** is the place for tea or cocktails.

The Brown Palace is convenient to a lot of downtown. (See the **Sixteenth Street Mall** below.)

Magnolia Hotel
818 Seventeenth St.
303-607-9000
www.magnoliahoteldenver.com

Convenient to downtown attractions (i.e., the **Sixteenth Street Mall, Coors Field**, the **Mile High Stadium**), this attractive property has a lot going for it. The staff are very friendly and helpful, and parking is on the premises—so convenient!

The following comments are based on my stay. The decor was more modern than traditional. The rooms were not fancy, floral, or frilly, but they were nice and comfortable. The lighting was fair, the clock was broken, and a bulb was out. My accommodations must have been considered a suite as all suites have kitchen accommodations. There is no turn down service at night, which is not a big deal! On the lower level, called the **Club**, there is a very nice complimentary breakfast bar. I have learned that in the Club, a pool table and a poker table have been added, and all the rooms have been renovated; the suites will follow suit. For guests, the drinks at **Harry's Bar** are discounted. Cookies and milk are served in the evenings. There were far more pluses than minuses. I look forward to seeing the refurbished rooms and suites at the Magnolia Hotel. I am certain that it is all wonderful. When I was there and as of this writing, the general manager is a woman. Yes! They do add a certain charm to a property.

I have stayed at the Magnolia Hotel in Dallas and in Omaha and recommend both.

The Oxford

1600 Seventeenth St.
303-628-5400
www.theoxfordhotel.com

I made another return visit to this historic Victorian boutique hotel and, as always, found it to be an antique gem with modern conveniences. Immediately upon arrival, as you check in at the antique original front desk, you sense old-world charm with quiet calm. The key to your room is a real key on a large, beautiful tassel. Nice!

The eighty guest rooms—no two are alike—are well appointed with several French and English antiques. I adored the small-tile bathroom floors, the pedestal sink, and the long bench for items. The bathtub was yellow in a black-and-white bathroom. The tub knobs were well marked, and the toilet seat was not a horseshoe shape. Yes! The bathroom soap was most pleasantly aromatic. The bed was very comfortable, and although the sheets didn't really fit tightly, a tag stated that they were 100 percent Egyptian cotton, but no thread count was given.

Now all has changed. There have been upgrades, new decor, and so forth. From the pictures I have seen, all has been done to perfection and in the proper way. Of course, each room has all the modern requirements mixed with antiques.

I love that the rug in the elevator states what day it is. How original! How easy it is to forget the day, especially when traveling. Complimentary morning coffee is served in the hallway on each floor and also in the lobby. All the oversized furniture is attractive and comfortable with new coverings.

The hotel is located conveniently to **Coors Field**, the **Pepsi Center**, and the **Denver Performing Arts Complex**; it is also just a few blocks from the **Sixteenth Street Mall**.

The Oxford Hotel was built in 1891 by the same architect who designed the Brown Palace a year later, making the Oxford Hotel Denver's oldest grand hotel. It was reported back then that the hotel was basically ahead of its time with gadgets and opulence, its own power plant, the most perfect steam heating, electric and gas lighting, and such. And on "each floor bathrooms had separate water closets with the latest improved sanitary appliances." The report also added that the kitchen was situated so that none of the cooking aromas could penetrate into the hotel. With everything from a barber shop, to a pharmacy, to a Western Union, to stables, to, of course, a saloon, the Oxford was really a city within a city. It had a "vertical railway," now called an elevator. It was, and today it still is, a tiny modern gem.

The Oxford Hotel today has true old-world charm. It is one of "Colorado's Most Romantic Hotels" and one of the "50 Best Hotels in the World," according to *Hemisphere Magazine*. The Oxford's card states, "Where the past and present join to perfection." I agree.

Be certain to take a tour of the hotel; see the oversized men's necessities downstairs and find out about the tunnels leading away from the hotel. All I add is, "Men will be men."

The hotel's Cadillac car with friendly driver is at your disposal, at no charge, to chauffeur you to any place within two miles. You can call for the car to come get you when you are ready to return to the Oxford. This is a wonderful service, particularly for women.

The **Cruise Room** (303-825-1107) off the hotel's lobby opened in 1933 and is in the style of the cocktail lounge on the famed *Queen Mary* cruise liner. It is art deco in style, and the atmosphere is absolutely friendly. Everyone always raves about the drinks, and I can attest to their quality, especially the lemon martini or was it a vodka gimlet? The chrome-with-red-leather seats add to the comfort of this bar, as do the delicious liquids.

McCormick's Fish House & Bar (303-825-1107) adjoins the hotel and Cruise Room. I have not eaten here, but from reports, McCormick's has maintained its acclamation of being a long-time national favorite. At the ever-lively front bar, a favorite for neighborhood residents as well as evening guests, in the 1970s you could often bump elbows with John Denver or Peter, Paul, and Mary. McCormick's is open seven days a week for lunch and dinner. Prices are sensible. McCormick's will also serve you in the Cruise Room.

Il Fornaio is also under the Oxford's roof. You can charge your meal to your room. I have not eaten there, but the sign says, "Serving Regional Selections in an Authentic Setting."

The award-winning **Oxford Spa & Salon** (303-628-5435) is adjacent to the hotel. A small, full-service spa, it is friendly, professional, and very convenient. The health club is free to all guests. Yoga, Pilates, and cardio classes are available. The decor has a western aura—earth tones and dark colors. Hotel guests receive a 10 percent discount for spa use and spa products. Go and enjoy!

Hotel Monaco Denver

1717 Champa St.
303-296-1717
www.monaco-denver.com

I have tried several times to stay at this colorful hotel, whose decor alone entices me. The hotel's mascot "Lillie," a Jack Russell terrier, is often in the front lobby to greet you. Perhaps one day I will be able to stay onsite and look the property over firsthand.

Panzano
909 Seventeenth St.
303-296-3525
www.panzano-denver.com

One of the many perks of research trips is the serendipities. The following is one of *the* best. Often one finds a restaurant where the food is excellent, but the attitude is shoddy and the service slack or the decor out of style. Not here! Panzano is close to perfect. Why don't I just say, "It is perfect!"

First visit: I first visited Panzano after a long drive, and a major meal was not under consideration. I was impressed that, despite my not wanting a big meal—perhaps just a salad—the attentions from the staff were most pleasant and understanding. The suggested salad was very delicious. The total atmosphere is wonderful. You can see the open brick oven where the breads are made daily. Warm breads are served immediately. Try not to eat too much bread (which is hard to do) as the meal, regardless of what you order, promises to be outstanding.

Second visit: This most special of Italian restaurants is under the aegis of creative, talented, hospitable, and knowledgeable executive chef Elise Wiggins. Upon entering you see the sparkling glassware, the bright white tablecloths, the dark wood furniture, the accessories, and the smiling personnel. Everything seems—and actually is—just right. Nothing is ostentatious or gimmicky.

Once seated, you begin a most positive gastronomic experience. Water of your choice is immediately offered, and breads are delivered.

Warning: I repeat, the breads are delicious, but do not consume too many. The best is yet to come.

Here is a summary of what I enjoyed: The tapenade was excellent. Not too salty and spread on the fabulous bread, it was just right. Chef Wiggins, knowing that I wanted to discover many aspects of her cooking skills, created a selection of small tastes of various appetizers. Each was excellent, although I think my favorite was the layered squash and vegetables with goat cheese.

As a main course, I enjoyed scaloppine di vitello: veal medallions with spinach, lemon, capers, and sun-dried tomatoes. It was probably the best veal, or close to it, that I have ever enjoyed. A sampling of the homemade gnocchi with wild mushrooms, sun-dried tomatoes, baby spinach, and gorgonzola cream proved delicious, and I am not a gorgonzola enthusiast. Dessert was a chocolate crème brulée. Whoa!

What an interesting conversation I had with Chef Wiggins as she described what I was eating. There was no question she knows her trade, and she is upbeat and fun. Here's a culinary tidbit she shared with me: When balsamic vinegar is aged like wine, it becomes delicately sweet.

Panzano = friendly and delicious perfection. Don't miss enjoying. The restaurant is open for breakfast, lunch, and dinner and for brunch on Saturday and Sunday. Call or check the Internet for hours.

Sixteenth Street Mall

This focal point has greatly improved since my first visit. It has clothing shops, chain stores, drug stores, and restaurants. Would I call it a must-do? More yes than no. Get your film developed, find a pair of comfortable shoes, buy a souvenir, have a good meal—yes. Maybe you'll get lucky and find something fantastic. Go there alone at night? Maybe not.

To Denver highway officials: Better signage is needed. You can see where downtown is from the tall buildings on the skyline, but if you are not from the area, it is not obvious which exit to take. Signage is also poor going to and coming from the airport. The natives know, but visitors need detailed and explicit signs. This trip I can say, "Thank you, OnStar, for guiding me."

LEAVING DENVER

Finding U.S. 36 out of Denver is not difficult. The highway between Boulder and Denver has become a major thoroughfare for commuters and visitors. There are major developments on both sides of the highway. The drive from Denver to Boulder takes about forty-five minutes, depending on traffic and snowstorms.

BOULDER
(POPULATION MORE THAN 105,000)

The first settlers came to Boulder around 1858, during the Pikes Peak gold rush. By 1860, Boulder had the first schoolhouse in Colorado, and the first frame house had been built. Prior to 1861, Colorado was part of Nebraska, and in 1862 Boulder County was formed. Boulder has not stopped "rushing" and building since those early days, and a list of all the city's "best of" awards would span pages. This is not a small town; yet, it has a small-town, friendly, open feeling, and of course it's very outdoorsy.

The drive into Boulder from Denver is scenic. Boulder is an attractive university town, full of the activity that its large, youthful population brings to the area. The **Flatirons** rise to over eight thousand feet above the city and still farther beyond, forming a dramatic backdrop. The snow-capped **Continental Divide** looms at over thirteen thousand feet. Cosmopolitan in a relaxed way, Boulder has a little bit of everything.

Hotel Boulderado
2115 Thirteenth St.

303-442-4344
www.boulderado.com

Its name an elision of Boulder and Colorado, this historic downtown hotel first opened in 1909. Had you checked in then, the rate would have been from $1 to $2.50 a night, depending on room size and conveniences. Visiting this landmark, you will feel like you are stepping back in time. The rates are slightly higher, and the conveniences are many. At this enjoyable property you will find an attractive, efficient staff whose goal to please is obvious.

During one of my visits, I discovered that sloppy (if any) attention had been given to my bedding. Once I notified the staff, the problem was quickly fixed, and the apologies were many.

Note: This can happen anywhere. I experienced similar at a multistar hotel. If you are in this situation, be certain to report the oversight. Many hotels have "room checkers," which is a good policy.

Parking is convenient. Often there are parking spaces by the hotel, but valet parking is also available.

Q's Restaurant (303-442-4880, www.qsboulder.com) is well appointed and superior, with an excellent menu and sensible prices. During happy hour, everything on the bar menu is half off. There is also the "Every Night Special": a five-course chef's tasting for $55 or five courses and five wines all-inclusive for $85.

The **Corner Bar** (303-442-4560), open from 11:30 a.m. to midnight, is an ideal place for whatever your gastronomic appetite desires. At the **Catacombs** (303-443-0486), one of Boulder's first liquor-licensed bars, music and libations are specials.

Pearl Street Pedestrian Mall

Within a very short walk of the Boulderado is the award-winning **Pearl Street Pedestrian Mall**. This attractive area has always been a favorite of mine. It is well laid out with a wonderful mix of shops, some quite pricey, but all with a vibrant, friendly atmosphere. You can enjoy the show either by people watching, window shopping, or store browsing. There are several street performers: Bongo the Balloon Man makes animal-balloon creations, and the Zip Code Man will guess your hometown when you tell him your zip code. Or watch in awe as the contortionist folds himself into a small box. There is definitely something for everyone.

Boulder Dushanbe Teahouse
1770 Thirteenth St.
303-442-4993
www.boulderteahouse.com

This real teahouse was a gift from Boulder's sister city, Dushanbe, Tajikistan. The only one in the Western Hemisphere, its main purpose is to make souls happy. Decorated by over forty native artisans over a three-year period, its vibrant colors and furnishings are outstanding. There are one hundred different types of teas and a full bar, and the teahouse is open for breakfast, lunch, and dinner. Your soul will be happy.

Boulder County Farmer's Market
Thirteenth St. between Arapahoe and Canyon
303-910-2236
www.boulderfarmers.org

This is a great place to stock up on the most delicious fresh edibles, as well as jellies, flowers, homemade items, and so forth. This farmer's market is a happening. I recommend, if available, the Colorado peaches. You will taste why with your first bite (see **Palisade**, Colorado).

Celestial Seasonings Tea Company
4600 Sleepytime Dr.
303-581-1531
www.celestialseasonings.com

Although I have not yet had the time to visit, I look forward to taking the forty-five-minute tour, seeing some of the 8 million tea bags made per day, and visiting the **Mint Room**! I hear the tour is most informative and fun, and I recommend it. I certainly recommend their teas.

Millennium Harvest House

1345 Twenty-eighth St.
303-443-3850
www.millenniumhotels.com/millenniumboulder

I found the staff very friendly and competent at this nice commercial hotel. There is a lot of activity. The hotel is convenient to many stores. My room was large, but the decor was dark. The bedside lamps are placed so high that turning them off is a big stretch. The bathroom had all the necessities and amenities.

The **Club Room** on the fourth floor provides a microwave, coffee, and depending on the time of day, pastries, cheese and crackers, and such. The ice machine is nearby. This is a friendly, professional hotel.

FYI: Boulder has all the chain stores and then some. It is a college town as well as an upscale mountain town, so anything you forget to pack you can get here.

ESTES PARK

The drive from Boulder to Estes Park is pleasant, and the road has definitely improved since my first visit several years ago.

Nearing Estes, you feel as if you are looking at a picture postcard. It is most attractive but soon you realize—particularly in the summer—that too many others have discovered Estes. **Elkhorn Avenue**, the main drag, is now jammed with trinket shops, taffy stores, moccasin and buckskin jacket stores, and endless T-shirt shops.

The Stanley
333 Wonderview Ave.
970-577-4000
www.stanleyhotel.com

F. O. Stanley, of Stanley Steamer fame, arrived in Estes Park in 1903. Realizing the potential of this beautiful area and knowing that it needed a major hotel, he purchased 160 acres and began his project.

It took two years to complete the main building, and as they say, the rest is history. By 1940, the year of his death, Stanley had not only built his grand hotel but created a sewer, power, and water company and the first bank in Estes.

The Stanley is a grand hotel. In years past, it suffered a decline, receiving few attentions. I am glad to report that upgrades and improvements have at last started and are succeeding.

Many types of rooms are available, with rates ranging from $119 to $1,500, depending on the season. Villas have also been built for rent or purchase.

The Stanley was featured in Steven King's *The Shining*, and it is said to have several haunted rooms. Visit this historic hotel.

Sweet Basilico Café
430 Prospect Village Dr.
970-586-3899
www.sweetbasilico.com

Owned by Raul and Shawn Perez, this is one of my very favorite small Italian restaurants. The food is wonderful. The Italian classics—lasagna, manicotti, eggplant parmesan, homemade focaccia—are absolutely delicious. The atmosphere is delightful, and the prices are right. Unless you plan to get there when they open, make a reservation. Enjoy.

GRAND JUNCTION

I-70 out of Denver takes you to Grand Junction in about four and a half hours. The excellent highway takes you through some of the most beautiful scenery in America. Be advised, however, that winter weather can cause considerable delays on Vail Pass and in the Eisenhower Tunnel. A flashlight or two, blankets, a small shovel, and heavy boots are recommended for the winter traveler. And bottles of water, always.

Grand Junction and the surrounding areas are unpretentious and friendly; the rock formations in canyon country are spectacular. I particularly recommend a drive through **Colorado National Monument** (970-858-3617, ext. 360; www.nps.gov/colm/index.htm), easily accessible from Grand Junction.

PALISADE

Palisade is within ten minutes of downtown Grand Junction. Take I-70 East.

With all due respect to the Peachtree State, you have not tasted peaches until you have bitten into a fresh peach from Palisade. Their taste is very different from that of any other peach. There are other delicious fruits from the area, so be sure to "fruit up" for delicious car treats. Don't leave the area without a trip to **Palisade Pride**, now part of Alida's Fruits.

Alida's Fruits
3402 C 1/2 Rd.
970-434-8769
www.alidasfruits.com

Don't you love that address? When I called to find out about Palisade Pride, the phone was answered by Alida herself. What a special conversation! One of the first things I learned was that Alida's is not really in Palisade but in **East Orchard Mesa**, just a short distance from Palisade and a stone's throw from the Colorado River. Get directions by calling, or see the map on the company's website.

After a rather lengthy conversation with Alida about her business and my project, I immediately visited the company website. It turns out that Robert "Farmer Bob" and Alida have grown and sold fruits and vegetables for approximately forty years. Their products are all about quality and freshness. I would bet that their produce gives a whole new meaning to the word "taste."

Note: When I called for the final updates, Farmer Bob answered the phone, and after a fun and interesting talk, we said, "Look forward to meeting you." It is on my agenda.

They produce superb dried fruits prepared without toxins. The dried peach slices and the tart cherries are hand coated with a vanilla cream confection, and the pears and apples are hand dipped in either light or dark chocolate and caramel coatings. These are unbelievably delicious. The fruit flavor remains but with the dab of that yummy white confection—oh my! These are my favorite, but I also exclaim approval for the chocolate fruits.

Call and place an order for these unbelievable fruits, or if you are in the area, a visit to their store is a must. Don't be surprised if you decide to make yourself a present of these delights.

Enstrom

701 Colorado Ave., Grand Junction
970-683-1000
www.enstrom.com

Enjoy a visit to Enstrom's, a fifty-year-old family business famous for its almond taffy, which is considered absolutely fantastic. Three generations have maintained the product, and they must be doing something right as Enstrom Candies produces over half a million pounds of almond toffee annually.

Chet Enstrom's hobby of making handcrafted almond toffee has become an irrefutable "must" for toffee aficionados. I have never read a bad review of these products. Chet's toffees were in demand by 1959, and by the late 1970s, production had reached over sixty-five thousand pounds. Today, this family business still produces small batches of seventy pounds each by hand. Here's to hobbies! Check the website for store locations throughout Colorado.

Note: The above two special shops might solve some Christmas shopping.

WYOMING

have crossed the state of Wyoming several different ways, and each is interesting. Wyoming is the ninth-largest state (in square miles) in the United States. Because of its elevation—sixty-seven hundred feet above sea level—the temperatures are cool to cold. Precipitations can and do vary greatly. There is a lot to do in Wyoming, particularly if you like the outdoors.

WAMSUTTER
(POPULATION APPROXIMATELY 240)

I had a friend with me on this trip, and seeing a sign for a café, we turned off I-80 to find ourselves on a very dusty road. The wind was blowing, making it hard to see with all the dust. Suddenly, a police car with very bright flashing lights and a noisy siren came up behind me.

"What have I done?" I asked my friend.

"I don't know," she replied.

Chief of Police Sergio came up and very nicely told me to get out of the car. He proceeded to tell me that I had neglected to stop at the stop sign. I explained that there was so much dust and wind that I hadn't seen it, and I didn't know this area. After I got my warning citation, we talked a bit. He told me about his family and his children's dirt bike. I told him about my project. We talked some more, and he said, "Use the citation as decoration on your refrigerator," and with that we said good-bye. Needless to say, I will always remember Wamsutter.

Heading north on I-25, there are several interesting stops.

CHEYENNE
(POPULATION MORE THAN 50,000)

This substantial metropolis is a civilized, clean, and friendly western town. It is one of the two largest cities in Wyoming.

CHUGWATER
(POPULATION APPROXIMATELY 250)

Big rock formations can be seen all around. There is a **Super 8 Motel** (www.super8.com) and much more!

Chugwater Chili Corporation
210 First St.
1-800-972-4454 (CHILI)
www.chugwaterchili.com

Country Girls Embroidery
1160 State Hwy. 313
307-422-3414
www.countrygirlsembroidery.com

Chugwater Dog Grooming and Boarding
140 S. Chugwater Hwy.
307-422-3217

Chugwater Soda Fountain
314 First St.
307-422-3222

Not bad for a tiny town. When I was there, town lots sold for $100. Can that be? Maybe my dyslexia left off a zero.

DOUGLAS
(POPULATION APPROXIMATELY 5,000)

This small town has lots of history, but nothing has brought it more notoriety than the birth of the jackalope. Brothers Douglas and Ralph Herrick had studied taxidermy by mail as teenagers. One day, on their return from hunting, they tossed a rabbit carcass into the taxidermy shop, and it slid right between a pair of antlers. Douglas's eyes brightened as he said, "Let's mount it that way!" And so was born a rabbit with antlers, to be forever known as the jackalope. These creatures have become part of the west on postcards, statues, pins—you name it. If you have been out west, perhaps you too have bought a souvenir featuring the jackalope, which the state of Wyoming trademarked.

Douglas has also been noted in Norman Crampton's *The 100 Best Small Towns in America*. In spite of—or perhaps because of—its size, the people of this town work together and strive to make it the best it can be.

CASPER
(POPULATION APPROXIMATELY 46,000)

This town has a **Hampton Inn** (www.hamptoninn.com), which I am pleased to note was managed by a woman when I was there. I found Casper to be a very friendly, nice place to visit. There was a lot going on, and I could see why it had won "best of" in several categories. The roads away from Casper and Cheyenne are strikingly beautiful, but services are few and far between. Even towns marked prominently on the map can consist of little more than a couple of intersections.

Driving Diva Tip: From Casper I left on I-25, then took Route 26/20. I recommend this drive.

POWDER RIVER (POPULATION 50)

Powder River has a post office.

HILAND (POPULATION 10)

I could not leave Hiland out! Way back when, it was so named because it was the highest point on the Wyoming section of the Chicago and Northwestern Railway. You can find it on a map, and the next time I am passing by, I plan to stop. It is about fifty miles west of Casper.

SHOSHONI (POPULATION LESS THAN 500)

The road is long and straight, when all of a sudden you round a bend and see a sign:

Welcome to
Shoshoni
Home of the Wyo. State
Old Time Fiddle Contest
Boysen Lake
Walleye Capital of Wyo.

Shoshoni means "little snow." At one time, this town had two thousand residents. The **Elkhorn Hotel** was the first business, and then the town grew so fast that people lived in tents. Fire burned the town in 1907 and 1908. Brick buildings replaced the wooden structures. Can you believe that in its heyday, Shoshoni had twenty-three saloons, two banks, two mercantile stores, livery and feed stables, and a newspaper? For its size, Shoshoni had more houses and restaurants than any other town in Wyoming.

Yellowstone Drug Store
502 E. Second St.
307-876-2539

Originally at 127 Main St., the Yellowstone Drug Store moved to its current location in 2009. When I arrived in Shoshoni, this corner emporium was in a white stucco-looking building with several types of windows, including double hung, oval, and triple wide. All styles were outlined in black. The parking lot was almost full. Once inside, I found a genuine soda fountain with swiveling stools. The floor space was full of round tables; the overhead florescent lights had no covers. One sign read, "Please order at the counter," but the truly revealing sign stated,

> In 2001 we dipped 15,339 gallons of ice cream!
> One-day record on 5-29-00
> 727 Shakes & Malts

My $4 shake was very thick and tasty (prices are probably higher now). The wonderful flavor certainly derived in part from the ambiance but also from the large amount of butterfat used in these creations. There are now sixty-two flavors to choose from! Other items besides ice cream shakes, such as souvenir trinkets, are sold at the drug store.

In Shoshoni I also discovered the B&K Shoreline Shop.

B&K Shoreline Shop
14 Bass Lake Rd.
307-857-0750

Here you will find an RV park, bar, liquor lounge, tackle, and more.

THERMOPOLIS
(POPULATION APPROXIMATELY 3,500)

I did not have time to stop, but . . .

FYI: The world's largest mineral hot springs are here at the foothills of *Owl Creek Mountains* and beside the *Big Horn River*. From reliable sources I hear this is a nice place to visit.

CODY

The road from Shoshoni to Cody is dotted on the atlas (signifying a AAA scenic byway). It is a nice drive. Arriving at the entrance to Cody, you realize you are stepping back into the Old West. It is also obvious that during the summer, there is a lot of tourism.

Cody is special and full of history and attractions that you will be glad to have experienced. Here are my discoveries, experiences, and critiques.

Buffalo Bill's Cody/Yellowstone Country

For more information about this area, visit www.yellowstone country.org.

Irma Hotel
1192 Sheridan Ave.
307-587-4221
www.irmahotel.com

Named after Buffalo Bill Cody's daughter, this wonderful hotel is a step back in time. William F. Cody, also known as Buffalo Bill, was probably the best-known person of his time. He stood in the foreground of important happenings that shaped the American West. In the 1880s he formed *Buffalo Bill's Wild West Show*, which toured the United States and Europe for thirty years. In 1895, Buffalo Bill founded Cody, Wyoming, and in 1902, he built the Irma Hotel. The Irma's ornate cherry wood back bar was a gift from Queen Victoria, who had it made in France.

With only forty rooms, this is not a big hotel, but the decor and spirit of its grand early days prevail. You can picture the European nobility who stayed here during their hunting trips. You can also feel the rough-and-ready spirit of showman Buffalo Bill. The hotel is a pleasant mix for all. Although the original hotel was built in 1902, additions were made in 1929 and 1976.

Small touches include lace curtains and tablecloths, floral wall paper, dark-wood furniture, metal headboards, high ceilings, hanging ceiling lights, and fringed lamp shades. Although you might not choose this wonderful décor for your own home, it provides a nice respite from the traditional.

Dining at the Irma is famous, be it at the **Restaurant Grill** or the **Buffet**. There is an abundance of food, and the prices are good.

The **Cody Gunfighters in Action** fight occurs each afternoon in front of the hotel. Fun!

Claudia Wade and Lee Anne Ackerman, who live in Cody and whose opinions I respect, recommended the following four lodgings.

Chamberlin Inn
1032 Twelfth St.
307-587-0202
www.chamberlininn.com

Agnes Chamberlin transplanted herself from Kansas and opened her first boardinghouse in 1903. She soon after became prominent and instrumental in the life and development of Cody. Her inn was the place to stay in the 1920s and 1930s, and the guest book was impressive, with authors, politicians, movie stars, and tycoons staying in this fine establishment.

Just a stone's throw from **Main Street**, this twenty-four-unit boutique hotel was totally renovated in 2005 and 2006. All reviews say this is a delightful property. One quote states, "Ernest Hemingway slept here—you should too."

Cody Legacy Inn and Suites

1801 Mountain View Dr.
307-587-6067
www.codylegacyinn.com

New, rustic, and cozy, this inn has large, inviting rooms. The list of amenities is long, and I particularly like the most appropriate lodgepole pine furniture.

Cody Cowboy Village

203 W. Yellowstone Ave.
307-587-7555
www.thecodycowboyvillage.com

Here you will find luxurious, new log cabins—so western! Featuring the "best beds in the West," this acclaimed village, near the rodeo grounds and about a mile from the museum (detailed below), is special.

The Cody

232 W. Yellowstone Ave.
307-587-5915
www.thecody.com

This brand-new, high-end hotel is, from all reports, soon to have its ranking stars—when a restaurant is added. In the meantime, it is an ideal place to stay. It is a green-friendly hotel.

Shopping

There are lots of shops on Cody's main drag, **Sheridan Avenue**. With everything from western-themed to modern stores, it is fun.

Maurice's
1101 Sheridan Ave.
307-527-5628

Here in Cody you will find one of the best chain stores where you can always find something sensibly priced. I am still wearing the shoes I purchased there.

The following two shops are operated by the Christ Episcopal Church to serve the Cody community and surrounding area.

Bargain Box
1644 Alger Ave.
307-587-6666

Bargain Box Furniture Store
1537 Beck Ave.
307-587-6333

Sightseeing and Dining

Cassie's Supper Club
214 Yellowstone Ave.
307-527-5500
www.cassies.com

You cannot be in Cody and not eat at Cassie's. The real Cassie was a madam. The present-day supper club was once a house of ill repute too. Those days are gone, and Cassie's now has delicious menu selections, wonderful western atmosphere, and live music every night in the summer for dancing.

Dinner was delicious. I shared a "Tumbleweed Onion" (breaded and deep fried!). I could not believe my ears when told to order prawns in Wyoming, but I did anyway, and they were so good. I split the entrée of prawns with my friend, who ordered steak, and what a steak it was. Everything was, I repeat, delicious. I have to confess that the cowboy sitting at the next table, who kept trying to catch my eye, was not bad for the ego. Cassie's . . . I plan to return!

Cody Trolley Tours
1192 Sheridan Ave. (Irma Hotel)
307-527-7043
www.codytrolleytours.com

Do not miss taking a Cody Trolley Tour—an hour full of interesting historic tidbits and fun comments. The guides are absolutely terrific. You will learn that the streets are so wide so that wide wagons could turn around. There are three *Sears Catalogue* homes, each originally purchased for $495. You'll learn how Buffalo Bill Cody and his wife got along and about Annie Oakley, who taught troops how to shoot. The presentation of the town's history is great.

Cody Stampede Rodeo
1031 Twelfth St.
307-587-5155 or 800-207-0744
www.codystampederodeo.com

One brochure states, "Rodeo Capital of the World, Cody Is Rodeo." This longest-running rodeo in the United States has been world famous since 1938. In June, July, and August, it takes place every night at 8:30 p.m. Real West, real cowboys, and real wild.

Dan Miller's Cowboy Music Revue
1171 Sheridan Ave.
307-272-7855
www.cowboymusicrevue.com

After hearing about Dan Miller and his show, I was ready to head for my seat in the audience. I'll go the next time I'm in Cody.

You can bring the whole family to this show. I hear that with each performance, it improves, and each show is wonderful.

Dan grew up on a dairy farm in Indiana, but his penchant for the theatrical world made him leave the cows for commercial endeavors in showbiz. His handsome, large physique (I saw pictures) definitely could find a place in the world of glitz—first Los Angeles and then on to Nashville. He was a natural in every way for TV. Lucky for Cody, Dan and his family moved here and brought his show along.

Buffalo Bill Historical Center
720 Sheridan Ave.
307-587-4771
www.bbhc.org

I had heard about this center and its six museums, but little did I realize that every rave review and glowing comment was absolutely true. It is hard to use so many superlatives and remain credible. This is considered America's finest western museum. Within its walls, you will find the **Buffalo Bill Museum**, the **Whitney Gallery of Western Art**, the **McCracken Research Library**, the **Plains Indian Museum**, the **Cody Firearms Museum**, and the **Draper Museum of Natural History**. Each is exceptional.

Adults will be honored to have the experience of viewing these exhibits, and children will be fascinated. Plan to spend some time here in a slow fashion. There are places to dine and shop.

While in Cody, I met the famous artist Harry Jackson, whose work is displayed at the Buffalo Bill Historical Center. At first I viewed the man as a scruffy western-looking gent, but I soon learned of his talents and visited with him at his studio. What a hoot. There must be something in the Cody air or water because, the first prominent American abstract painter, Jackson Pollock, was born in Cody.

Meeteetse Chocolatier
1943 State St., Meeteetse
307-868-2567
www.meeteetsechocolatier.com

I am anxious to visit this town, just thirty minutes from Cody, where in 2000 the population was 351 and now, who knows? It has a great story. Bronco rider Tim Kellogg needed a new saddle. They were expensive, costing $1,400 and up. His mother suggested that he make and sell some of his grandmother's chocolates at the **Cody Stampede** to raise some funds. Like most sons and daughters, his first answer to this parental suggestion was no! Mother prevailed and got a booth at the stampede, and just to keep mother happy, Tim made the chocolates. As it turned out, he could not keep an adequate supply on hand. Each day they sold out pronto. And so it started. Remember, always listen to your mother! And the rest is history. Look this little emporium up on the Internet. You'll see Tim in front of his store. Then check out the list of items and the in-store events. What a decadent discovery! I look forward to visiting.

FYI: These decadent delights contain *no* sugar, additives, or preservatives.

Driving Diva Suggestion: Read and research all about Yellowstone National Park *before* arriving. It is awesome, and there are so many things to see.

YELLOWSTONE NATIONAL PARK

Leave Cody via Highway 20 to Highway 14/16, where you can enter Yellowstone at the east entrance.

Driving Diva Factoid: All of Yellowstone National Park is in Wyoming except a small part, which Wikipedia states is in Idaho. West Yellowstone is in Montana.

Awesome, fantastic, breathtaking, unbelievable, amazing, enormous, incredible: Those are just some of the adjectives you will apply to this great place. Take time to plan your Yellowstone experience. There is a tremendous amount to see and do here. It was over 640,000 years ago that the climactic event that formed Yellowstone took place.

There are several different entrances into the park. The well-marked roads in Yellowstone make a big loop. You should plot your route in the park and drive and enjoy.

Yellowstone has 300 miles of roads and 950 miles of hiking trails. It is imperative that rules and regulations be adhered to. Remember that you are on the turf of the Yellowstone animals. They do not mind if you look and photograph, but don't get too close. Just because you think they are engrossed in their eating, don't be a fool. They know just where you are and can get angry in a split second. Do not gamble!

Old Faithful is the most predictable and most publicized of all the geysers. It erupts faithfully, every sixty-three to seventy-five minutes, discharging about three to eight thousand gallons of water with a temperature of 204 degrees Fahrenheit. The water reaches a height of 90 to 184 feet.

Although most everyone talks about Old Faithful and waits to see this geyser perform, a bigger and more spectacular geyser, **Grand Geyser**, is not too far away. This one requires patience, but it is worth the wait. The Grand Geyser usually goes off about every twelve hours, but its timing is not exact. It erupts with a broad fountain spray, whereas Old Faithful erupts in a hose-like, cone-type spray. There are two smaller geysers on each side of Grand Geyser called the **Vent Geyser** and the **Turban Geyser**. These smaller geysers are connected hydrodynamically. When Vent Geyser starts to rumble, that usually indicates that Grand is about to do its performance. Then, Turban starts, and the show really begins. Grand Geyser reaches heights of 150 to 200 feet. Not to be outdone, the smaller geysers will continue to erupt and play for about an hour after Grand has finished. Sometimes, without any indication, Grand will show off with another eruption that is often higher and stronger than the first. It is worth the wait to see.

Yellowstone's Lower Falls and Upper Falls are beautiful. **Canyon Village** is the perfect place to take a deep breath, get a beverage, "see a man about a horse" (use the facilities), and shop for souvenirs.

You will also see the **Fountain Paint Pot area**, as well as hot springs, mud pots, fumaroles, spectacular waterfalls, flora and fauna, and on and on. There is no end to what you will encounter in Yellowstone. Remember to help preserve this magnificent wonderland, and don't do anything stupid because, remember, you are on the animals' turf.

Driving Diva Factoid: In 1872 President Ulysses S. Grant signed the legislation to create Yellowstone as the world's first national park.

Hotels

Your budget will determine where you lodge. There is something for everyone, including **Old Faithful Inn, Lake Yellowstone Hotel and Cabins,** and **Mammoth Hot Springs Hotel and Cabins** (866-439-7375, www.yellowstonenationalparklodges.com). These three grand hotels of Yellowstone are wonderful, unique, comfortable, and clean. There are also cabin and lodge accommodations available. Be sure to make your reservations early.

Old Faithful Inn is extraordinary. Built in 1903, it has sixty-five-foot ceilings, massive fireplaces, lodgepole pine railings, and more. When you enter, you will feel dwarfed by it all. The Old Faithful Inn is just a short distance from **Old Faithful Geyser**.

Reservations are required in the wonderful, well-run, full-service dining rooms, which I adore. There are also cafeterias and fast food options. Some of the lodges have special dining functions, such as the **Old West Dinner Cookout** at **Roosevelt Lodge**, which I hear is a special event.

Driving Diva Tip: Remember to keep your national park pass with you so you can reenter the parks.

GRAND TETONS NATIONAL PARK

It is a pleasant experience to drive south toward **Jackson** out of Yellowstone for an afternoon of discoveries and to view the **Tetons** from a different perspective. If you start early, it is not a problem to get to Jackson for the day and back to Yellowstone before dark. Preferably, spend time in the Jackson area.

The Tetons are a spectacular mountain range and so distinctive that you won't mix them up with any other. **Grand Teton National Park** (www.nps.gov/grte) is located just south of Yellowstone and north of Jackson. These impressive mountains rose millions of years ago when the earth's crust cracked along the fault.

I had been in **Jackson Hole** several times and seen the area, but never from this vantage point. As you look out over the dark blue of **Jackson Lake**, dotted with a few anchored boats, the massive snow-capped Tetons in the background are indeed a beautiful sight.

Leeks Marina and Pizzeria
89 National Park Rd.
303-543-2494

What a delightful place to lunch. It is a beautiful setting, especially if you sit on the porch overlooking the marina. Everything is delicious and sensibly priced. It is extremely female friendly.

JACKSON (POPULATION APPROXIMATELY 9,000)

More than twenty-five years ago, my older son went to camp in Jackson (Teton Valley Ranch Camp) and subsequently became a counselor. He always raved about the spectacular scenery and how fantastic rafting on the **Snake River**, as well as the hiking and horseback riding, were. I didn't doubt him, but only when I saw the area with my own eyes did I realize how true his words were. Camp life in these surroundings is a special experience.

Jackson is well-heeled, and the residents act accordingly. It is an attractive western area, with nature, wildlife, and physical activity a part of each resident's lifestyle. In the winter, skiing is very popular. The bold Tetons are your constant companions.

Jackson in the summer is filled with tourists, but I have not found it too objectionable. The natives might not agree. My summer experiences in Jackson were always fun and interesting.

Driving Diva Factoid: Jackson is the name of the actual town, while the valley is called Jackson Hole.

In the past several years, the cultural environment has improved and grown in Jackson. A good example is the Grand Teton Music Festival.

Grand Teton Music Festival
4015 N. Lake Creek Dr., No. 100, Wilson
307-733-3050
www.gtmf.org

The festival started in 1962 and struggled until it achieved today's prominence. For many years, the performances were held under a tent, but then in 1974 **Walk Festival Hall** was opened.

Visitors Center
25 S. Willow, Ste. 10
307-732-0629
www.gtnpf.org

Opened in the summer of 2007, this multi-million-dollar structure is grand. The big glass windows frame the Teton Range, providing a splendid backdrop to the great exhibits.

There are many western presentations in Jackson to enjoy, including the world's longest-running shoot-out, which is held six times a week in the **Jackson Town Square**. On the third Saturday in May, there is the world's only public auction of elk antlers. This too takes place in the square. The **National Elk Refuge** (307-733-9212, www.fws.gov/nationalelkrefuge) is located on the north edge of town. The Boy Scouts collect shed antlers, which are then auctioned; the proceeds go to the elk-feeding program. (I adore such events and programs.) Like every tourist, you must have your picture taken at one of the four famous **Antler Arches** in downtown Jackson.

To list all the eateries and lodgings in Jackson would take pages. Suffice it to say, there is something for everyone, and, of course, you can always picnic or camp out, if that is your desire.

Parkway Inn

125 N. Jackson St.
307-733-3143
www.parkwayinn.com

This is very convenient to town and to many of the local events. The on-site parking is easy. The decor in the rooms is pleasing, with attractive antiques and handmade quilts on the beds. A delicious complimentary breakfast is served in the breakfast lounge. Everyone seems to meet here and discuss his or her Wyoming agenda.

There are many upscale hotels to choose from if your budget permits.

The private homes and ranches are impressive with primarily western decor. I enjoyed seeing the homes, viewing the area, and visiting with people—especially school chums. But this water lover began to feel a tiny bit landlocked after a while, even with all the beautiful lakes and the Snake River.

Regardless, this awesome area is a should- and must-see.

Reel Women Inc.

PO Box 24, Wilson
307-413-6671 or 208-787-2657
reel-women.com

I could not leave this tidbit out. I insert this here as so much of Reel Women Inc.'s activity takes place in Jackson Hole. The mailing address is above.

Lori-Ann Murphy, founder and instructor, runs this fly-fishing school. Here you will find everything pertinent to the sport and its adventures. Lori-Ann is an advisor for the Orvis Company and consulted for Meryl Streep and Kevin Bacon in the movie *The River Wild*. She has won awards and can often be found at sport shows and banquets, demonstrating and speaking about her passion— fly-fishing. The popular women's fly-fishing school is held in Jackson Hole. There are various other fishing trips. If time permits, take a two-day course. And don't you love the name Reel Women Inc.?

IMPORTANT DRIVING INFORMATION

Leaving Jackson, heading west, you will go through **Wilson**. The road west from Wilson into Idaho, the **Teton Pass**, is a brake burner for a short time, but it is beautiful. Listen for road updates, and pay careful attention.

MONTANA

The largest of the Rocky Mountain states, Montana is truly beautiful and runs all the way from **Glacier National Park** in the north to the Montana side of **Yellowstone National Park** in the south.

Driving Diva Factoid: The very real town of *West Yellowstone* is in Montana, which is not to be confused with Yellowstone in Wyoming.

THREE FORKS
(POPULATION APPROXIMATELY 1,500)

On your way to or from Yellowstone or Glacier national parks, or if you just happen to be in the area, Three Forks is a must-stop. It may not be just around the corner, but you'll wish it was. You will have a very delicious experience.

Wheat Montana Farms and Bakery

10778 Hwy. 287
800-535-2798
www.wheatmontana.com

Driving in Montana for long stretches, you will notice the huge grain farms, which serve to get you in the mood to stop at Wheat Montana. Here, you will find almost everything that has to do with wheat—flour, grains, cereals, legumes, and seeds. You'll also find their cookbook, bread machine mixes, wheat chili mix, aprons, and more. In the bakery department, you can get possibly one of the best sandwiches you will ever consume. Now you will know what bread is supposed to taste like! Try their products even if you have to obtain them by mail.

For three generations the Folkvord family has been involved with grain production. Their operation now includes twelve thousand acres of the most productive soil in Montana. At five thousand feet above sea level, it is the highest elevation at which grain is grown in North America. Elevation, weather, and attention to quality versus quantity all enhance this fine product.

Depending on the time of year, as you drive you will see huge parcels of land crowned with waving grains—not unlike a graceful dance—that seem to stretch all the way to the horizon. You'll see a line of combines harvesting grain. The sight is awesome. It looks choreographed, and in a way it is.

Driving Diva Factoid: If you store grains in a plastic pail with an oxygen absorber in a temperature-stable environment, the grains should last six to eight years, and perhaps even longer. Flour or any other processed product should be used within a year (info from www.wheatmontana .com).

The interstate as you head north is long and straight and goes on and on and on. Because of the beauty that surrounds you, you may get a bit weary, but only briefly, as the land and sky are awesome, and you do not want to miss a single cloud or gentle breeze.

As you drive along I-15, you can't help but wonder how often the inhabitants of these big ranches visit their neighbors. How often do they go shopping? How close is the grocery store? Neighbors are not close by for borrowing a quick cup a sugar. If you go to a barber, by the time you get home, it's almost time for another trim!

Driving in Montana is an experience—one that you will want to have many times.

GREAT FALLS
(POPULATION APPROXIMATELY 55,000)

You can take I-15 north to **Shelby**, then take Highway 2 to **Browning**, and then drive on into **Glacier**. Or right outside of Great Falls, you can take Highway 89 to Browning and then drive on into Glacier. Either way, the countryside is magnificent, and as you near Glacier, you begin to feel the aura of the fantastic national park you are about to enter. It is awesome and magical.

GLACIER NATIONAL PARK

Entering Glacier National Park, you embark on the experience of a lifetime. There is so much to see. The following are my discoveries and highlights, but do your own research to learn as much as you can before you visit this magnificent place.

I read a Glacier logo and it proved so accurate: "Experience a Dream, with Your Eyes Wide Open."

Places to Stay in the Park

Glacier Park Lodge
1 Midvale Rd., East Glacier Park
406-226-5600
www.glacierparkinc.com

This establishment is large and impressive.

Many Glacier Hotel

774 Railroad St., Columbia Falls

406-732-4411

www.glacierparkinc.com

This establishment is also large and impressive.

Swiftcurrent Motor Inn and Cabins

406-732-5531

www.glacierparkinc.com

This establishment is rustic and wonderful.

Lake MacDonald Lodge

406-888-5431

www.glacierparkinc.com

This lodge is delightful.

Izaak Walton Inn

290 Izaak Walton Inn Rd., Essex

406-888-5700

www.izaakwaltoninn.com

This establishment is charming and attractive.

I have stayed and dined at Glacier Park Lodge, Many Glacier Hotel, and the Swiftcurrent Motor Inn. What wonderful places! They are perfect and not pretentious. But that describes Glacier in general.

Lake MacDonald Lodge and all the places are very friendly. Prices vary, but they're worth every penny. All the wonderful lodges have restaurants and a most special ambiance.

Bears: Remember that you are on their turf. Respect the bears, and keep your distance. They may look and act docile, but that can change in a flash. You cannot run fast enough to escape their reach. Wildlife abounds: Enjoy, respect, photograph, remember, and then have the joy of reflecting.

Must-do's

Red Bus Tours

406-892-2525

www.glacierparkinc.com

The Red Bus Tours use bright red motor coaches built originally in 1936 by the White Motor Company. Today, the legacy continues, and the coaches have been upgraded and refurbished by the Ford Motor Company. The drivers, known as "jammers," originally got their nickname because they had to jam the gears as they traveled the roads. The Red Bus Tour is a big must-do, so make reservations. The fee is sensible.

The Sun Road

This is part of the Red Bus Tour, but you can also drive it yourself. Fifty-two-miles-long, it is a bit of a challenge and can be a white-knuckle experience in places. I definitely recommend leaving your car and letting the experienced "jammers" drive, answer questions, and show you the sights.

The Red Bus Tours make various stops along the way. These red buses have canvas roll-back tops that allow for unbelievable views as you feast your eyes on awesomeness. You will go along the **Garden Wall**, cross the **Continental Divide** at **Logan Pass** (elevation 6,646 feet), and descend to **St. Mary Lake**. This road is an absolute engineering feat.

Driving Diva Factoid: Take a sweater. Although there are blankets in the bus, a sweater will also feel good as the temperature drops in the afternoon, and the canvas tops are closed. If you are driving, you should try to go in July or August, when the roads are at their best. Snow can come very early in Glacier.

FYI: By 2030, there is a good possibility that all the glaciers in Glacier National Park will have melted!

Many Glacier Boat Tours

Seeing Glacier's beauty from the water is another special experience. There is a fee, and spaces are limited. Make a reservation (406-257-2426).

Eateries near Glacier Park

Serrano's Mexican Restaurant
29 Dawson Ave., East Glacier
406-226-9293
www.serranosmexican.com

This restaurant is nonsmoking, informal, and sensibly priced.

Babb Bar Cattle Baron Supper Club
Hwy. 89, Babb
406-732-4033

This is a real western restaurant serving what some claim is "the best beef in the West." My beef dinner was very good. The large restaurant is on the second floor over the bar. The staff really gets a daily workout going up and down the steps and back and forth to the kitchen. You must be hungry when you dine, and don't rush as it is deliciously special.

I didn't see anything else in Babb (population approximately 500), so maybe the Babb Bar Cattle Baron Supper Club *is* Babb.

Whistle Stop
1024 U.S. Hwy. 49, East Glacier
406-226-9292

The sign adds "World Famous" to the name. Go hungry and be prepared for a unique breakfast experience! I recommend you split whatever you order. You'll be lucky if you are hungry again by dinner time. It is not fancy and not to be missed.

Park Café & Grocery
U.S. Hwy. 89, St. Mary
406-732-4482
www.parkcafe.us

Located at the East Glacier entrance to Glacier National Park, this colorful, noisy, crowded, and popular café is known for its delicious pies. My favorite was a blueberry, blackberry, and raspberry mix called Razzleberry. The establishment serves about forty pies per day! Go and enjoy. You might have blue teeth for a while, but it's oh so worth it! The café's motto on a tie-dyed shirt read, "Pies for Strength."

Two Sisters
U.S. Hwy. 89, Babb, four miles north of St. Mary
406-732-5535

This funky, fun place is delicious and offers reasonable prices. Try the burger with Creole sauce, followed by a piece of buttermilk chocolate cake.

Museums

Blackfeet Heritage Center & Art Gallery
333 Central Ave. W., Browning
406-338-5661
www.siyehdevelopment.com/heritage.html

Promoting the heritage of Native Americans, this gallery is well worth the stop. It is not large, but you will learn a lot.

Museum of the Plains Indians
U.S. Hwy. 2 and 89 West, Browning
406-338-2230
www.browningmontana.com/museum.html

The hours vary by season. You will find an interesting and varied display of arts by the Northern Plains Indians. The array of historic clothing, weapons, household items, and daily goods is informative. The exhibitions and sale items by outstanding contemporary Indian artisans are impressive.

Driving Diva Tip: There is so much to see and do in Glacier, it would be a good idea to plan your itinerary with professionals at the National Park Service or your hotel. Also, get suggestions from others who have been to Glacier.

FYI: Working at one of the national parks is a wonderful experience. I hope to do so in a few years. There are all types of jobs for all ages. I think mine will be in the *Glacier Gift Shop* (www.glaciergiftshop.com). It has to be a rewarding, interesting way to spend the summer.

LEAVING GLACIER: GOING WEST

The roads out of Glacier are good. Highway 2 takes you into **Whitefish** (population approximately 5,032) and then into **Kalispell,** which is the largest town in the Flathead valley. Big Sky country, as this Montana area is termed, is rapidly gaining in popularity.

KALISPELL
(POPULATION APPROXIMATELY 17,149)

Main Street Kalispell

There are many old, original buildings, lots of shops, and lots of stoplights on **Main Street**. I discovered another **Wheat Montana Bakery** (www.wheatmontana.com) here!

Apple Barrel
3250 U.S. Hwy. 2 E.
406-755-7753

This place was very friendly and sold very fresh produce.

50,000 Silver Dollar Bar
Frontage Rd. W., Haugan
406-678-4242

Exit 16 off I-90, which is about ten miles east of the Idaho border and ninety miles east of Spokane, is the perfect place to stop. Here you will find the $50,000 Silver Dollar Bar, one of those "should I really stop here?" kinds of places. The answer is yes! It is a wonderful spot with all sorts of sensibly priced items. The food area and ladies room were clean. The employees were friendly. The food prices were reasonable and the food good. Also Montana's largest gift shop, it sells lots of trinkets of all varieties and prices. I have also learned that this fun stop is a third-generation enterprise.

Driving Diva Tip: This is not a quick in and out unless you make it so. Plan accordingly.

GRASSRANGE
(POPULATION APPROXIMATELY 144)

One trip, leaving Glacier, I took I-15 at Shelby and then headed south to Great Falls, where I got on U.S. 87 South. After getting gas in **Lewiston**, I came upon Grassrange, where a country store loomed temptingly. What a delight this two-part establishment turned out to be! The store half is on one side, overseen by men. The restaurant half is on the other side, and it, of course, is run by women. When I arrived, the homemade sweet buns were just coming out of the oven. Wow! It was a wonderful stop. If you are ever in Grassrange, be sure to stop. You will be welcomed and just might learn a thing or two.

MAMMOTH HOT SPRINGS

Mammoth Hot Springs Hotel
100 Grand Loop Rd., Yellowstone National Park
307-344-7311

Another good road trip is to travel from Glacier to the Montana-Wyoming border, where you will find the Mammoth Hot Springs Hotel in Wyoming. This is such a delight! Each time I stay there, I discover more and more. The scenery is beautiful, and the elk casually grazing around the property form natural props. There are many types of accommodations, all most comfortable.

Suggestion: Find the *hot pots*. You will see cars parked along the side of the road in Montana. There is a shed where you can change into your bathing suit and put on your wading sneakers or such—which hopefully you have not forgotten! You can then go carefully (the rocks are very slippery) into the very warm spring and waterfall pool. It is fabulous! What a day!

For more details on the Mammoth Hot Springs, see the Wyoming chapter.

GARDINER (POPULATION 852)

The original entrance to Yellowstone National Park—and the only entrance open year-round—is in Gardiner. The famous **Roosevelt Arch**, dedicated by Teddy Roosevelt in 1903, is prominent; it can be seen from two miles outside of town. Aside from walking and sightseeing, there are hiking, biking, and rafting in this beautiful area. From my very first visit, the unique charm and total realness got me.

Gardiner is less than a ten-minute drive from Mammoth Hot Springs Hotel in Wyoming. Remember to look for animals, *big* animals, which are often on the road.

Gardiner is one of those towns that, at first glance, you are not quite sure why you are there, but then within minutes you are glad you came. This tiny hippie town is rustic and low-key, but with hints of real savvy. Situated in **Paradise Valley** with the **Yellowstone River** running right through it, this little place is worth a visit.

Go to Gardiner in the late morning, and plan to have lunch at Helen's.

Helen's Corral Drive-in
711 Scott St. W.
406-848-7627

Get the full aura of the area, park your car in town, and walk to Helen's Corral Drive-in, "Best Food in the West, est. 1960." Get directions from any Gardiner native. Everyone knows Helen Gould. Helen's was recommended to me by the gas station attendant, who recommended the "must-have": Helen's buffalo burger. As the menu states, "One size only, all burgers are one half pound! All burgers come loaded unless you tell us different! Baskets include a small salad and French fries, no substitutions."

Walking to Helen's, you will see most of Gardiner. When you are told that Helen's is just down the block, do not be surprised if you don't see it right away. Its outside decor is not elaborate. Arriving at Helen's, I introduced myself to the man who was both cooking and hosting. As I was to discover, he was Helen's son, Steve, who is the cook. Spencer, Helen's grandson, is also involved in this family enterprise.

One buffalo burger was ordered, as was the recommended milk shake, which proved very thick and delicious. Helen appeared and sat down to talk. Hopefully you will have the same unforgettable pleasure. She is a Gardiner treasure.

The walk back to your car is vital, because you need a bit of exercise after a meal at Helen's.

FYI: There were other restaurants in Gardiner, although with each visit it is obvious that they come and go.

As of 2006, I heard that a unique ice cream counter and embroidery store had closed. I enjoyed my initial discovery so much that I had to include it. Stitch-Niche was started by the Hofmanns, with an ice cream counter on one side and clothing and custom embroidery on the other. Mr. Hoffman made all sorts of ice cream delights, including an egg cream, big ice cream cones, and twenty-five-cent tiny ice cream cones. What, you ask, is an egg cream? It's an ice cream soda without ice cream. It is so New York City, and here I was enjoying one in Gardiner, Montana! Custom embroidery could be done overnight and at any time. Sadly, Mr. Hoffman passed away, and the last time I was in Gardiner, Joni Hoffman was managing both sides of the business, which I learned have now closed.

WEST YELLOWSTONE
(POPULATION APPROXIMATELY 1,177)

It is easy to get the Yellowstones confused. West Yellowstone, Montana, just outside the west entrance of Yellowstone National Park, is a very western town with great restaurants and shops and nice people. It is nothing fancy, but it is an enjoyable must-see if you like to experience the real life of such places. I am not necessarily talking about relocating; just try it for a little time, and you might be surprised.

Stage Coach Inn
209 Madison Ave.
406-646-7381
www.yellowstoneinn.com

This centrally located inn is most attractive, casual, and definitely female friendly. It has all the standard things you might need, including a coin-operated laundry and poker games with licensed dealers. (What a combo!) The atmosphere is friendly western. "Fancy" is not an adjective that applies. The lobby is "award winning" with its wing-shaped stairs that fan out to the left and right. In the center is a large western-style painting with a story: As an unfaithful husband came down the stairs, the wife shot at him and missed; therefore, there is a hole in the painting. Oh, those western events.

Restaurants

Bullwinkle's
115 N. Canyon
406-646-7974

The service was excellent and friendly, the food good, and the prices sensible. The entrée of buffalo steak was delicious. At one point, the wrong entrée was brought to someone at the table. There was an immediate apology, the wrong entrée was left on the table for all to try, and the correct meal was brought immediately. That is the way such a mistake should be handled!

Uncle Laurie's Riverside Café
237 Firehole Ave.
406-646-7040

This café doubles as an espresso bar and serves breakfast, lunch, and homemade pies and desserts. And it delivers! I enjoyed a good breakfast at the counter, talking with the pretty chef and a policeman who was also having breakfast.

Shops

Yellowstone Silver Co.
110 Canyon St.
406-646-7512

This western jewelry shop is run by a very friendly mother and son duo, who gave me suggestions about places to see.

Theater

Playmill Theatre of West Yellowstone
29 Madison Ave.
406-646-7757
www.playmill.com

In 2011 they celebrated their forty-seventh season, and the schedule of shows is impressive.

IDAHO

Heading west from Montana on I-90 toward Spokane, you are in Idaho for a very short time, but you pass through wonderful towns like **Mullan** (population 840), **Wallace** (population 1,000), and beautiful **Coeur d'Alene** (population 24,000), a place high on my must-visit list. Idaho is a big and beautiful state. I feel outdoorsy just saying the name.

On my first visit to Idaho, I visited **Sun Valley** with my parents and brother. I was very young, but I remember liking everywhere we went. I also remember seeing sage brush for the first time.

Many years later, I visited a classmate in **Boise**. I drove over the **Teton Pass**, passed through **Victor**, **Driggs**, and **Idaho Falls**, and took I-15 to I-86, then I-84 into Boise. (Victor and Driggs have become popular places to live for the young-and-active crowd seeking to avoid the high cost of living in nearby **Jackson Hole**.) Victor is home to **Reel Women Inc.**, purveyors of fly-fishing adventures for women (see the Wyoming chapter).

I was surprised to find that Boise was so big. The area is beautiful. I visited the impressive Boise State University and also discovered that Boise is home to one of my very favorite grocery stores: **Albertson's**. My classmate, whom I was visiting, took me to the antique area and around Boise. She lived in **Eagle**, which is an absolutely beautiful, bucolic area. The roads are slightly confusing, at least to this visitor, so I suggest (once again) that you get explicit directions.

There is obviously a lot to see and do in Boise. Later I looked up Boise on the Internet. In so many categories, it rates "best of" or "best for" or in the top ten. I was impressed, but then, I have been impressed by all of Idaho. I can honestly and unquestionably say, Idaho is a must-revisit.

UTAH

While driving into Utah on I-80 from the east, you'll notice the landscape changes dramatically from high plains to huge red rock formations. The traffic changes dramatically too, as you approach **Salt Lake City**. During my first few drives through Salt Lake, the roads always seemed to be under construction. Now, I am told, construction is finished, and the roads are good.

Beautiful as it may be, Utah has a few "our way" laws. The liquor laws were peculiar, and from all I have read and been told as of this writing, the "membership law" has been rescinded. This said, some rules still hold true, so be aware.

INTERSTATE 80 AND THE SALT FLATS

I-80, a very straight, long road, goes across the state. Driving it at night, I felt alone, and often I actually was. Every so often, an eighteen-wheeler went jetting by, but that was about it. You must do this fascinating fifty-mile stretch once. Some people talk about the smells; others relate how barren it is. Regardless, you should visit this unique area.

Driving Diva Factoid: Going west in the late afternoon, the sun is in your eyes—for too long. A full gas tank and cell phone are imperative.

The **Great Salt Lake** is six times saltier than the ocean. You will want to stop and feel the coarse salt—even take a bit of it with you. For as far as you can see, it will just be white, white salt. In some parts, you can walk onto this salty terrain but not without foot protection. It is a special experience.

WENDOVER
(POPULATION APPROXIMATELY 1,000)

Civilization returns in Wendover, Utah, which is a stone's throw from **Wendover West**, Nevada, a neon-lit gambling town. Wendover, Utah, is Utah-subdued: no gambling and, of course, the Utah laws. These two towns are so close together, I have heard they share high schools (see Wendover West, Nevada).

PARK CITY

A short distance from **Provo** and Salt Lake City is Park City, which has become more universally known due to the **Sundance Film Festival**.

Sundance Institute
1825 Three Kings Dr.
435-658-3456
www.sundance.org

Getting to Sundance is an easy and beautiful drive, which I did in the summer. I am sure it has its winter charm and challenges, too, with snow conditions that often prevail.

Sundance Resort and Institute

8841 N. Alpine Loop Rd.

800-892-1600

www.sundanceresort.com

Family-oriented, safe, and beautiful, this is a community for art and nature. I consider it a wonderful place simply to escape to and even reconnect with yourself. The various accommodations are handsome. The log cabin look is rustic-posh, with bright, colorful Indian blankets popping out at you from natural-wood backgrounds. Of course, there are fireplaces. Be it the private rooms or the public areas, nothing is not well appointed and beautiful at Sundance.

Robert Redford purchased this land in 1969, and with determination he started Sundance, a community for those who appreciate nature. The arts are present, as are the sports. There is plenty of skiing, fly-fishing, hiking, snowboarding, and horseback riding.

When one checks in, the room key is attached to a small flashlight. This is a clue. The accommodations are snuggled into the woods. It can be a very dark walk from your car to the front door of your accommodations. The flashlight is a must! Thank you, Sundance organizers!

The shops are appealing, and the collection of merchandise is attractive and very tempting. The restaurants are excellent. Remember, you are in Utah and check for any Utah rules.

Restaurants: The multi-award-winning **Tree Room** (435-649-9108) is attractive and romantic, with excellent food. The wonderful Native American art displayed on the walls, from what I understand, is from Mr. Redford's private collection.

The thoroughly enjoyable **Foundry Grill** (866-932-2295) is open for breakfast, lunch, and dinner six days a week. On Sundays, there is brunch and dinner. This is more casual dining.

The **Owl Bar** (801-223-4222) is a private club. Here, you will feel like you are in a different place and time, even before you start imbibing. Don't be surprised if you see a familiar theater face. On the weekends local musicians perform, and the bar doesn't close until midnight.

Downtown Park City

The charming historic **Main Street** (800-453-1369) retains its old mining-town ambiance. The majority of buildings were built in the late 1800s and early 1900s. This is a town full of shops, galleries, and restaurants—and in high season, people. Although it's only seven blocks long, you should put on your walking boots or shoes and tour. Be sure to get a map and a listing of all that is going on. You do not want to miss out.

Zoom
660 Main St.
435-649-9108
www.zoomparkcity.com

Robert Redford opened this restaurant in 1995. All the Sundance-Redford restaurants are award winning.

Sundance Film Festival

The prestigious Sundance Film Festival is held in Park City in January, when the quiet little town becomes Hollywood alive with hope from all connected with the event. There are seminars, screenings, and exhibits.

Constructive Observation: Calling the resort, sometimes it takes a while for the phone to be answered.

Confession: I visited Park City/Sundance Resort when I was just beginning to discover, visit, and review places across the United States. I was a novice from head to toe. I look forward to returning to the area and viewing it with a more mature eye.

BRYCE, ZION, AND ARCHES NATIONAL PARKS

The road you take to get to these treasures is up to you—just be sure you do so. The national parks are managed and run extremely well. Each is a gem and should not be missed.

Bryce National Park

This colorful collection of rock spikes is hard to describe and equally hard to fathom when you are face-to-face with these vast formations. The rock formations are called hoodoos, and the areas they are clustered in are called amphitheaters.

You will have to plan ahead and make reservations when going to Bryce. Visiting spur of the moment, I lucked out and was able to get a room at the Lodge at Bryce Canyon.

Lodge at Bryce Canyon
PO Box 640041, Bryce
435-834-8700
www.brycecanyonforever.com

There is a restaurant, a gift shop, and a post office. There is a lot to do at Bryce, including hiking, fishing, horseback riding, and all those adventurous activities. Perfect!

Zion National Park

What a wonder! There is much to do here, and planning is key to your venture. The mile-long **Zion Mount Carmel Tunnel** has specific requirements for entrance. Be sure to check, particularly if you have a large vehicle.

Zion means "place of refuge." The huge rock formations towering over you are awesome. Like each national park, Zion is in a category by itself. I could only describe it as I saw it.

Although there are many places to stay outside of the park, the Zion Lodge is the only one of its kind in the park.

Zion Lodge
PO Box 925, Springdale
435-772-7700
www.zionlodge.com

You can see the park by taking one of the **shuttle buses** (www .zionpark.com/shuttle_bus_service.htm), but of course driving the area is a special experience. There are highways and byways to drive, as well, of course, as all the endeavors for the athlete, including climbing, backpacking, horseback riding, water sports, and more. You will see people climbing the rocks, and their feats are impressive.

Arches National Park

Located five miles north of **Moab** on Highway 191, **Arches** is another spectacular national park to visit. It is open all year, except on December 25. It is large and contains all the literature and documentaries you need to get an in-depth appreciation of Arches. There is no food sold in the park, and there is no lodging (you stay in Moab). Throughout the park, restrooms and water are available.

The way to see this park is via car. The roads are excellent. Allow an hour plus, plus, plus, because you will want to get out and very slowly ingest the beautiful sandstone arches. There are over two thousand. The park encompasses more than seventy-six thousand acres. Some of the arches are massive; some look fragile—as if you might be able to push them over. Not hardly! You are looking at over a million years' worth of carving. I had no intention to stay as long as I did, but getting out of the car to sit and look out over the vast, barren terrain to let the music of the wind blow around me, I was taken into a private place that I was slow to leave.

Driving Diva Input: Put your two index fingers together, tips just touching. Arch your fingers and hold them under a light. This is an inkling of what the arches look like.

Early homesteaders tried to live in this barren, albeit beautiful, setting. Indeed, it was a challenge as you will learn when you stop at **Wolfe Ranch** and learn the details. There is truly something for everyone of all ages at Arches.

MOAB

Moab is a necessity if you are going to be in the area. Investigate its potentials carefully; a lot is available. I was surprised to find this vibrant little oasis that welcomes almost 1 million tourists a year. Its lushness stems from its being situated on the banks of the **Colorado River**. Moab is the perfect focal point for your excursions in the nearby national parks and surrounding areas.

ARIZONA

PHOENIX AND SCOTTSDALE

Taking I-8 from San Diego to I-10 (as I did), and then into Phoenix/ Scottsdale, is quite direct, but it still takes about seven long hours. It's not a bad drive, and there are several places to stop and get gas—I emphasize that there are not many but several. It's a landscape of heat, dust, and rocks—which in their own way can be very attractive. The temperature will change drastically along the way. When I left San Diego, it was 71 degrees; by the time I reached Yuma, 180 miles away, the temperature was a very hot and dry 118 degrees. This drive requires a full gas tank (top it off whenever there's an opportunity), water (of course), a charged cell phone, and cream for your face. Yes, the sun will find your face through the windshield.

YUMA (POPULATION APPROXIMATELY 60,000)

This is possibly the hottest, driest town in the United States, though those in **Gila Bend** may beg to differ. Yuma is a real town, where you can stretch, eat, get gas, and possibly feel hotter than you have ever felt in your life. I did find a strip mall with one of those "you might find anything here" stores, which I call "gypsy stores" because they are liable to have moved by the time you read this.

DATELAND

Between Yuma and Gila Bend there is really a whole lot of nothing. Dateland is just a spot on the map, but it is an authentic place to stop. I recommend that you do. There is a mini market with gas, postcards, restrooms, trinkets, and telephones, as well as a restaurant, gift shop, and bus stop. The restaurant is spotless, and everyone is friendly. Appropriately, a lot of dates are grown in the area. The specialty is the fact that they grow "the world's finest Medjool dates." At the restaurant, you can get dates of all varieties (except the two-legged kind), like date milk shakes and cream pies. I would suggest being very careful about eating too many dates, as delicious as they are, before returning to your drive in the heat. When traveling (especially in high heat), I like to keep my stomach rather empty, but from all reports, I hear that the date milk shakes are excellent.

Date Data: Many consider dates nature's candy. They are low in fat and sodium, contain no cholesterol, are high in fiber and magnesium, contain more potassium than bananas, and are rich in iron.

Note: In the 1940s, Gen. George Patton had two desert training camps here, and in 1942 three airstrips were built for training B-25 bombers. Most of this is gone, although due to the hot desert heat, the military still uses the Dateland area for training troops going to Iraq.

GILA BEND

On entering the town, you'll see a sign reading,

Gila Bend
Welcomes You
Home of 1700 Friendly People
And 5 Old Crabs Ele. 737

The name Gila Bend comes from the fact that the **Gila River** makes a 90-degree "bend" to the north here. Gila Bend is about fifty miles southwest of Phoenix; a shortcut to the metropolis is to take Route 85 at Gila Bend north to I-10. I have done this several times, and Route 85 is a good road, though without the services of an interstate.

About forty miles outside of Phoenix, there is one of the largest prisons imaginable, including a large juvenile correctional center, where a road sign reads, "Do Not Stop for Hitchhikers." Hmmm.

PHOENIX AND SCOTTSDALE

Phoenix and Scottsdale are so close together that they practically lie on top of one another. A thriving oasis in the middle of the dessert, Phoenix is not difficult to navigate. The key is to become familiar with the main thoroughfares and keep an eye on "the Camel," imposing **Mount Camelback**, as a point of reference.

Whether a camel or a camelette . . . at first it might be hard to discern. The camel is "seated" on all fours. Focus and you will soon see it. It's an excellent landmark.

The Phoenix/Scottsdale area is a veritable heaven on earth for women, with its spas, restaurants, golf courses, pools, and shopping. Here are my recommendations, based on my several visits to this fabulous desert oasis.

Hotels

Royal Palms Hotel

5200 E. Camelback Rd.

800-672-6011

www.royalpalmshotel.com

What a fabulous oasis it is! From the second you see this gem, you know it is special. Immediately you get a feeling of intimacy and quiet delight. As you drive the small, circular cobblestone driveway and park your car, attired attendants greet you with a smile, even in 110-degree heat.

When you enter, you feel like you are walking into a private home—no, a mansion—which the Royal Palms once was. Its history from home to hotel is interesting:

> In the early 1920s, New York financier Delos Cooke pursued his dream to build a winter home in Phoenix and commissioned the building of a mansion in the grand Spanish colonial style. A world traveler, Delos and his wife, Florence, filled their mansion with wondrous treasures from their travels around the world.
>
> After Cooke's untimely death in 1931, the home was sold to a series of private parties, who added various rooms, including an in-house chapel. After World War II, a group of investors purchased the Cooke property with the intention of developing a first-class resort. A new era for the estate began.
>
> Named for the regal, towering trees lining each side of the entryway, the Royal Palms Inn opened to guests in the winter of 1948. It became a destination of choice for discriminating travelers from around the world, including celebrities such as Groucho Marx and Helena Rubenstein.
>
> In 1995, local Arizona businessman Fred Unger purchased the landmark property and went about the task of restoring Royal Palms to its original charm and elegance. Today, after a multi-million-dollar restoration, the preservation of this historic property has been assured.

There are rooms, suites, casitas, deluxe casitas, a camelback villa, and a honeymoon villa. I was traveling in the summer and was upgraded to a magnificent deluxe casita. The room was absolutely charming and cozy with its wrought iron bed frame, fireplace, private patio, and custom-designed furniture. Though wonderful, it needed a bit of fine tuning: The oversize stuffed chairs could have used an ottoman between them; the switch on the bed lamps was not an easy reach; the door on the TV entertainment center didn't fold back all the way. These little things could easily be corrected.

A Female Tidbit: If you have a private patio, you can rinse out your items and hang them discreetly on a patio chair, where they will dry almost instantly. Don't leave them out at night, because that's when the sprinklers go on.

Everyone at the Royal Palms was extremely friendly, capable, and knowledgeable. The courtyard and all the inside areas and gardens are beautiful.

The heavenly **Alvadora Spa** is what I call a boutique spa—small, intimate, and serene. You definitely do not feel like a number lost among pseudo smiles. The technician who gave me an "Orange Blossom Body Buff" was skilled and professional and generally seemed to care about what she was doing and how I was feeling. I recommend this treatment without a doubt. In the spa world, there are many kinds of treatments applied by technicians whose experience varies, from the perfunctory body rub with smelly oil and several minutes of gonging sounds to oils carefully applied until you are comfortably in la-la land. The Alvadora was definitely in the latter category; providing one of the best spa treatments I've received. Prices can range from $30 to $400 for a four-hour spa package. (An 18 percent gratuity is automatically added to your bill.) There are many different options, so study the (then) difficult-to-read brochure carefully. You have nothing to think about except you and your experience. Alvadora proves that size doesn't matter when it comes to a first-rate experience.

The Royal Palms's principal restaurant, **T. Cook's**, features not just a maître d' but a "director of romance." Even if romance is not on the evening's agenda, the director oversees everything with enthusiasm and his restaurant gamesmanship. My dining experience at T. Cook's was exceptional. I enjoyed soft-shell crab with sweet pepper relish and warm bacon dressing; toasted beet and chèvre salad with watercress, mâche, and walnut vinaigrette; spit-roasted chicken with baby green beans, creminis, and beurre rouge. Ice cream was my dessert, and it was served on appropriately chilled plates. Hot plates, cold plates, large plates, small plates, decorated plates—it was truly a delicious dinner delight, and the presentations were perfect. Prices are sensible. T. Cook's is very popular, so reservations are recommended.

T. Cook's also has outdoor patio dining—perhaps not a great idea in midsummer, though the area is cooled by a misting system. This makes alfresco dining bearable with a fun twist. Forget your hair! The bar at T. Cook's is in the courtyard. There is bar seating for about thirteen, in addition to several overstuffed leather chairs and a 1930s-style sofa. Music from the baby grand piano fills the air. The **Cigar Room** is located at the bar and seats approximately twelve people in plush chairs and sofas over a red leather floor. I did not see any "men only" signs, so ladies too can enjoy.

Royal Palms offers cold bottled water on departure—a classy gesture befitting a classy place.

The Phoenician

6000 E. Camelback Rd.
480-941-8200
www.thephoenician.com

You hear about some places over and over again until they develop a sort of legendary status in your mind. The Phoenician lives up to its reputation and more.

Though huge, slick, and glamorous, the Phoenician is not intimidating. The complex is well run, pleasant, and inviting, even though it sprawls over 250 acres, contains 654 rooms, and boasts

27 holes of championship golf, 12 tennis courts, 9 heated pools, and a 165-foot waterslide (which this mother thoroughly enjoyed after several moments of hesitation).

Note: Foot protection is vital by the pools due to the heat of the walkways.

The Phoenician is indeed big but not gaudy. The art is tasteful, and the decor is well designed. It is not hard to find your way around once you get your bearings, but the staff is most helpful if you get lost. I stayed in the **Canyon Building**, which is kind of a resort within the resort. Just a few steps outside my room was the pool for the building, where I enjoyed a delightful late-night swim under the stars. Conveniently, the Canyon Building also has its own self-park garage downstairs.

The first night I had drinks at the **Thirsty Camel Lounge** with then director of public relations Debora Bridges, who gave me an outstanding verbal tour of the property. (She definitely knows her profession.) The Thirsty Camel is the perfect spot to wind down, with its spectacular views and relaxing classical music in the background.

Dinner was at **Mary Elaine's**, located on the top level of the main building. The views are magnificent, and the attention to detail was to the max. Then women would receive a "perch" on which to place their purses.

During dinner I met Greg Tresner, the master sommelier, who succinctly and interestingly explained the wines being served.

FYI: There are only forty-two master sommeliers in the United States and ninety-seven worldwide, as noted in *Arizona Food & Lifestyle*.

Update: After nearly twenty years, **J&G Steakhouse** (480-214-8000) has replaced Mary Elaine's, but not a morsel of excellence has been diminished. The sommelier is still present, but the pocket-book perch is gone. From what I have learned, this is a most special eating experience. It is a Jean-George Vongerichten creation.

Il Terrazo (480-423-2530), featuring American Italian cuisine, is another dining area serving breakfast, lunch, dinner, and an excellent Sunday brunch. Casual dining can be found at the **Relish Burger Bistro**, overlooking the championship golf course.

I had an excellent facial at the **spa** (800-843-2392), and there are numerous choices. The space is big, gracious, and appealing.

My experience at the Phoenician was very memorable. You will feel at home and comfortable in spite of its size. You will enjoy.

Arizona Biltmore and Spa

2400 E. Missouri Ave.
602-955-6600 or 800-950-0086
www.arizonabiltmore.com

Designed by consulting architect Frank Lloyd Wright and opened in 1929, the Arizona Biltmore was later bought by William Wrigley Jr. For the next forty-four years, the Wrigley family owned and operated this unique property. In 1973 it was sold to Talley Industries. There have been several expansions and renovations to the Arizona Biltmore, but it has always retained its special style. In spite of its size, you will not feel overwhelmed here, though more signage would definitely help to keep you from getting lost in the maze of corridors. The **spa** (602-381-7632) is most pleasant, and one of the unique features of the resort is a giant chessboard cut into the lawn. The resort has three restaurants: the **Café** for casual, healthy eating; **Frank & Alberts**; and **Wright's** (602-381-7632), the resort's signature restaurant, where I found the food and ambiance exceptional.

This property, known as the "Jewel of the Desert," has 738 guest rooms, eight swimming pools, seven tennis courts, six restaurants and lounges, and a full spa, salon, and fitness center. There are two eighteen-hole championship golf courses, the **Links** and the **Adobe**, and an eighteen-hole putting course. Everything you could possibly want can be found at this magnificent resort, though it is anything but glitzy. The Wright-influenced design is subdued but attractive, and the landscaping is superb. The resort was recently added to the Waldorf-Astoria Collection in the Hilton Hotel system.

Driving Diva Factoid: Irving Berlin composed "White Christmas" sitting poolside at the Arizona Biltmore.

Even at the height (and in the heat) of summer, the Arizona Biltmore is a busy place, hosting business meetings as well as family vacations.

Camelback Inn Marriott Resort and Spa
5402 E. Lincoln Dr.
480-948-1700 or 800-242-2635 (CAMEL)
www.camelbackinn.com

Upscale but relaxing, accommodations here consist of extremely attractive casitas, some of which are in fact duplexes, with the bedroom and bath on the loft level and the living room, dining and kitchen areas, and powder room on the lower level. Walk in the gardens. Perhaps the cacti will be blooming. This is a nice oasis.

Phoenix-Scottsdale Shopping

This area is notoriously upscale, but I have found a good diversity of stores from consignment shops to the usual big-box outlets.

Camelback Colonnade
1919 Camelback Rd.
602-953-6412
www.camelbackcolonnade.com

Here you'll find **Last Chance** (602-248-2843), a huge Nordstrom's outlet and shopper's paradise. It consists of Nordstrom's "mistakes" (Yes!). Overbought clothing lines that are now being liquidated are available at fabulous sale prices, and you will not believe how much there is to choose from. Have fun!

A must-stop for any shopper is a complex of stores on the 2000 block of **East Camelback:**

My Sister's Closet, My Sister's Attic, and Well Suited

2033 E. Camelback Rd.

602-954-6080

My Sister's Closet (www.mysisterscloset.com) has recycled designer apparel; My Sister's Attic (www.mysistersattic.com) has recycled home furnishings; Well Suited (www.shopwellsuited.com) has clothing for men. The stores are operated by Eco-Chic Consignment Inc., whose philosophy is "recycled stuff for humans and their homes." (I confess, I left a few pennies at My Sister's Closet.)

Driving Diva Observation: When you enter freeways or highways in Arizona (and possibly in other states as well), a caution light blinks red or green, telling you if cars are approaching on the road—so you know whether to enter or wait. This is excellent. Of course, you need the input from your eyes as well.

SOUTH OF PHOENIX

Heading southeast out of Phoenix toward **Tucson** and **Green Valley** on Route 10, one comes across a number of curiosities, such as the ominously imposing **Picacho State Prison**, where once again you are urged not to pick up hitchhikers.

Rooster Cogburn's Ostrich Ranch

17599 E. Peak Ln., Picacho

520-466-3658

www.roostercogburn.com

This is the largest ostrich ranch in the United States. Have you ever fed an ostrich? It's a hoot. You buy the proper ostrich food for a very small amount of money, then go feed these funny-looking birds. At first I thought they would bite the hand that was trying to feed them, but no. A quick thrust of the neck over the high fence, and the food is safely plucked away from you. D. C., Lucille, and Danna Cogburn own and operate the ranch; Lucille was there when I visited. Most friendly and knowledgeable, Lucille can tell you everything you ever wanted to know about ostriches (and then some). The ranch sells everything from ostrich eggs to ostrich feather dusters.

Note: Rooster Cogburn's is closed on Wednesdays. If you miss visiting, you can look the ranch up on the Internet.

TUCSON

One of the oldest cities in the United States, Tucson has a lot going on. I spent a short time there, but without a doubt, it is vibrant, artistic, interesting, and historic. I should go back.

FYI: From firsthand experiences, I report that St. Mary's Hospital is more than first rate.

St. Mary's Hospital
1601 W. Saint Mary's Rd.
520-872-3000
www.carondelet.org

I hope you do not need it, but I provide the information just in case.

GREEN VALLEY AND AMADO

Green Valley, a growing suburb of Tucson, is charming, friendly, clean, and attractive. A few miles south of Green Valley on I-19 is

Amado, the place the Hollywood crowd would getaway to in the 1930s. If you exit at **Arivaca Road**, you will see a huge concrete cow's skull that marks the entrance of a cantina, the Longhorn Bar & Grill.

Longhorn Bar & Grill

28851 S. Nogales Hwy.
520-398-3955
www.longhornamadoaz.com

Rumor has it that the nightly specials are terrific.

Across the way is the popular and famous Cow Palace Restaurant.

Cow Palace Restaurant

28802 S. Nogales Hwy.
520-398-1999
www.cowpalacerestaurant.com

You can't miss it. The building is red and white with a cow statue on the roof. Opened in 1920, the palace was frequented by such celebrities as John Wayne and the unique Griz Green, the Gabby Hayes look-alike who was an occasional movie extra.

PRESCOTT AND JEROME: NORTH OF PHOENIX

Prescott (pronounced "press-kit") is charming, and it's hard not to feel welcome in this rather upscale western town. Boasting gentle seasons, recreational activities of all types, and major cultural events, it is home to the world's oldest rodeo as well as Prescott College. There are wonderful antique stores, craft shops, and boutiques. A memorable Prescott experience is an evening gathering in the town square by **Courthouse Plaza**. One night there might be square dancing; the next night there will be something else.

There's a lot of history in Prescott; over 450 buildings are on the National Register of Historic Places. **Whiskey Row** (www.whiskeyrow.us) is directly across from the Courthouse Plaza.

Hotel St. Michael
205 W. Gurley St.
928-776-1999
www.stmichaelhotel.com

The old Hotel St. Michael is a true step back in time.

Palace Restaurant and Saloon
120 South Montezuma
928-541-1996
www.historicpalace.com

The Palace Restaurant has a friendly western ambience and excellent food.

Hassayampa Inn
122 E. Gurley St.
928-778-9434
www.hassayampainn.com

This sixty-eight-room historic property sits right on the street and is full of charm. Built in 1927, it is not without modern amenities. Nothing is pretentious at the Hassayampa Inn; everything seems just right. A meal in the three-star **Peacock Dining Room** (928-777-9563) is a delicious delight. I enjoyed every second at the inn and in Prescott.

Driving Diva Alert: Route 89A from Jerome to Prescott is a true white-knuckle experience. Route 89A is probably the worst road I have ever driven on.

JEROME (POPULATION APPROXIMATELY 450)

Jerome, positioned on a steep hill, was a booming mining town of nearly fifteen thousand people in the 1880s. It had the largest copper mine in Arizona, and people came from all over to find work. In 1918, a fire broke out in the eighty-eight miles of underground tunnels, leading to the safer practice of open-pit mining. However, continual dynamiting cracked Jerome's buildings so much that the town actually began to shift, with the jail sliding some 225 feet. (It can now be found across the road from its original site.) In 1953, only fifty residents remained, but by the 1960s, Jerome's renaissance was underway. An artists' colony of sorts established itself, and the stalwart residents joined in rebuilding the town. Today it is a must-visit and touts itself as "American's Most Vertical City" and the "Largest Ghost Town." There are all sorts of shops and places to dine. I must return to Jerome as the reviews claim the food is excellent at all the restaurants and the ambiance fun and friendly. Three names must be mentioned:

Asylum Restaurant
200 Hill St.
928-639-3197
www.theasylum.biz

Belgian Jennie's Bordello Pizzeria
412 Main St.
928-639-3141

Mile High Inn and Grill
309 Main St.
928-634-5094
www.milehighgrillandinn.com

Also a consideration would be to indulge in a glass of wine at the Jerome Winery while some local music plays in the background.

Jerome Winery
403 Clark St.
928-639-9067
www.jeromewinery.com

GRAND CANYON

At least once in a lifetime, one should visit the world's biggest hole in the ground—an unbelievable 277 miles long and 18 miles wide with an average depth of 1 mile. Because of the shifting light, the Grand Canyon looks like it is always changing. The colors within the canyon glow and at times seem almost neon-like. In spite of its size, there is a breathtaking quiet to the canyon. There are many lodges to stay at on the **South Rim**, but reservations are a must and should be made far in advance. The rooms are not fancy, but they are very comfortable. The El Tovar Hotel has the more formal dining.

El Tovar Hotel
10 Albright Ave.
888-297-2757
www.grandcanyonlodges.com/el-tovar-409.html

Bright Angel Lodge & Cabins
219–221 Village Loop Dr.
520-638-2631
www.grandcanyonlodges.com/bright-angel-lodge-408.html

When I checked into the Bright Angel Lodge, I was asked if I would like a wake-up call so that I could see the sunrise over the rim the next morning. Of course I would, and it was well worth getting up for. What a fantastic experience! I am still talking about it and telling everyone to do likewise. Be sure you do not miss this unbelievable, beautiful, awesome sight.

The experience: What was that early-morning experience like? First of all, it was chilly, even in the summer. It is quiet and cold, and people are ambling, many with arms crossed over chest to keep in warmth, waiting for the first glow of dawn and eventual warming rays. Silently, it suddenly starts. The sky lightens, and the rocks start to take on their early dawn colors. Gradually, a huge orb starts to inch its way upward as this world awakens. It is not hard to realize why the early inhabitants of the area thought the sun was a magical, mystical entity. You might find yourself agreeing.

There is a lot to do at the Grand Canyon, such as hiking, taking helicopter or mule rides, or just meditating on stone and light. I thought it might be easy to walk a tiny way down the canyon and look up. Not for this mother! Once the guardrail was no more, that took care of my walk. I even tried to go down a ways on my backside. No way. I hear from my younger son, who has hiked the canyon several times, that it is a magnificent experience. I'm sure it is, and I'll just take his word for it.

As of 2011, the entrance fee into the park is $25 per vehicle (including all passengers) or $12 per individual, which provides you with a seven-day pass. Pick up a senior citizen lifetime pass for all national parks if you're eligible. Your camping fees are additional to the entrance fee and are charged by the night. Hotel reservations are handled by Xanterra Parks & Resorts (303-297-2757, www .grandcanyonlodges.com). Rates range from approximately $50 to $325.

Note: For those with respiratory and heart problems, the altitude of the Grand Canyon's rims ranges from seven to eight thousand feet, so consult with your doctor before visiting.

NEVADA

FYI: Wendover West, Nevada, and Wendover, Utah, are two towns with the same name on the border of these two states.

- - - - - - - - - - - - - - - - -

Arriving in Nevada from Salt Lake City, Utah, you will have spent a very long time crossing the salt flats—something you should do at least once. (See the Utah chapter for details.)

- - - - - - - - - - - - - - - - -

WENDOVER WEST

Wendover West, being the first city in Nevada along I-80, is a big gambling town. Even so, women can feel relatively secure, although this is not Mayberry by any means. It is important to be alert, look like you know what you are doing (even if you don't), and know where you are going. Drinks are often free in the casinos, but don't be too tempted.

Wendover Nugget Hotel (formerly the State Line Hotel)
101 Wendover Blvd.
775-664-2221
www.wendovernugget.com

Comfortable and even sort of cozy, despite its size of more than eight hundred rooms, the Wendover Nugget was, most of all, clean and friendly—not fancy, not plush, but nice.

Discoveries: Wendover West

There are lots of other hotels and motels, as well as the usual fast fooders. Pawnshops come in several varieties: very professional establishments, rough shops that are willing to take your blood if that is all you have to offer, and friendly places that are fun to look around in and maybe find a treasure or two. If you spend even a short time in a pawnshop in a gambling town, you will see amazing things. I think some desperate people would remove the fillings from their teeth if they could pawn them for just one more try with Lady Luck.

Wendover West to Reno is a long drive and will take you at least eight or nine hours, but it should be done at least once. Although the highway is excellent, I would not recommend driving I-80 across Nevada at night. There are long, desolate stretches, and if you were to need help (heaven forbid!), you could have a real problem. A cell phone is imperative. The road is dusty, windy, and full of trucks; the topography is barren, flat, and at times monotonous, but it does have an aura that you should experience.

ELKO (POPULATION MORE THAN 14,000)

This is the first real town you will come to. It has all the usual retail chain stores. (I even found one of my favorites, **Maurice's** [www .maurices.com].) Elko would be a good place to stay overnight if you wanted to divide the trek across the state. It is a beautiful area for wildlife and outdoor sports.

RENO (POPULATION MORE THAN 133,000)

Reno looks like a major metropolis after Elko. It's a busy and crowded place, full of casinos, pawnshops, and all the riffraff they attract. Although there are many hotels, I played it safe and stayed at the Hilton, which is now the Grand Sierra Resort & Casino.

Grand Sierra Resort & Casino (formerly Hilton Reno)
2500 E. Second St.
775-789-2000
www.grandsierraresort.com

With two thousand rooms, this hotel is big! From all I saw, the property is very professionally managed. Do not expect warm and fuzzy service, but you are of course in a gambling mecca. My room was comfortable, and I was to learn that all the rooms are oversized, encompassing 425 square feet. Accommodations are sensibly priced. Of course, getting a guest on property is key for gambling returns, and with a bit of time and research, I would presume that deals are available. The resort is on 142 acres, and there is a lot to do aside from gambling. Entertainment abounds. There is a fifty-lane championship bowling facility and an indoor golf simulator, a mini go-cart ride, swimming, and more, including a variety of places to eat. From the Grand Sierra, discovering the area is easy and convenient.

PS: Interestingly, before 1844 Reno was inhabited by the Paiute and Washoe Indians. In 1859 Charles Fuller of Pine Grove, California, put in a toll bridge across the *Truckee River* and then the *Comstock Lode* was discovered in *Virginia City*, one of the largest strikes in the world. And so, the population explosion began, putting Reno firmly on the map. In 1886, the University of Nevada moved from Elko to Reno. Gambling had its ups and downs, but in 1879 it was legalized, only to be banned in 1910. Finally, in 1931, for tourism and economic reasons, Nevada legalized gambling. All this, mixed with the establishment of the quickie divorce, got Reno moving on the fast track. It is interesting to visit Reno, even if you are not a gambler.

LAKE TAHOE

The drive into Tahoe from Reno on U.S. 395 can be a slight brake burner, but do not fear; just be aware and alert. People are generally patient with those who drive slower than the natives, but look out for passing cars.

Tahoe is now very in with the new Silicon Valley money barons, and price doesn't seem to be much of an object. It's no wonder the barons choose this stunningly beautiful area. I immediately was impressed and would go back in a heartbeat.

Lake Tahoe is huge and straddles both Nevada and California. **Incline Village** is the Nevada side of Tahoe.

Hyatt Regency Lake Tahoe Resort, Spa, and Casino
111 Country Club Dr., Incline Village
775-832-1234
www.laketahoe.hyatt.com

This is a wonderful place to stay, with its lakeside beach and mountain backdrop. When I was there, the beach attendant was most considerate in reminding bathers of the intense sun at that altitude (six thousand feet) and to apply sunscreen accordingly. Nearby are plenty of restaurants, a very nice grocery store, and a post office. Perhaps I will discover more of this beautiful area in the not-too-distant future. Hopefully, development will take place in proper increments in Tahoe. The resources are there; hopefully the powers that be will not get hoodwinked or greedy.

Note: If you are heading west out of Tahoe into California, be sure to top up the gas tank. There are not a lot of gas stations along this section of I-80.

LAS VEGAS

I-15 will take you to the ultimate neon city, the one and only Las Vegas. Whatever you have read or seen about Las Vegas will pale in comparison to seeing it firsthand. And because of the crowds, the money changing hands, the shows, the gambling of all sorts, and everything else that happens in Las Vegas, it is actually a relatively safe place for a woman to visit on her own. Police, security guards, and video cameras are everywhere.

Las Vegas has also become something of a destination for families. There are plenty of things for children to do. It's best to plan well ahead for a stay in Las Vegas. Hotels sell out for the weekends, as do tickets to popular shows. Obtain information and input from others who have been to this city. On my most recent trip, I spent one very full day in Las Vegas. A possible return trip for discoveries, shows, restaurants, and such could be on the agenda.

In 1978 the largest hotel at that time was built, the twenty-six-story, 5,690-room MGM Grand.

MGM Grand Hotel & Casino
3799 Las Vegas Blvd. S.
702-891-7777 or 877-880-0880
www.mgmgrand.com

Travel Tip: If you're driving to Los Angeles, avoid leaving Las Vegas on a Sunday afternoon. The interstate is a parking lot all the way to the coast.

Note: Less than a two-hour drive from Las Vegas is unbelievable *Death Valley*, which should not be missed. (See the California chapter for details.)

WASHINGTON

Taking I-90 into Spokane from Montana you are in Idaho for less than ninety miles. Then Washington State welcomes you.

SPOKANE
(POPULATION APPROXIMATELY 178,000)

I arrived in Spokane at about 7:30 p.m. It was still light, and I immediately liked something about the city. I have continued to tout it—a wonderful discovery.

Davenport Hotel
10 S. Post St.

509-455-8888

www.davenporthotel.com

Beautiful, stylish, and classy are understatements for this magnificent, historic hotel founded circa 1890 by Louis Davenport, the ultimate perfectionist: "He insisted on fresh flowers throughout the hotel, flatware be aligned one thumb knuckle from the table edge and money be washed and pressed before being given in change."

He sold his hotel in 1945 and took his magic with him when he left. The Davenport just was not the same and finally closed in 1985. For the next fifteen years, it was doubtful that it would ever regain its status in the hotel world. Perhaps demolition would be the answer.

In 2000, thanks to local (and farsighted) entrepreneurs Mr. and Mrs. W. Worthy, the Davenport was saved and is once again glorious and glowing. Perhaps the money isn't washed and the one-knuckle rule no longer applies, but, as Mr. Worthy, states, "We in essence have a brand-new hotel that's hidden in a 100-year-old body." To which I add, they have done a great job!

One feels an immediate warmth on entering the hotel. It is female friendly, and old-world charm is evident. The lobby is beautiful in every way.

My room accommodations were attractive, comfortable, and not overly decorated. The massive mahogany headboards are impressive and give stature to the high beds. Steps at each side aid with getting into the bed. The bedding is excellent and the bed comfortable.

The spotlighting above the beds is nice, and there is also a lamp between the beds. The overhead air vent should have a deflector as those "breezes" blowing above sleepers can cause all sorts of cricks in the neck and headaches. The entertainment center is well placed, and there is a desk for "work."

The bathroom area is divided into three parts. The separate vanity area has only one sink—not the worst thing in the world and fine if you are alone. There is a large tub, large separate shower, and a doorless cubbyhole for the toilet. Door please! Dispensers for soap and shampoo in the shower area and by the tub are convenient.

Each night when I was there, I had the delicious pleasure of enjoying a soft chocolate–peanut butter delight left next to the bed. Now, I learn that The Davenport's turndown service includes one ounce of soft peanut brittle and a one-ounce piece of soft chocolate–peanut brittle. I look forward to tasting!

Spa Paradiso (509-747-3529, www.spaparadiso.com) at the Davenport is good and professional. I enjoyed my spa experience. The staff was friendly, receptive, and knowledgeable—three adjectives that do not always apply to one spa! Be sure to look at the suggested packages in the spa brochure. I found these extremely well priced.

Do not miss visiting; better, stay at the Davenport. It is a special experience at a most special property.

The **Davenport Hotel Tower** is open. Across the street from the historic Davenport, it has 328 rooms, twenty-one floors, and all the amenities, bells, and whistles you could possible need or want. It is ideal for corporate meetings. The decor in many of the areas is safari themed—a first for Spokane, or so I was told. I look forward to visiting the Davenport Hotel Tower.

While walking and discovering, I found Spokane an ultraclean city—even the alleyways were clean. The streets are wide, the area uncongested, and the people friendly and open. I was impressed.

Spokane's city planners seem to have thought out how the city could best expand and how the expansions would work not only on paper but in real life. So many planners seem to look at development and expansion only from the drawing board perspective.

The area around the Davenport Hotel is interesting, with a lot going on. Be sure to get a map! Though it's a walkable area, street sense and awareness must prevail, particularly at night. If you are alone, know where you are going, and let the concierge know your plans. There were a few street children in groups along the sides of buildings in the downtown area. (Hippies still remain.)

The River Park Square

There are many shops to visit, but if you're not shopping, then there is the well-planned **Riverfront Park** by the **Spokane River**. The park has a wonderful antique carousel if the child in you, or with you, needs attention.

There is also the upscale Spokane Valley Mall, with all the usual stores.

Spokane Valley Mall
14700 E. Indiana Ave.
509-926-3700
www.spokanevalleymall.com

Spokane Steam Plant into Steam Plant Square
159 S. Lincoln
509-624-8050
www.steamplantsquare.com

This steam plant heated downtown Spokane until 1986. A most adventurous undertaking was the transformation of the original. It is fascinating to see the boilers, catwalks, and coal bunkers once essential to the working plant, which now houses a state-of-the-art technology center. There is also the Steam Plant Grill, serving beers brewed onsite by the **Coeur d'Alene Brewing Company**.

Steam Plant Grill
159 S. Lincoln
509-777-3900
www.steamplantgrill.com

The far-sighted creation of Ron and Julie Wells, the grill allows diners to enjoy excellent food in a unique environment—the steam plant. In opening this grill, the owners did not have to concern themselves with decor. Open for lunch and dinner, this great place is within walking distance of the Davenport. Read the history of the steam plant, which was in operation for over seventy years, then sat idle for ten until it was realized that its eighty thousand square feet could be used for offices, retail space, and the Steam Plant Grill. Applause! Congratulations for the renaissance of the original steam plant.

Italian Kitchen
113 N. Bernard St.
509-363-1210
www.italiankitchenspokane.com

This delicious little restaurant is within walking distance of the Davenport (a bit farther than the Steam Plant Grill). I thoroughly enjoyed dinner, the friendly staff, and the reasonable prices. I have learned that the Italian Kitchen has new owners since I visited but has not lost any of what I discovered. Delicious!

There is obviously a lot to see in and learn about Spokane. I would definitely put it on my revisit list. The city seems to be doing things well—learning from other places that might not have taken the time to plan as carefully.

SEATTLE

Taking I-90 West to Seattle, you drive about four hours on a good interstate. **Moses Lake** is the first real city, with gas stations, food outlets, and the like.

About thirty minutes outside Seattle, you can stop and stretch at North Bend Premium Outlets.

North Bend Premium Outlets
461 South Fork Ave. SW
425-888-4505
www.premiumoutlets.com

I-90 to **Mount Baker Ridge Tunnel** takes you into downtown Seattle.

There is so much to see and do in Seattle, a thriving big city. Read up on its many attractions, and plan accordingly. I had heard a lot about Seattle—all good, all correct! Seattle is special.

Tacoma Art Museum
1701 Pacific Ave., Tacoma
253.272.4258
www.tacomaartmuseum.org

Alexis Hotel

1007 First Ave.
206-624-4844
www.alexishotel.com

It is as this boutique hotel's slogan states, "A Work of Art." The Alexis offers a special, wonderful experience for all. It is definitely female friendly.

The outside greeting was welcoming, and I had no qualms about turning my car over to the attendant.

On entering the hotel, I was greeted by a huge, awesome, very colorful Dale Chihuly. His glass art is fabulous! This impressive piece was only on loan, however, and is not in residence at the Alexis at present.

FYI: In *Tacoma*, Washington, you can take a walking tour that takes you through the *Dale Chihuly Glass Collection* for $16 per person (in 2011). Children are free.

The Alexis lobby decor is subdued but extremely tasteful. The front desk staff were attractive but, more importantly, alert and efficient. My room was a beautifully appointed suite with a kitchen. The cozy and inviting bedroom had a queen-size bed with crisp, white Egyptian cotton linens. The white Egyptian cotton duvet covering the down comforter was only luxurious. Everything was immaculate. I saw other rooms, but regardless of size, they did not diminish in quality. As of 2007, all guest rooms and hallways were refurbished. Specialty suites named for celebrities are theme decorated with their namesakes' respective claims to fame. My suite contained books of all varieties—many signed by the authors when at the hotel.

In the late afternoon, complimentary wines are served in the lobby—a nice inclusion. Women even solo do not hesitate to attend and to talk with other guests. I met a couple from my home area.

For a special dining experience at the Alexis, visit the Library Bistro (whispering not required).

Library Bistro
92 Madison St.
206-624-3646
www.librarybistro.com

The Library Bistro now serves only breakfast and Saturday and Sunday brunch, as well as personally prepared, private dining menus. When I was there, I enjoyed a long, delicious dinner. The salad, main course, and dessert could not have been better. Most memorable was the appetizer, a small serving of macaroni and cheese with thinly sliced apples. The sauce on the macaroni was very creamy and just right—upscale soul food.

Now there is also the Bookstore Bar for lunch and dinner. I am certain that every morsel is delicious.

Bookstore Bar
1007 First Ave.
206-382-1506
www.librarybistro.com

When I was at the Alexis, the general manager was a woman, and I always like to tout females who are in command. As of this writing, the Alexis has another female GM, Jenne Neptune. She is lucky to be at such a special property.

The Alexis is a Kimpton Hotel. Although, try as I might, I have not stayed in many. From what I have heard, they stand for superb quality.

Staying at the Alexis allows you to walk to many of Seattle's famed attractions. Strolling through the neighborhood around the Alexis is a must—but more of a must is an excellent pair of walking shoes.

Pikes Place Market
1531 Western Ave.
206-682-7453
www.pikeplacemarket.com

This wonderful market is a cheerfully noisy happening. Here, both people and produce thrive. You'll find all the fresh fruits and vegetables you can imagine, as well as freshly baked pastries of all varieties and sizes. A morning walk for a very fresh pastry and coffee is a nice way to start the day. You may not want any fresh fish (or even like fish), but the famous fish throwing and chanting is a must-see and will cause you to smile and laugh. Trinket vendors and the like seem to be everywhere. Take some fresh fruit back to your room or for your trip. This unique nine-acre market was started in 1907 to bring farmers and consumers together. There are many restaurants. Musicians perform a variety of sounds and tempos. At the market, there are "permanent" vendors who have a set spot; others can rent one of the two hundred table spaces by the day. Are you running out of room in your car? Have you made too many purchases along the way? Maybe you can rent a table for the day to sell those spur-of-the-moment items you're no longer sure you need. Just a thought.

Pioneer Square

The historic district of Seattle is called Pioneer Square. This ninety-acre area has art centers of all varieties and sizes, museums, shops, restaurants, bars, and such. There are also spots to be aware of as the homeless and undecided folk frequent the area. Be alert.

Bill Speidel's Underground Tour
608 First Ave.
206-682-4646
www.undergroundtour.com

I did this when I was tired and my feet numb. Although I recommend taking the one-and-a-half-hour underground tour, don't do it under the conditions I did. In 2011, tickets cost $16 for adults, $13 for students and senior citizens, and $8 for children (the tour isn't recommend for those age six and under). The tour actually takes you underground to see the sights under the Seattle streets and sidewalks. You are actually walking on what were once the main streets of old Seattle. The informative, interesting, and humorous tour begins inside the saloon, **Doc Maynard's Public House**. You will eventually proceed down the equivalent six uneven flights of stairs. (It did not seem that many to me.) Wear appropriate shoes or sneakers. It is damp and cool in this subterranean city, so a sweater will be appreciated. You will learn about the coining of the term *skid row* and also the association between the Seattle underground and toilets. The guide on my tour was informative, handsome, fun, and very creative in his presentations.

Note: This tour is not for the claustrophobic, although it is definitely not like going into a cave or a natural cavern. It is just under and around underground. This area is within walking distance of the Alexis, and there are lots of shops—again of all varieties.

Waterfront Seafood Grill

2801 Alaskan Way
206-956-9171
www.elgaucho.com/waterfrontpier70/home.htm

This nice restaurant was filled with young people. The attention to service and food was right. The view overlooking the waterfront and of the surrounding tables was most pleasant. The latter made you realize that you are not, and probably never were, like the young people of today. (Can't have everything!) The recent reviews—since I was there—are so excellent that I look forward to returning.

BAINBRIDGE ISLAND

When planning the visit to Seattle, I read up on the city and collected info from friends, but no one mentioned Bainbridge Island. What a treasure I was to discover! It is a real island reached by a ferry from the **Ferry Terminal** (801 Alaskan Way, Pier 52), which is also within walking distance of the Alexis. The ticket price is very reasonable, and senior citizens get a discounted rate. Arriving on Bainbridge Island after a peaceful, relaxing, thirty-five-minute ride, you will find that the popular modes of travel are bicycle or walking, although you can ferry over in your car.

I could have spent a day or more (preferably the later) in this charming oasis. The island is approximately five miles wide and ten miles long, which computes to approximately 17,778 acres or twenty-eight square miles. Walking shoes are a must. The main drag, so to speak, is **Winslow Way**. When you arrive on the island, go to the chamber of commerce for a map and personal information.

Chamber of Commerce

395 Winslow Way E.
206-842-3700
www.bainbridgechamber.com

As for my finds and discoveries on Bainbridge Island, the list would be long. The following are those on the very top of my list.

Within a few minutes on Bainbridge Island, I felt a pulling sensation in my torso. Remember, I had not known about this island twenty-four hours prior to my arrival, much less set foot on it. What did I find?

Bargain Boutique

572 Winslow Way E.
206-842-5567

This fantastic boutique of bargains is filled with both consignment and donated items. The store is clean and the personnel friendly. Merchandize was excellent and sensibly priced. When I left, there were a few empty spots on the shelves. Yes! Proceeds go to the children's hospital, which I read has similar stores in other parts of Washington.

Closet Transfer
562 Bjune Dr. SE
206-842-1515

Enjoy this consignment shop discovery!

Heart
181 Winslow Way E.
206-842-0688

Heart's motto is "Clothes & Accessories for the Way We Live." Hours: Monday through Saturday, 10 a.m. to 6 p.m.; Sunday, 11 a.m. to 5 p.m.

Doozie
554 Winslow Way E.
206-842-3439

This store of "Fantastic Affordable Finds" might have just what you've been seeking for your nest.

Berry Patch & Contents
278 Winslow Way E.
206-842-3593

With all sorts of "Essentials for Your Home," Berry Patch indeed offers a large variety.

Pastiche
119 Winslow Way E.
206-842-6019

Pastiche has antiques and fine collectables.

Ester's Fabrics
181 Winslow Way E., Ste. D
206-842-2261
www.esthersfabrics.com

The oldest fabric shop in the state of Washington, Ester's provides a collection of fabrics of all—and I do mean all—varieties.

You'll discover bolts of fabric finds, imported ribbons, vintage fabrics, and more. All the choices will test your decision-making skills. Ester's has a big oil-cloth selection and items for any craft project. I just wish the shop wasn't quite so far away. Take your pictures and measurements—for sure.

Streamline Diner
397 Winslow Way E.
206-842-8595

What a discovery! Lunch included an exceptional homemade squash soup. There are no faults in the fare at this diner, and the pastries are too good. The service was efficient and friendly and the prices reasonable. Streamline Diner, I am looking forward to my next delicious visit.

Blackbird Bakery
210 Winslow Way E.
206-780-1322

Just follow your nose and pick up a treat—for energy's sake—as you shop the shops on Winslow Way.

On Bainbridge, you find shops of all varieties and price points. They are primarily on Winslow Way or just around the corner on a side street.

Wear your walking shoes. Have fun finding all sorts of delights on this fantastic island.

I adored Bainbridge Island and look forward to returning.

By the time I got back on the ferry to the mainland, I confess I was tempted to lay down on one of the long ferry benches. Instead, I enjoyed a coke and just sat, slightly numb, and watched the view as the impressive skyline of Seattle came closer.

Seattle is on my ever-expanding revisit list.

I-5 South is not difficult to find when you are leaving Seattle.

***

Tidbit: I passed seventeen hundred bicyclers! (At least, that's how many I was told there were.) I later found out they were from the *Seattle*

Bicycle Club and were on their way to Portland! Bicycling is great, and I do enjoy riding short distances, but to get to Portland, I am glad I am driving a car.

KALAMA (POPULATION LESS THAN 2,000)

To get to Kalama, take Exit 30 off of I-5.

I had never heard of Kalama had not planned to stop there— but am delighted I did as I now know about this charming town. The land area is 2.3 square miles, and the average cost of a house in 2003 was about $119,000.

Kalama is about three hours south of Seattle and about thirty-five miles from Portland, Oregon. As the Kalama sign said, "Antique Capital District," the car, of course, turned off the highway. (Advertising pays!).

Quaint shops line the few immediately visible blocks of Kalama. Here is a list of delightful places I discovered and are hopefully still there.

Heritage Square: Antiques & Dealers
176 N. First St.
360-673-3980

There are lots of miscellaneous antiques, as well as a soda fountain of sorts, where the attendant, Lisa, fixed a great latte.

Columbia Antiques & Collectibles Mall
364 N. First St.
360-673-5400

You'll find fifty dealers with a mixture of collectibles.

Antique Deli & Pastry Shoppe
413 N. First St.
360-673-3310
www.kalamaonline.com/antique-mall-deli

You will find the homemade breads, pies, and other selections hard to resist. It's not pricey, delicious, and very friendly.

I recommend making Kalama a stop on your road trip. Plan to spend quite a few minutes.

OREGON

-5 is a good road. Getting to downtown Portland was a little tricky, but in the process, I saw the scope of this large and diverse city. In one direction, the skyline had beautiful mountains; in another, there was significant view of the river. I discovered a waterfront teaming with life and a variety of shops. For a while Portland was known as America's best-kept secret, and not too long ago, *Money* magazine ranked it the second-best big city to live in. No question it is an outdoor city, with the **Mount Hood** glacier always looming. There is a restriction on building heights so that Mount Hood's dominance cannot be usurped.

PORTLAND
(POPULATION APPROXIMATELY 529,000)

When learning about Portland, I read that it is a city designed for walking. This is apparent in that the blocks are smaller than in a lot of other cities. *Public Art: Walking Tour* is a very handy book.

Portland covers 134.3 square miles. It is on Pacific time, so if you are from the East, you can gain two or three hours in your life. Temperature-wise, summer highs are near 80 degrees, and at night, the highs are near 60 degrees. The winters are not freezing—cold yes, freezing no. Portland is busy but also rather relaxed. There is a lot going on, so do your homework and choose your destinations. It is easy to walk by something you should know about.

Heathman Hotel

1001 SW Broadway at Salmon
503-241-4100
www.heathmanhotel.com

This award-winning hotel is located downtown in the **Cultural District**. An old-world hotel with charm and character, the Heathman is right in the center of things, so you might have to juggle a little traffic.

The doorman was competent and friendly. The lobby has two separate desks for check-in, which was efficient. Though not fancy, the property is first-rate, with an art deco style. The hotel's colors are dark browns, interspersed with bright purple and orange accents and scattered animal-print fabrics.

My room was attractive and comfortable. The TV pulled out of a cabinet and was conveniently placed for one bed, though not really for the second. The bedroom window faced a brick wall of the building next door. Instead of blocking off the window, the management had painted the wall itself with an attractive mural, making the view semiattractive in its own way. I can think of many places that should do this—so simple, yet such a big improvement.

The hotel's hallways seemed narrow, which is fine and typical of old properties. Long decorative mirrors in the hallways are especially handy for those last-minute fixes.

I liked the bottle of water on the bed at turndown. There is also a large lending library, and guests have access to a four-hundred-title movie library.

Jazz is an integral part of evenings at the Heathman. It is pleasant to sit in the **Tea Court** and wind down from your day's activities. Also the **L'Heure de Plasir** (happy hour) is ever popular. There are specials both for imbibing and dining. The **Heathman Restaurant** is open for breakfast, lunch, and dinner. Be certain to try the salmon hash at breakfast. The blueberry muffins were light and excellent. When I was there, Philippe Boulot headed the culinary team, and his credentials are long and impressive.

It won't be hard to enjoy the Heathman. The Heathman's motto is "Where Service Is Still an Art." Applause! Applause! A sister property opened in Kirkland, Washington, in 2007.

Pioneer Place
700 SW Fifth Ave.
503-228-5800
www.pioneerplace.com

Within a short distance (perhaps a few blocks), you'll find Pioneer Place, an upscale shopping area. I won't list the shops, as they come and go, but I am certain high class will remain.

Things to Know: The *Portland Light Rail* is a bargain. This can take you to many sights and discoveries. On busy corners, there are kiosks staffed with young, enthusiastic, knowledgeable people who are there to help you discover Portland. More cities should have this service.

On weekends there is the *flea market and street fair*, with lots of things to buy. When I was there I purchased a magical pixie-dust amulet. An amulet is a magical object worn to guide energy to the person wearing it. Have I had any magical pixie-dust experiences, you ask? Not that I know of, but then, I must confess, I have not been wearing it. Must do so, just in case.

Portland Classical Chinese Garden
239 NW Everett St.
503-228-8131
www.portlandchinesegarden.org

Here you'll find impressive, quiet beauty and, to quote their brochure, "Never Twice the Same."

Waterfront

The walk to the waterfront is nice but also sketchy, as there are permanent stragglers in various clusters or prone positions.

McCormick & Schmick

0309 SW Montgomery
503-220-1865
www.mccormickandschmicks.com

I had looked forward to dining at McCormick & Schmick's, but the reception there was nil. Was it female scoffing or lack of experience? Regardless, after waiting and even walking around, I walked out.

Newport Bay at Riverplace

425 SW Montgomery St.
503-227-3474
www.newportbay.com

Newport Bay proved delightful, with delicious fare and sensible prices. In spite of the wind, I sat outside overlooking the water, and it was most attractive. The attendants were upbeat and friendly.

Across the street from the Heathman is the Metro Café, a restaurant deli of sorts.

Metro Café

1000 SW Broadway
503-242-2435

I was able to get (from a most attentive young man named Matt) half a sandwich and a drink along with a big cookie. I took the morsels back to my room and just kicked back and planned the next day. Sometimes an easy meal hits the spot.

There is a lot to Portland. It would take a few days to see it. I am glad to have been there, and perhaps another visit will take place.

Driving Diva Tip: Leave Portland and head south. Taking 26 West to 6 West, weave through *Tillamook State Forest* (www.tillamookforest center.org). The roads are beautiful, and if you stay on them, you will eventually reach the Pacific Ocean.

Oh My! Always keep your eyes open for signs (and things) that hint at something special. Driving on Wilson River Loop Road, I saw a sign for Bullshit Road. (Excuse me, Mother!) Sometimes you just luck out. I saw another sign on an old schoolhouse for Latimer Quilt and Textile Center. I decided to park the car and walked up to the door with great anticipation. I was sad to find that it was closed on that day, but I heard voices from inside. Of course, I knocked anyway, and the door was opened by a most attractive lady. There were several other ladies near the door too as a meeting had just adjourned. They let me in and what an event!

Latimer Quilt & Textile Center
2105 Wilson River Loop Rd., Tillamook
503-842-8622
www.latimerquiltandtextile.com

The displayed quilts (some hanging, some folded) were beautiful. The prices for the art were sensible. One could purchase quilting products or join a class. Related items were also for sale. Be sure to check this center out in person or electronically.

I learned that the building (circa 1940) had been a school for grades one through eight. Thirteen years before, it had been too dilapidated and about to fall down. Then a few determined women got together and developed this most special, creative, vibrant quilting center. Latimer Quilt and Textile Center is a must-see.

I reluctantly left, but not before I purchased an Over-the-Hill Voodoo Doll. The tag states, "Stick pin in whatever area is giving you problems. Instant relief! Use more pins as necessary." Also, the ladies had enjoyed refreshments and goodies during their meeting. I was offered a delicious homemade lemon tart. Thank you, Latimer Quilt and Textile Ladies, for a wonderful visit! A true serendipity.

Tillamook Cheese Visitors Center
4175 Hwy. 101 N., Tillamook
503-815-1300
www.tillamookcheese.com

Judging by the size of the center and the number of cars and buses in the parking lot, this is a well-known destination. I am delighted to have made the discovery. Here you will find 78 million pounds of legendary Tillamook cheese to be delivered throughout the world. At the center, you can see cheese in the making, sample some tasty goodness, be tempted in the gift shop, eat lunch at the deli, and then sample some of the famous ice cream. The center is pristine and the staff very friendly. I asked what makes Tillamook cheese different, and they told me it was the fact that everything is aged naturally. The recipe is over one hundred years old. **The Creamery Café** is very popular. If I had only been hungry! Alert: The Tillamook fudge is made with Tillamook butter and comes in forty-three flavors. You might have to wait your turn to purchase, but you won't be alone, and from all I hear, it is worth the wait.

The population of Tillamook is approximately four thousand. According to a brochure, there are a lot of area attractions, including the Pioneer Museum, the Tillamook Air Museum, camping, clamming, crabbing, hiking, and walking the beaches.

Pioneer Museum
2106 Second St.
503-842-4553
www.tcpm.org

Tillamook Air Museum
6030 Hangar Rd.
503-842-1130
www.tillamookair.com

One of the most unusual events I have ever heard of is at the Tillamook county fair in August. It is called **Pig N Ford Races** (www.pig-n-ford.com). Basically, the participants line up. At the signal, they rush over to some pigpens, grab one squeaking pig, run to their respective Model Ts at another starting line, put the pig in the car, and race to the finish line. I think you get the gist of this zany event. I just thought it was worth mentioning,

Creekside Restaurant

I-5, Exit 99, Canyonville
541-839-3110

The Creekside Restaurant in the **Seven Feathers Truck and Travel Center** (541-839-3100, www.i5exit99.com) in Canyonville (population approximately 1,200) was large, very clean, pleasant, friendly, and sensibly priced.

ASHLAND
(POPULATION APPROXIMATELY 20,000)

Road construction had lengthened the driving time, and it was late. Driving into town, I realized I was in a charming area as the streets were clean, and everything looked well kept. As the afternoon sky darkened, there was a glow all around. For a town its size, Ashland is full of wonderful discoveries and places.

Ashland Springs Hotel

212 E. Main St.
541-488-1700
www.ashlandspringshotel.com

I had heard so much about the restored Ashland Springs Hotel and was anxious to see the property firsthand. I had no problem finding it. It is the tallest structure in town with an impressive white facade.

Upon entering I knew I would not be disappointed. The Ashland Springs had the right environment mixed with a relaxed decor of overstuffed chairs and sofas. Tall potted palm trees added definition to areas in the big room. The large collection of sea shells mixed well. It was all charming. My room was most relaxing, clean, and cozy. There were pastel colors, a comfortable bed and sitting area, and a nice bathroom. It wasn't fancy but just right.

An excellent complimentary breakfast with plentiful fresh fruit was served on the mezzanine. For the first time, I ate pluots, a cross between a plum and an apricot. Delicious! There were hard-boiled eggs, various cereals, and yummy muffins. The coffee was also delicious. You sit at small, bistro-like tables, and there is no excuse not to talk to other guests as the entire ambiance lends itself to doing so.

The hotel is downtown, so walking around and exploring is easy. There are shops, restaurants, and the standard town emporiums.

At one time, the hotel bar was the longest in Oregon. The attractive decorative accents include movie items from the 1950s. The Ashland Springs Hotel is a charmer, a boutique hotel you will enjoy. Although I didn't fully realize it when planning this trip, Ashland hosts the famous Oregon Shakespeare Festival, which is within walking distance of the Ashland Springs Hotel.

Oregon Shakespeare Festival

15 S. Pioneer St.
541-482-2111
www.osfashland.org

Spur-of-the-moment tickets are not to be counted on, as I found out. Investigate this special theater. Everyone I spoke to raved about it.

Southern Oregon University, with fifty-five hundred students, is in Ashland. The entire population of Ashland is about 20,000. I mention this because towns with a major academic contingent have added agendas, not to mention many young people.

Discoveries

Déjà Vu Fashion Consignment Shoppe
1644 Ashland St., Unit 3
541-522-0720

I found some goodies here!

Pilaf Global Pantry World Food
225 Water St.
541-488-4433

As this establishment is 100 percent vegetarian, it makes a nice change from more usual menus. It is pleasant and not that expensive.

Blue Giraffe Day Spa Salon
51 Water St.
541-488-3335
www.bluegiraffespa.com

About one block from the **Plaza on Ashland Creek**, this downtown spa can be a little hard to find as it is behind and around the block. It is by a real creek so—as I was told—follow the sound of the water. The decor is attractive and inviting, and there are many types of treatments to choose from. Since I was there, the spa has expanded, as has the variety of treatments. Go and enjoy over and over.

MEDFORD
(POPULATION APPROXIMATELY 63,000)

When in Ashland, be sure to take a less-than-fifteen-minute drive to Medford. This town has the major stores, grocery chains, and so forth.

Harry & David
1314 Center Dr., Medford
541-864-2278 or 877-322-1200
www.harryanddavid.com

Medford is the corporate headquarters of Harry & David, purveyors of superb and delicious products. From Harry & David, you can order the fantastic Royal Riviera pears. A most informative tour is given of the plant's facilities. You will realize by tour's end that there is no doubt about the professed quality and caliber of the products. The strict quality control that has made Harry & David a leader in the field is evident even to the casual visitor. At the end of the tour, you are given a sample of one of the company's products. I was given a tiny box with a couple of galettes and a mini mint, which were delicious. If you can't visit the site, order from the catalogue or keep an eye out for some of the retail shops.

Leaving Ashland, it is easy to get back on I-5 South. In less than an hour, you are in California.

CALIFORNIA

On the road from Ashland Springs, Oregon, past spectacular Mount Shasta and Lake Shasta, farm fields gave way to congestion, ultimately landing me in . . .

BERKELEY AND OAKLAND

Claremont Hotel Club & Spa
41 Tunnel Rd., Berkeley
510-843-3000 or 800-551-7266
www.claremontresort.com

The Claremont opened in 1915 as a "retreat for wealthy San Franciscans," according to the brochure. It is a huge, bright-white edifice that sits atop a hill overlooking the San Francisco Bay. Finding the place wasn't easy, and when I called for directions, the person on the phone practically had to form a committee to advise me on how to get there (an all-too-common problem at some hotels).

Once there, I was immediately greeted by well-attired, friendly attendants who happily granted my request to park my car close by. The entrance to the resort is impressive and tempting at the same time as you walk past a long hall filled with tantalizing shops and boutiques. I nearly had heart failure on checking in, though, when I was told that I didn't have a reservation! The tune changed when I presented my confirmation number. A must-have!

This is a huge place, and I have to comment (again) that I do not think present-day hoteliers realize that one of their main responsibilities is to provide legible, frequent signage. As I followed the bellman to my room, I made mental notes as to the location of the pool area, sport spa, and even the elevators. Walking down the inside hallways, I knew I would have difficulty finding my way out (which proved true several times during my stay). Maybe I should have left a trail of birdseed.

My room was attractive, in restful, warm, beige colors. There were two double beds, a large TV/entertainment center, and a bar in a nook. All the rooms have been renovated, I am sure in a most California-attractive fashion. I had a great view of San Francisco and the bay, particularly as the sun was setting and the night lights came on.

The bathroom was well done: double vanity, toilet and shower in separate areas, bright heat lamps, and phone by the toilet (minus points, though, for the horseshoe toilet seat.)

A visit to the pool area was first on the agenda (sandals and cover-up recommended). It took a bit of exploring to get there. Your hotel key and hotel card must be presented at the pool desk. It's a nice big area with a lap pool and a children's pool. Because of its proximity to neighboring cities, the Claremont is full of families visiting for weekends and holidays. The pool areas are well laid out, so you do not feel that children have the run of the place. The chaises are close together, but not too close. At the poolside Bayview Café, you can eat indoors or out or by your chaise.

I dined at the resort's **Paragon Bar & Café** (510-549-8585), which had a nice ambiance and adequate food and service. I ate breakfast at another restaurant at the resort, Jordan's, now **Meritage**, and was somewhat disappointed. First, I was misled about the orange juice being fresh (fresh out of a container maybe), the ketchup tasted like tomato paste, the coffee was too strong, and the buffet was nothing to write home about. (To make amends, the next morning the maître d' proudly presented me with real fresh-squeezed orange juice. I didn't think that would be a good time to mention that the silver needed polishing as well.) From all reports, fine tuning has been done, but I am relating what I experienced.

The twenty-thousand-square-foot **Spa Claremont** offers every possible treatment you can imagine. Although a busy place, this beautiful area will melt you "like buttah" the moment you walk in. Among the many options are the "Thai Journey," "Mayan Temple Journey," "Zen Trilogy Body Wrap," "LA Stone Therapy," "Rosemary Citron Dead Sea Salt Scrub," "Coconut Body Polish," and more. The spa is open to the public, so call ahead for your appointment. Like I said, it's a busy place.

Visit this huge, impressive, historic property, and, even better, stay a night or two.

Around Berkeley

Downtown Berkeley and the University of California are about a mile downhill from the Claremont. Around the campus, I was amazed, even shocked, by the large number of hippies who seemed to inhabit the sidewalks. These were no flower children at a Grateful Dead concert but rather young people in a near-indigent condition. Blame it on my mature eyes, but the thought that one of these homo sapiens could have been the child of someone I knew was unsettling. I felt for both the children and their parents. This is not a part of town where you'd want to park your car and go for a light stroll—at least, not when I was there and from what I was told.

Around Fourth Street, though, a very nice area has shops of all varieties, art galleries, and restaurants. There were many eateries to choose from, but because I was there early, some weren't open yet. I ended up at a place called Crepevine.

Crepevine
1600 Shattuck Ave., Berkeley
510-705-1836
www.crepevine.com

Crepevine was delicious, inexpensive, and clean. (I hope it is still there!)

Going in the other direction (uphill) from the Claremont, you enter a very nice area with beautiful Victorian homes and fantastic views. It's well worth a drive-through.

UKIAH

Vichy Springs Resort & Spa
2605 Vichy Springs Rd.
707-462-9515
www.vichysprings.com

Two hours north of San Francisco you will find this oasis. To paraphrase comments I have read, arriving at Vichy Springs you feel as if you are miles from any worries in a most tranquil setting. This 150-year-old Hot Springs Resort and Spa, with twenty-six rooms and cottages, is California Landmark 980. Here you will find the only natural, warm, carbonated mineral baths in North America, a hot soaking pool, an Olympic-size swimming pool, and seven hundred acres for walking, hiking, or strolling. The costs are sensible, the waters superb, and the atmosphere delightful. I am soon on my way to soak, enjoy, and discover.

Wine Train
1275 McKinstry St., Napa
707-253-2111
www.winetrain.com

One hour north of San Francisco is the Wine Train. Taking this perfectly restored train, with dining and lounge cars, is an adventure, and what a way to see the beautiful wine country of Napa valley. Round-trip takes about three hours and covers thirty-six miles. There are three options for travel, the most popular being the one where you ride in the car with the vista dome. You can dine in gourmet style, with three- to five-course menus, and enjoy wine, wine, wine. Each of the three price options is well worth it. The scenery probably becomes more beautiful (if possible) with each sip. I am anxious to find out.

SAN FRANCISCO

San Francisco is a gem of a city, although many years ago, when I first visited, it seemed less crowded and sparkled more than it did on my last visit. There is plenty to see and do in San Francisco, but remember to bring really good walking shoes (maybe even hiking shoes) as the hills of the city can be a challenge.

Driving Diva Alert: When parking on a steep downhill slope, point your front tires toward the curb; point them away from the curb when you are parking on an uphill slope. This will prevent your car from joining the traffic without you.

San Francisco is, for the most part, pretty and friendly, but it is a big town and has some areas that you should definitely stay out of, such as the Tenderloin District and the area south of Mission Street. So much for a minus or two. There are hundreds of pluses.

The buses are good and clean, and the people are friendly. Have the necessary fare, and a handy bus map helps.

Prescott Hotel
545 Post St.
415-563-0303
www.prescotthotel.com

Lucky and delighted was how I felt about staying at this wonderful property. I would not call it a boutique hotel since it's a bit more grand than that, with 164 upscale guest rooms. The Prescott is centrally located and convenient to nearly everything. As I arrived early and my room wasn't ready, I had my car parked, stored my bags, and struck out into the city with a map and a lunch recommendation. More on the Prescott experience below.

Plouf

40 Belden Pl.

415-986-6491

www.belden-place.com/plouf

Plouf refers to "the sound a stone makes when it drops into a French stream." Within walking distance of the Prescott, it's a great place to eat! I dined alfresco in the alley adjacent to the inside dining area. Although it was packed, it didn't feel crowded because of how the long tables were arranged. This very nice seafood bistro is trendy and quite French, and the food is delicious in a garlicky sort of way. (That is meant to be a compliment.) The service is fast, and the challenge is not to spoil your appetite by eating all the delicious, garlicky, broth-soaked baguettes promptly put under your nose when you sit down. The prices are sensible and the atmosphere delightful.

I decided to walk off my lunch by strolling around **Union Square** (www.unionsquareshop.com) with its mixture of famous brand-name shops, the not-so-well-known stores, and the "I don't know how they stay in business" shops. Before too long, I found myself in **Chinatown** (www.sanfranciscochinatown.com), where I purchased a very un-Chinese item (though it might have been made in China—aren't most things?), which I highly recommend: a very large, strong plastic bag with a zipper on top that folds down to a manageable size.

Returning to the Prescott, I was glad to get into my room, rest, and organize for a bit. I was staying on the Club Level, which features complimentary beverages and hors d'oeuvres served by the exceptional Neoo. Amusing and warm, Neoo always remembers what you liked to drink.

See below for the restaurant at the Prescott and more.

I really wanted to discover the areas and shops of San Francisco
that are not featured in the usual travel brochures.

Ferry Building Marketplace
One Ferry Building
415-983-8030
www.ferrybuildingmarketplace.com

Along the **Embarcadero** (www.embarcaderocenter.com) at the
foot of Market Street, this fabulous open market has fine fresh
vegetables, flowers, homemade items, and other delicacies. Street
merchants also offer attractive jewelry, clothing, and even cooking demonstrations.

Fun Out-of-the-Way Shops and Places

Taking the No. 1 California bus or the No. 38 Geary bus and following the recommendation of some locals, my next destination was
Clement and Thirty-first streets.

Kimberley's Consignment
3020 Clement St.
415-752-2223
www.kimberleyssf.com

I had the feeling that this probably wasn't an ordinary thrift
store, and, indeed, as I discovered, there were few real jump-out
bargains. Persistent visits would probably lead to the discovery of
bargains. The owner admitted, "Yes, we are high-end, but then, our
items are high-end." She told me that they are the oldest shop of
its kind in San Francisco—Kimberley's had been run by her late
mother.

Jane Consignment
2249 Clement St.

415-751-5511

www.jane-consignment.com

Less than ten blocks away is the more reasonably priced Jane Consignment, "A Breath of Fresh Wear," owned by Jane Wilson. The store is a little funky, but you will find bargains, and Jane is delightful.

Tandoori Mahal
941 Kearney St.

415-951-0505

www.tandoorimahalsf.com

Not too far from Jane's, I had lunch at this inviting Indian restaurant. The host and hostess didn't speak much English, but we communicated just fine using a little sign language. They pointed to a table covered with a crisp, white tablecloth (good sign) and then to a savory buffet. Though lunch was modest—two small appetizers and tea—Tandoori Mahal hit the spot.

After lunch, I took the No. 2 Clement Street bus to Fillmore Street in order to rest my aching feet. I had been warned that this part of town might be a huge temptation for me, with its many bookstores, health and beauty shops, bakeries, restaurants, and the mother lode for the Driving Diva: consignment shops! Within a few blocks I found a Junior League Store with first-rate items at sensible prices.

Next-to-New Junior League Shop
2226 Fillmore St.

415-567-1628

Victorian House Thrift Shop
2033 Fillmore St.

415-567-3149

This shop aids the California Pacific Medical Center.

Seconds-to-Go Resale Shop
2252 Fillmore St.
415-563-7306

This shop benefits the scholarship funds at the Schools of the Scared Heart.

One of the shops had a beautiful, huge screen that I not only wanted but actually needed, and the price was right. But I never could have wrestled it onto a bus or into a cab. Sigh.

The Fillmore area is definitely a place to spend the day . . . many times over and over.

Back at the Prescott, a bit weary but anticipating my dinner experience, I got a second wind, changed attire, and was ready to dine. I was anxious to experience the excellent Postrio.

Postrio
545 Post St.
415-776-7825
www.postrio.com

I report here what I enjoyed then. Upon entering, one descends a small flight of stairs into the restaurant. I was personally greeted by then general manager James Minch, whose professionalism, hospitality, and recommendations guided me through a most memorable meal: gazpacho for starters, then ginger shrimp curry over rice with coconut, garbanzo nuts, and lotus root. His wine choices were especially good, and dessert was downright decadent. Save both your pennies and your appetite for Postrio.

Sidebar: James Minch, after many years at Postrio, has gone to Spruce.

Spruce
3640 Sacramento St.
415-931-5100
www.sprucesf.com

It is called a neighborhood restaurant with an upscale, sophisticated ambiance and menu. I look forward to a visit.

Hotel Majestic
1500 Sutter St.
415-441-1100
www.thehotelmajestic.com

Located in Pacific Heights. this charming and attractive hotel is a true gem. Originally a private residence built in 1902 by Milton Schmidt, a railroad magnate and member of the California State Legislature, it became the Hotel Majestic when Schmidt sold it in 1904. Untouched by the earthquake of 1906, it remains San Francisco's longest continuously operated hotel. To add to its charm, the Majestic is a bit away from downtown, which makes parking easy and convenient in the hotel's covered garage on the next block. Ghosts are said to inhabit the hotel, and in one room, the bathtub mysteriously fills with water all on its own—or so I have been told.

The outside of the hotel was painted in an attractive, subtle mix of colors.

The well-known **Café Majestic** (415-441-1280) is a favorite, and the **Butterfly Lounge** is a popular place to rendezvous. Regardless, visit and, if possible, stay at this special place.

The Prescott and the Majestic are two of many small hotels in San Francisco, but you if want the "grand hotel" experience, even if you can only afford to have dinner, I can personally recommend the Ritz, the Mark Hopkins, and the Stanford Court.

The Ritz
600 Stockton St.
415-296-7465
www.ritzcarlton.com

The Ritz is, well, ritzy, and if a dinner in the Dining Room is not in the budget, a small munch at the Terrace will do just fine.

Mark Hopkins

One Nob Hill

877-270-1390

www.intercontinentalmarkhopkins.com

This fine hotel's Top of the Mark restaurant features a bar with a spectacular, panoramic view of the city. The cost of this view is approximately $10 for a glass of Chablis.

Stanford Court

905 California St.

415-989-3500

www.marriott.com

This hotel is comfortable and attractive, though in recent years, it seems to have become a bit more hectic and commercial since I stayed there on my first book tour.

HEADING SOUTH

Several highways head south out of San Francisco, the most expedient (for getting to Los Angeles) being I-5. More attractive alternatives are U.S. Route 101, which weaves in and out of farmlands, or the famed Pacific Coast Highway, Highway 1. When I first asked someone about Highway 1 way back when, I was told you really have to be careful because the road was so windy that you'd see your own exhaust pipe much of the way. From the first very sharp curve onward, though, Highway 1 is not as bad as described. It is well maintained, though you do have to keep a lookout for speeders and passers, and driving at night is not recommended. Head-on collisions are all too common on the highway, which was designed for slower automobiles. It took eighteen years of construction before it was completed in 1937.

The weather can change drastically along Highway 1, so pack for cold as well as warm conditions. The early-morning fog rolls in and is quite beautiful, albeit damp and chilly and a hindrance to visibility. By noon or so, the fog has rolled on, and the day warms.

You can exist in many different ways in Big Sur, and if you choose to do nothing except look, you will still come away with enhanced experiences that you will remember well and with pleasure.

There's a lot of development along the Santa Lucia Mountains side of the highway and somewhat less on the ocean side, where the Pacific throbs and bangs and rolls against the shoreline.

Swanton Berry Farm
Two miles north of Davenport on Hwy. 1
831-469-8804
www.swantonberryfarm.com

About seventy miles south of San Francisco along Highway 1 is Swanton Berry Farm, home to some of the best strawberries I've ever tasted. The farm opened in 1983 with two acres and today has eighty acres of not only strawberries but also blackberries, artichokes, broccoli, cauliflower, and other vegetables—all grown organically. There are two farms: the Farm Stand and Swanton's Coastways, where you can pick strawberries, blackberries, kiwis, and ollalieberries. Don't believe that anything you purchase (except for perhaps vegetables) will last till you get home; my strawberries were gone by the time I reached Carmel.

CARMEL

Charming, tony, and attractive, Carmel is the type of place where you do not want to see cutoffs, tank tops, or flip-flops. Homes are known by name and have no numbered addresses, which enhances the town's residential character. Still, streets and shops (as well as the beach at the edge of town) tend to be filled with tourists visiting for weekends and holidays.

I found lots of shops, restaurants, and antique stores amid the many New York brokerage offices.

Villeroy & Boch
Ocean Ave. between Dolores and Lincoln, South Side
831-624-8210

At Villeroy & Boch, I did purchase an unusual metal candleholder that was on sale.

As befits a town whose mayor at one time was actor Clint Eastwood, Carmel boasts several fine resorts and inns.

Quail Lodge
8000 Valley Greens Dr.
831-620-8866
www.quaillodge.com

I visited this most accommodating property a few years ago. My accommodations consisted of two rooms: a large sitting area with a fireplace and an equally large bedroom, both well appointed in earth tones. Everything about the bathroom was perfect, from the beautiful bathrobes, to the heated floor and towel bars, to the huge tub.

I took full advantage of the amenities, soaking in the large tub, then wrapping myself in a bathrobe and plopping down on the sofa to read about the Quail Lodge's golf course (831-620-8808), home to the California Women's State Amateur Championship each December. Forward to now: The lodge per se is closed, and it is now more a semiprivate golf club.

There are two places to eat at the Quail Golf Club: **Edgar's** (831-620-8910) in the golf club house, which is open to the public, and there is also and the **Covey Restaurant**. Quail's future is to be decided. I only hope this attractive property enjoys a timely renaissance.

Bernardus Lodge
415 W. Carmel Valley Rd.
831-658-3400
www.bernardus.com

The Bernardus is near perfection. From the moment I arrived, I knew I was in for an extraordinary experience. As soon as I pulled up in front of the lodge, I was greeted warmly, and my bags were whisked away with the promise that they'd be taken to my room. Nestled into a terraced hill directly in front of where you park, the Bernardus makes you feel as if you are visiting a very spacious, perfectly appointed, private home.

Two concierges, each with his own computer and seated behind a large table, attended to my check in. After an exchange of greetings, a waiting attendant stood to show me to my room. A welcoming glass of wine (from the lodge's own vineyards, no less!) was offered, along with an invitation to tour the property. I followed the attendant through the main building and out into the garden, where sounds from running fountains filled the air. The pool and spa area were to the left, and in the area to the right, one could enjoy casual outdoor dining warmed by a large fireplace.

My room was understated, rustic but elegant, with special attention to many details. Welcoming complimentary estate wines, soft drinks, pastries, and cheese awaited on a table; elsewhere, there were fresh flowers and a bowl of fruit. Also, there was a large TV, CD player, coffeemaker, and tea server. Imported linens and down comforters graced the bed. In the bathroom, I found coral-colored toilet paper and Kleenex, a loofah sponge, bath salts, a scale, and a huge tub. The overstuffed chairs and sofa and the armoires were perfectly proportioned. From a balcony, I could overlook the manicured gardens. Heaven!

Bernardus Pon, creator of the acclaimed **Bernardus Winery and Vineyard** (800-223-2533), established Bernardus Lodge in 1999, with the goal of combining exemplary hospitality with exceptional epicurean experiences. Mission accomplished! The wines are delicious and form a great marriage with a meal. I wondered if the Bernardus's signature restaurant, **Marinus** (831-658-3595), could possibly live up to its fantastic reputation and many awards. The answer was yes.

The dining room is not large, but large enough. Since I do adore a perfectly set table, I appreciated the crisp, white linens, polished silverware, and sparkling goblets. And the food . . . where do I begin? I started with the superb portobello soup, then tried the foie gras over lobster in a pastry shell. My main course was lobster with mango and prosciutto; dessert was a simple homemade ice cream. All the vegetables and fruits used are grown on property. Cal Stamenov is the executive chef and culinary director of Marinus, and my meal proved that his culinary talents are indisputable. I didn't merely walk back to my room. I floated.

The turndown service is as you would expect and then some: How about a half bottle of wine and some treats from the chef for a night cap? Though tempted, I did not succumb. The imported linens, feather bed, and down comforter were quite enough to send me into dreamland.

The Spa at Bernardus Lodge (831-658-3560) is small but pleasant. Candlelight in the hallways contributes to the atmosphere, as does the fact that you have to be eighteen to use the spa. The facilities are what you would expect, with a large waiting room (called a warming room) with fruits, teas, and refreshing cucumber water. I had a "Wellbeing Massage"—nothing out of the ordinary but still very pleasant.

The pool area just outside the spa is a perfect place to relax, whether you've had a treatment or not. I tried to continue my feeling of well-being as I stretched out on a comfortable chaise and let the Carmel sun warm my oil-filled pores and massaged body. The sound of running fountains was nice background music that added to the ambiance.

Alas, before I knew it, my stay was over, and my bags were being taken to my waiting car. Everyone I passed on the way out bade me farewell. The attendant who had put my bags in the car had also placed a bottle of water in the front seat—a thoughtful parting gift from a most special place.

BIG SUR

Beginning south of Carmel is legendary Big Sur, the rugged shoreline where author and resident Henry Miller claimed that he first "learned to say amen" (whether as a spiritual incantation or an exclamation of relief at having survived the drive is not known).

Big Sur is a ninety-mile stretch of awesome coastline. There are pull-outs where you can stop, view, rest, take a deep breath, and so forth. There is no charge to use them, so do so whenever needed. At designated places, you can climb down to the beach. I hear the walk is worth it, but having looked at some of the paths, I guarantee it is not for bad knees or hips under any circumstances. Remember, if you go down, you have to come back up!

Again: Do not fear this highway, just respect it, maintain a sensible speed, and enjoy.

Driving Diva Factoid: It was not until the 1950s that electricity arrived in Big Sur, and it still does not exist in some of the more challenging rural areas.

Nepenthe Restaurant
48510 Hwy. 1
831-667-2345
www.nepenthebigsur.com

I have heard that the name *Nepenthe* means either "isle of no care" or "no sorrow." *Webster's* defines it as a potion used in ancient times to induce forgetfulness of pain or sorrow or anything capable of causing oblivion of grief or suffering. This legendary restaurant was started over fifty years ago by Lolly and Bill Fassett, who from the start aspired to give their guests excellent service in a special and relaxed atmosphere. It's special, indeed, because you are hanging over a cliff above the pounding Pacific Ocean! The view is wonderful, except when the fog rolls in, and when I was there, there was more fog than view, but I waited a while and saw more view. Regardless of the fickle weather, I recommend Nepenthe and compliment its third-generation owners, who maintain their grandparents' original vision for the place. Be prepared to wait for a good seat around sunset though. And, as at many other such special places, you pay for the view.

I was told to watch for the elephant seals frolicking in the ocean around Big Sur, and sure enough, there they were. They're big animals, but surprisingly nimble. As they frolicked, they looked quite adoringly toward one another, rubbing their snouts and heads together.

Hearst Castle
750 Hearst Castle Rd., San Simeon
800-444-4445
www.hearstcastle.com

The unbelievable former private residence of publishing tycoon William Randolph Hearst is farther down on Highway 1 at San Simeon. The name Hearst Castle is no misnomer and may in fact understate the scale of the property, which, in addition to the main house (La Casa Grande), also includes an eighteen-room guesthouse. This beautiful and grand castle was the "hideaway" Hearst used for his supposedly clandestine romance with actress Marion Davies, perhaps the worst-kept secret in America in the 1920s and 1930s.

The guided tours are very well done and well worth the price of admission ($25 for adults and $12 for children in 2011). You take a designated bus up the hill past what looks like an African savannah: Hearst had his own zoo at San Simeon, and many descendants of the original zebras, elk, goats, llamas, and deer survive on the 250,000 acres that the Hearst family eventually donated to the state of California.

Hearst Castle was designed by architect Julia Morgan, a petite but formidable and highly talented female and one of the first women to graduate with a degree in civil engineering from the University of California, Berkeley. Construction began in 1919 and lasted until 1947.

San Simeon Pines

7200 Moonstone Beach Dr., Cambria
805-927-4648
www.sspines.com

After visiting the Castle, I had intended to stay here, but I was ahead of schedule and decided to proceed to my next destination. The people at San Simeon Pines were very gracious, and the Pines are a must if you are ever in the area.

Morro Bay

Inn at Morro Bay

60 State Park Rd., Morro Bay
800-321-9566
www.innatmorrobay.com

It was a little after twilight when I drove into the circular driveway. The lights were twinkling, and I could see the bay on the other side of the building. My room, on the bay side with parking right in front, was simple, but comfortable and clean, and with a wonderful view—from what I could discern. I was delighted to be where I was.

I asked for a good, easy-to-reach restaurant, and the staff recommended the Great American Fish Company.

Great American Fish Company

1185 Embarcadero
805-772-4407

Dinner proved to be fine—nothing fancy. I ordered the "senior portion," which does not mean large but rather that the patron is over thirty-nine and a half. It was just right. More restaurants should have such an option.

Waking early the next morning, I discovered what I had not seen in the dark. Whoa! The inn's brochure describes the surrounding area better than I possibly could: "To the north stands a grove of 100-year-old cypress trees. To the south lies **Morro Bay National Estuary** [www.mbnep.org]. To the east stretches the 18-hole bay-view **Morro Bay Golf Course** [www.centralcoastgolf.com]. And directly out front—in the bay—rises the 20-million-year-old, six-story, former volcano given the name **Morro Rock** [www.morrobay.com/rock .htm] in 1542 by explorer Juan Rodriguez Cabrillo." I later learned that *morro* is the Spanish word for a Moorish turban.

After a light breakfast, and surmising that Morro Bay was probably just another beach community, I set out and discovered not only how very wrong my assumptions were but how very wrong a published review of a place can be. This particular review stated that there was not much to do aside from gawk at Morro Rock and the monstrous oceanfront electrical plant across the water from it.

Driving Diva Observation: Some people cannot see real beauty if there is an obstacle nearby.

It turns out that there is a lot to do in this seaside community. A short drive from the inn is the main drag, Morro Bay Boulevard, where I found La Petite and, next door, the Queen's Closet.

La Petite
317 Morro Bay Blvd.
805-772-2361

This is a boutique store.

Queen's Closet
325 Morro Bay Blvd.
805-772-4288

The Queen's Closet sells plus-sized apparel. Fortunately (then!), I didn't qualify to shop there. I learned that it had been in existence for thirty-seven years under three owners.

You wouldn't think of recommending a fabric shop as a destination point for a road trip, but the Cotton Ball actually got me twice!

Cotton Ball

1199 Main St.
800-895-7402
www.thecottonball.com

This fabulous fabric and trimming shop also has craft supplies and a garden courtyard in the back filled with decorative items. It's a treasure trove!

Forcing myself out of the shop and onward, I discovered these spots.

Best Friends

480 Morro Bay Blvd.
805-772-2002

This shop sells gifts and home decor.

Art Effects Gallery

435 Morro Bay Blvd.
805-772-5159
www.arteffectsonline.com

Kathleen McCarthy designs handmade lampshades of a theatrical nature.

Lina G's All the Trimmings

468 Morro Bay Blvd.
805-772-7759

This interesting shop has an abundant supply and variety of trimmings and accessories.

Taco Temple

2680 Main St.
805-772-4965

Taco Temple is a popular eating place. Initially, I was hesitant to visit, but the promise of a California fusion menu lured me in. The card reads, "Taco Temple: Tacos, Burritos, Tostadas: The Freshest California Style Mexican Food on the Coast. Working Chefs & Owners: Adam & Dawnelle." Taco Temple is small and nothing fancy, but the food is fabulous and the atmosphere friendly. It was wonderful! I wanted to order one of everything. Nothing on the select lunch menu was then over $8.95.

Back at the Inn at Morro Bay, a most attractive restaurant is the **Orchid** (805-772-2238, ext. 1711). I dined there following drinks and hors d'oeuvres with one of the inn's executives. With Morro Bay in the background and an abundance of orchids, the setting was delightful and the dinner delicious. Be sure the Inn at Morro Bay and the Orchid are on your agenda. There is also the **Bay Club** for casual dining: breakfast, happy hour, and dinner from 5 p.m. to 9 p.m.

SAN LUIS OBISPO

Madonna Inn
100 Madonna Rd.
800-543-9666
www.madonnainn.com

One cannot go to San Luis Obispo without at least stopping to take a look at the world-famous Madonna Inn. On the recommendation of friends who told me I would really be "in for something" if I stayed there, I booked a room and gave the place a try. My, my! I hadn't quite prepared myself for this unique, funky, and wonderful find. Built, owned, and operated by Alex and Phyllis Madonna— Alex being the architect and wife Phyllis the interior designer—the place is the ultimate in California kitsch—nice, original kitsch. (Is that an oxymoron?) The Madonnas opened the first twelve rooms in 1958, but demand was so high that they quickly added another twenty-eight. In 1960 they started construction of the main inn, which now comprises 109 rooms. What makes the inn so unique? For one thing, no two rooms are alike, and they are all themed, from the Cave Man Room, with its rock walls, to the Safari Room, described as a "lively African setting with a jungle twist." Where else can you stay in a bright red room with two king-size beds, Victorian furnishings, a seven-foot bathtub (so you know the bathroom isn't small), and a huge rock fireplace that looks like it was designed by Fred Flintstone? The enormous living room also includes a small sink, refrigerator, and coffeemaker. Not that I am recommending it, but a family of ten with sleeping bags would have plenty of room in the Travelers Suite, as my accommodation was named.

The big, main dining room at the Madonna Inn is the **Gold Rush Steakhouse** (805-784-2433). Funky, slightly glitzy, sparkling, and more, it is not unattractive. How would you describe a dining room where you are greeted by the "swinging girl," who has been swinging from the genuine oak branches overlooking the dining room since it opened? A love of pink helps, as there are tufted pink-leather seats, pink tablecloths, and a pink floral-patterned carpet. The ceiling is filled with hundreds of little twinkling lights, which also cover plants throughout the room. Believe it or not, it all works. I had a delicious steak dinner in this twinkling room, and for dessert, a slice of one of the inn's famous three-layer cakes did the trick. Oh so good!

Driving Diva Factoid: According to the Madonna Inn brochure, "The twenty-foot gold tree fixture in the main dining room was made from electrical conduit, left over from building projects, as well as some left over copper."

The **Silver Bar** (805-784-2432), which also doubles as the morning meeting place for coffee and a Danish, continues the red-and-pink theme.

At the **Bakery & Pastry Shop** (805-784-2437), a more casual meal can be had, and it is most popular with tourists as well as the locals.

A large sign proclaiming, "Let's Eat and Be Forever Happy," greets you upon your entry—so Madonna Inn! I could wax on about the delicious choices on the menu. I settled for a Monte Cristo and coconut pie. While I was eating, someone came up behind me and asked, "Is everything all right?" Turns out it was Mr. Madonna himself! We quickly conversed, and he introduced me to his buddy Harry Henderson, sitting a seat down from me.

FYI: As for individual bakery goods, the early bird definitely catches the worm here, as many of the best and most popular items disappear quickly. The bakery aficionados are there very early.

Shopping options at the Madonna Inn include, for ladies, the **My Favorite Things Boutique** (805-784-2441)—lucky me! I just happened to be there when there was a sale!—and the Brass Tower Men's Store, both of which are well and selectively stocked. I learn now that they have been combined.

FYI: One of their signature items is pink sugar. You can get it in a shaker or by the pound. Next time, at least a dozen will be in my car. Fun!

Believe it or not, a local attraction for women is the Wine Cellar Waterfall Men's Room. Yes, I did say men's room. I'll leave it at that. Perhaps it presents an ingenious way to avoid left-up toilet seats and unattractive splashes. (Of course, make sure that there aren't any men in there before you go in.)

A Mother's Question: What's a good way to "train" little boys?

Speaking of "facilities," the ladies room is brightly colored, and a sign above the vanity reminds, "Your beauty is your smile"! The restroom also had a small basin and toilet for little ladies. Adorable!

The Spa at Madonna Inn is just up the hill. If you want to pamper yourself, be sure to make an appointment ahead of time. I found my treatment relaxing and pleasant.

Driving Diva Factoid: In April 2004, Alex Madonna passed away due to a heart attack. He was eighty-five. It was obvious he had lived a full and creative life, starting his construction business before he graduated from high school. After serving in the army during World War II, he returned to build or repave most of Highway 101. He constructed the bridge over Twitchell Reservoir, which *Bridges Magazine* named the most beautiful bridge in the country in 1958, the same year the Madonnas opened the Madonna Inn. The rest is history. I feel honored to have met this unique gentleman. I look forward to a revisit and to seeing Mrs. Madonna, her daughter, and her staff. Also, Harry Henderson has passed away. Thank you for special and wonderful memories.

Just up the road, actually across from the Madonna Inn, is the Madonna Plaza.

Madonna Plaza Shopping Center
271 Madonna Rd.
805-544-5710

The standard shops are there, and it's very convenient to the inn.

Downtown San Luis Obispo

Downtown San Luis Obispo is just a few minutes away by car from the Madonna Inn.

Smokin' Mo's BBQ
1005 Monterey St.
805-544-6193
www.smokinmosbbq.com

I recommend Mo's for lunch. Once I parked the car, I simply followed the aroma. Since it was a little early for lunch, I had a chance to look around. I discovered that when Mo decided to find out what barbecue was all about, he and a buddy traveled across the country to research the cuisine. They visited ten states and over eighty barbecue restaurants, purchasing chairs and taking pictures of cooks. These things now decorate the restaurant that the two buddies built from the ground up. Their goal was to be the finest barbecue restaurant in the West. Whether or not they succeeded, I cannot say, but on the day I ate there, it certainly was. You can purchase some of the sauces to take home, and there are now Mo's in Pismo Beach, Huntington Beach, and Chico.

Fortified with barbecue, I left Mo's to explore the town. I discovered a gem of a place, well cared for and not terribly congested. The main shopping street is Higuera. Here are some of my finds:

Creamery
470 Higuera St.
805-544-1446

This real creamery has unbelievable homemade ice cream. I'm not an ice cream freak, but this place could have made anyone a convert.

Finders Keepers
1124 Garden St.
805-541-5282

This consignment boutique was attractive and well kept. A major discovery was Brio Caffe.

Brio Caffe: Cucina Italiana
1203 Marsh St.
805-541-5282

The husband-and-wife team of Manny and Rebecca Estrella have created a treasure. It is not fancy-schmancy, but everything is made from scratch with the freshest foods. The most expensive item on the lunch menu was linguini pescatore: sautéed shrimp, garlic, fresh tomatoes, basil, and button mushrooms tossed with linguine for $10.95. Most lunch items were from $5.25 to $8.35. Everything just right and delicious.

SANTA BARBARA

I have been to Santa Barbara several times, making new discoveries with each visit.

Bacara Resort and Spa
8301 Hollister Ave.
805-968-0100
www.bacararesort.com

This is the type of place whose advertisements ooze glamour, luxury, and style. The male and female models smile and hold their champagne glasses out to you, she of the buffed nails (no fake claws), dark lipstick, full eyebrows, Marcel hairdo, and small breasts, attired in an evening gown that skins the body and draped in diamonds that sparkle right off the page. Am I envious of her body? Well, a little, but after many pregnancies, I wouldn't exchange my rewards for a figure like that. But perhaps Bacara could work a little magic on me.

Bacara is not right in Santa Barbara, but more toward Goleta, about fifteen minutes from downtown. I had to use my OnStar to find it, though I confess that I drove by the entrance twice. It was not well marked.

A huge event was in progress when I arrived, and attendants were all over the place. I parked the car and went in the first big doorway I saw. I waited in line to check in, which was done in a rather haphazard but friendly way.

The property is so large that golf carts are often used to get to the rooms. The bellman was most helpful in getting me to my accommodations and showing me where the pool, spa, and restaurants were. The room was most attractive with an inviting porch. The walls were very light beige with dark brown ceiling beams. The furniture was mahogany. The ultrawhite bedspread, king bed, oversized pillows, and blue-print quilt were all appealing. There was also a big basket of extra towels. So much for the highlights of Bacara.

Finding my way around the property was a challenge as the signage is extremely poor. I got lost going up and down hilly pathways until I hitched a ride on a golf cart.

The shops at Bacara are quite fancy but offered nothing to drool over. A father and daughter I met in one of the shops agreed with me. He was ready to treat and spoil his daughter.

There are two main restaurants at Bacara: **Miro** (805-571-4204) and the **Bistro** (805-571-4217). Miro was closed, so my only choice was the Bistro, which definitely was not a winner. The service was poor, hot soup arrived cold, and my serving of gnocchi was microscopic. The portions were lost on the plate, and when I discussed the matter with the waitress, she brought two more thimble-sized gnocchi. The father and daughter I spoke with in the shop stopped by the table and reported a similarly unimpressive dining experience.

The next night I was to dine with the public relations manager, again at the Bistro, but she was a no-show. However, the chef, David Garwacki, made up for it in the nicest way by joining me at my table and recommending a fantastic meal. Thank you, Chef Garwacki.

There is no question that Bacara is an outstanding property, but the management has some work to do. The pool, which looks huge in the brochures, is not so huge, and the beach is not the cleanest. The seaweed and tar are natural but could, and should, be skimmed. My spa experience there was *almost* alright. The facilities were what you would expect, but the personnel at the check-in desk (at least when I stood there) could use a little more training. My appointment was changed, as was the treatment I was supposed to have. Maybe they were just having a bad day.

I didn't leave Bacara looking like anyone in the resort's ads, but at least I could say that I'd been there. Maybe things will be a little more together next time, if there is a next time.

News as of 2011: No details but Bacara is now under new ownership.

Downtown Santa Barbara

Downtown Santa Barbara is filled with boutiques, restaurants, and a brokerage house or three—or four. The people are attractive and wealthy. Following a devastating earthquake in 1925, the city was largely rebuilt in a Spanish-Moorish style, which contributes to its charm. Chic shops and alfresco dining seem to dominate. The beach and marina are a short walk downhill.

Above downtown is the so-called Riviera.

El Encanto Hotel and Garden Villas
2020 Alameda Padro Serra
805-568-1357
www.elencantohotel.com

A charming, enchanting, lush hideaway on a hillside overlooking the Pacific Ocean in the distance, El Encanto has eighty-four beautifully appointed cottages and villas snuggled into its gardens. It would be easy to do what film star Hedy Lamarr did: move in permanently.

A few years ago I was lucky enough to stay in one of the cottages. The living room had a fireplace and other comfortable furnishings, and my bedroom was cozy. It was oh so nice!

Recently the property was purchased by the elite Orient Express Group, which closed the hotel for restoration and enhancements. It plans to open again. I can imagine it will only be perfect.

Montecito Inn
1295 Coast Village Rd.
805-969-7854
www.montecitoinn.com

Just south of Santa Barbara, this inn is another treasure. Financed by a group of investors headed by screen legend Charlie Chaplin, the Montecito Inn opened in 1928 at a cost of $300,000. It was called "the cream of the coast," and the first guests included the movie world's elite, including Carole Lombard, Wallace Beery, Norma Shearer, Janet Gaynor, Marion Davies, and others. Bertrand Harmer was the original architect of this three-story Mediterranean-style building, which had an earthquake-resistant roof.

As times progressed, a driveway into the enclosed parking facility was built, and later a pool, spa, and sauna were added to the rear of the building. A wishing well (lost during construction) was the inspiration for Richard Rodgers's song "There's a Small Hotel."

I've never stayed at the Montecito Inn, but I've seen the rooms and facilities. Everything is quaint and elegant without overdoing it.

The **Montecito Cafe** (805-969-3392) is on the main floor, snuggled into a corner of the hotel and facing the street. If the hotel is a treasure then the café is a gem; my lunch there was delicious. Lemon grilled chicken is one of the most popular items. Proprietors Mark and Margaret Huston obviously know what they are doing. The service was excellent, the food delicious, and the ambiance just right. Tables were close together but not offensively so. Better yet, prices were sensible.

OJAI

South of Santa Barbara and east into the mountains is the town of Ojai (pronounced "oh-hi").

Ojai Valley Inn and Spa
905 Country Club Rd.
805-646-1111
www.ojairesort.com

I had heard about Ojai but never visited this place, which people had described as special. Learning of my book project, the public relations department informed me that the Ojai property was under major renovation and that both accommodations and services would be limited. No problem—I had heard so much about Ojai and wanted to include it in the book. The staff went out of their way to make everything just right and to squeeze as much as possible into my brief visit. They succeeded.

This is Southern California at its finest. In 1922, Edward Libbey (as in the well-known glass company) purchased 220 acres of this beautiful valley to share with his friends. He commissioned California architect Wallace Neff to design a country club with a golf course . . . and, as they say, the rest is history.

Driving Diva Factoid: Ojai means "the nest" or "moon," and for years it was home to the Chumash Indians. They believed, as some people still do, that the east-west-lying valley had mystical powers. Film director Frank Capra chose the Ojai valley to film the movie *Lost Horizon* with Ronald Coleman.

Everything from the time I arrived on property was programmed—and nicely so. I was grateful since there was a lot to get in during my brief visit. Upon arriving, I was instructed to check in, leave my bag, change, swim, steam, soak, and eat.

I wanted to sample Spa Ojai's treatments, and the staff scheduled what they thought would be best. I was to have a "Kuyam" (pronounced "koo-yahm") at 1 p.m. and a "Zen Shiatsu" massage at 3 p.m. It sounded wonderful. (Would my sons recognize me if they saw me at 4:30?)

Oh my! The Kuyam is Spa Ojai's signature mud treatment. You leave your robe outside, go into a room, take a seat, and apply Moor mud to your body. I'm sure a spa professional would explain Kuyam differently, but I'm going to relate how I experienced it.

There were six to eight ladies—all strangers to each other—in their birthday suits. (In California you never know what to expect, so I was glad we were all women.) We were seated in a warm, aromatic room, each with our bowl of mud. Some of the ladies smiled, some frowned, and some just wore quizzical expressions on their faces. I can tell you that being nude in a group like this was not everyone's cup of mud. I applied the Moor mud as instructed to as much of my body as possible. It did not feel particularly glamorous, but I was hopeful. The mud seemed to be doing something to my skin as it firmed up—that is, as the mud firmed up. Soon we were guided in meditation, which was pleasant and definitely different. Then the room began to fill with herb-scented steam released from vents for "inhalation therapy."

A Swiss shower to wash off the Moor mud followed this part of the treatment. Let me tell you, this mud does not willingly come off the body, especially when it gets into the body's crevices. (Mine are more like ravines.) This is followed by a second shower for final cleansing; then, you are lotioned, wrapped in a warm linen sheet, and taken to the outdoor loggia to reflect. The price is what you would expect, and yes, I would do it again, just in case it takes two sessions to improve the body, mind, and those crevices.

The scheduled Zen Shiatsu message was most pleasant. This treatment is meant to stimulate and restore balance to the body by releasing blockages along the energy pathways. It involved moderate-to-strong touch using *shi* (finger) and *atsu* (pressure). A nonoil treatment, Shiatsu promotes overall well-being by restoring vitality to your body as well as relieving stress, muscular discomfort, and fatigue.

The thirty-one-thousand-square-foot Spa Ojai includes every type of spa amenity you can imagine. This professionally run spa is for women and men who aim to improve themselves via several types of treatments and through cardiovascular fitness, as well as yoga and meditation. Reservations are a must, since this award-winning spa is also open to outside guests.

The Ojai Valley Inn and Spa is a 308-room resort on 220 acres. Walking the grounds is magical. Do you know another place that "encourages guests to gather fresh herbs in the garden for a wreathmaking class"? The standard sports are all offered, but I chose to go horseback riding, which proved relaxing and scenic. I had ridden quite a bit in younger days, so this was pretty easy.

The signature restaurant is **Maravilla**, serving exceptional California cuisine with a view of the Topatopa Mountains. The **Oak Grill** serves classic American cuisine, and you can eat inside or on the terrace, where the magnificent oaks keep you company. **Café Verde** is in the spa. **Jimmy's Pub** has an upscale bar menu and is a popular sports bar on property.

I was particularly impressed by how the Ojai Valley Inn and Spa treated its employees. As I mentioned, the property was undergoing major renovation when I was there. Usually when this occurs, staff members are laid off temporarily—but not at Ojai. In order to keep unneeded staff members employed during the renovation, the resort offered training in construction skills such as hanging sheet rock, painting, and plastering so that these staff members could participate in the work and keep that paycheck coming in. I found this exceptionally thoughtful of the owners, the Crown family, and the workers I spoke with took great pride in what they were doing and told me how much they enjoyed being part of the renovations. Applause! Applause!

Driving Diva Update: The Ojai Valley Inn and Spa received AAA's Five Diamond Award in 2007.

Addendum: The owners of Ojai Valley Inn and Spa built Casa Elar, a beautiful Tuscan-style villa. Its provenance alone reveals that Casa Elar is exceptional. There are two suites downstairs and a master suite upstairs, as well as a private massage room, elevator, great room, entertainment room, and so much more. The gourmet kitchen and extra rooms, private pool and spa, and shaded terrace with stone pizza oven and gas BBQ all overlook the valley. You can rent this spectacular oasis, and there is no doubt you will have a fantastic experience.

Suzanne's Cuisine

502 W. Ojai Ave.

805-640-1961

www.suzannescuisine.com

We enjoyed dinner at Suzanne's Cuisine, which is located a short drive off property. Opening this special "cuisine" in 1992, Suzanne had become a gourmet fixture and Ojai star by 2000. Her menu is exceptional; only the finest items and freshest herbs are used to create her specialties. The interior of this restaurant is calming and understated. Suzanne was previously an interior decorator, and her decorating talents have not been lost here. One could say that this restaurant gem is a family affair. Daughter Sandra, who has an MBA in finance and marketing, now runs the business side as well as lunchtime. Mother tends to other things until the evening, when she is back at the helm.

Three of us dined together. Among the superb courses we shared were crab and corn cakes with white sauce, shrimp and mango salad, fried crab cake balls with hoisin sauce, halibut, lamb chops, shrimp with ginger sauce, coffee ice cream with Kahlua and chocolate syrup, and coconut ice cream. Everything about Suzanne's is gem quality, and you will agree. Enjoy.

At first glance, the town of Ojai itself doesn't seem that impressive, but during the very short drive to Suzanne's, I was surprised by all that I saw. Then the next day I saw more. It was Sunday, and the **farmers' market** (www.ojaicertifiedfarmersmarket.com) was bustling, as were several attractive, upscale shops. While most places weren't for the bargain hunter, I did find a consignment shop. It is fun to look.

I look forward to revisiting this fabulous place—Ojai.

ON THE ROAD AGAIN

Seventeen miles northwest of Los Angeles, but somehow still "in" LA, is the magnificent Getty Center.

Getty Center
1200 Getty Center Dr.
301-440-7330
www.getty.edu

Admission is free, although, before 5 p.m., parking will set you back $15 per car (in 2011). Situated high atop a mountain overlooking the San Diego Freeway, the Getty Center is a wonderful place to visit, even if you're not an art aficionado.

You park your car and take a tram up to the center's Arrival Plaza, some 881 feet above sea level. I would suggest getting the "Map and Guide" folder and the "Architecture & Gardens" folder, both of which are extremely helpful and easy to read.

Driving Diva Factoid: The Getty Center uses 164,648 square feet of exterior glass, and the travertine used on the buildings—one hundred shiploads' worth—is from the same quarry as that used to build the Colosseum and the colonnade of St. Peter's Basilica.

There are three different eateries at the Getty: fine dining on the plaza level at the **Restaurant** (310-440-6810; reservations recommended), cafeteria-style dining on the lower level in the **Cafe at the Getty Center**, and coffee, lunch, and snacks at the **Garden Terrace Cafe**, also on the lower level but with outdoor seating only.

SANTA MONICA

Ten miles from the Getty Center is Santa Monica, where hardly an inch of prime oceanfront property has gone undeveloped. Famous for its fabulous beach, pier with arcade, famous 1922 merry-go-round, and chic celebrity inhabitants, it had a surprising number of squatting people on and around the beach: bodybuilders (male and female), jugglers, guitar players, and what I call meditators and contemplators (people staring into space or chanting). It was more bizarre than dangerous, but as a woman, I wouldn't strike up an impromptu conversation with any of these characters. (A friend of mine's daughter once ran away to Santa Monica, causing my friend to fly post haste to get the daughter back and on her medication. From what I saw, it is not a place you would want your child to escape to with or without her meds!)

Now to the beautiful, attractive, funky, and delightful finds I made in Santa Monica.

Georgian Hotel
1415 Ocean Ave.
310-395-9945
www.georgianhotel.com

Built as a hideaway for the stars in 1933, the Georgian takes you back into another era. I found it just as the brochure described it: a light blue edifice with a wonderful big porch facing the ocean. Entering the lobby, you can just picture the dignified participants in one of those clandestine affairs of yore. After checking in, I was shown to the mahogany-paneled elevator, where, lo and behold, there was a real, live elevator operator.

My room was comfortable, although darkish in decor. The bathroom was "original," but the nice touch was the rubber ducky by the tub, and the accommodations were clean and comfortable.

The wonderful porch is the highlight of the Georgian Hotel. You can sit and watch the beach scene as you enjoy breakfast—such an excellent way to start the day. (The hotel's restaurant is the **Veranda**, and the original **Speakeasy** is now used for special events.)

Driving Diva Update: Since I visited, the Georgian has been renovated and the elevator replaced, presumably putting its operator out of work.

Montana Avenue

In Santa Monica, Montana Avenue (www.montanaave.com) is ten blocks of eclectic, upscale boutiques, coffee shops, cafés, and restaurants. Take your time. There is a lot to see. The Third Street Promenade is a wide, bustling, three-block stretch open only to pedestrians. It contains over fifteen movie theaters, a collection of shops and restaurants, and hordes of people. There is a lot of street entertainment on the promenade, such as dancers, magicians, fortune tellers, and the like.

LOS ANGELES

Thirteen miles from Santa Monica is downtown Los Angeles. There are several ways to get there, but my favorite is Wilshire Boulevard.

Where else to stay in downtown LA but the fabulous Millennium Biltmore Hotel?

Millennium Biltmore Hotel
506 S. Grand Ave.
213-624-1011
www.millenniumhotels.com/Biltmore

Built in 1923, this grand dame is indeed a magnificent beauty. Touted as the "toast of the coast," this impressive building was designed by Schultz and Weaver (designers of the Waldorf Astoria, among other prominent properties). The nearly seven hundred rooms (of all types and sizes) are very comfortable. When I stayed there, I was upgraded to a suite, so I had a lot of room. The decor was appropriate for a historic hotel, mixing the new with the old. The ballroom, known as the Biltmore Bowl, hosted the Academy Awards in the 1930s and 1940s, and the lobby is adorned with photographs from that era.

Tea is served daily in the beautiful **Rendezvous Court** (213-612-1562), which was at one time the hotel's main lobby. This afternoon tradition lasts from 2 to 5p.m.; champagne, sherry, and kir are also on offer. This is a great respite after a busy morning, but I don't recommend having tea late in the day if a big dinner is planned. The Rendezvous Court also has a bar. The **Gallery Bar** and **Cognac Room** are very cosmopolitan and a wonderful place to meet someone for drinks. Both are also congenial if you are alone. When I was there, I exchanged much chatter with the bartender about my hotel adventures, past and present. A couple drinks and the evening was a wrap—and delightfully so.

Dining at the Biltmore has always been exceptional. **Smeraldi's Restaurant** (213-612-1562) serves breakfast, lunch, and dinner and specializes in Californian Mediterranean cuisine. There is also **Sai Sai Restaurant** (213-624-1100) with its sushi bar and modern Asian cuisine.

The Biltmore used to have something called the chef's dinner, for which you were invited to dine in the kitchen. I was delighted to receive such an invitation. The original china, crystal, and silverware were used, and not a thing was left undone. The menu card for my chef's dinner read, "Le Grand Menu (Inspired by the Spartan's Award Dinner 1946 with a 21st century twist)."

The chef outdid himself, and my dinner dates—the then general manager, his wife, the public relations manger, and a few other personnel—all combined to make it a very memorable evening.

The Biltmore is located downtown and, some say, off LA's beaten path. But there is still a lot going on in the area.

Museum of Contemporary Art
250 S. Grand Ave.
213-626-6222
www.moca.org

The museum also has a sensibly priced café.

Walt Disney Concert Hall
111 S. Grand Ave.
323-850-2000
www.laphil.com

Home to the Los Angeles Philharmonic, the hall is about half a mile from the Biltmore.

Staples Center
1111 S. Figueroa St.

213-742-7340
www.staplescenter.com

Home of the Lakers, the arena is just five minutes from the Biltmore.

Conveniently, the Pershing Square metro station is across the street from the Biltmore.

Broadway is also just a short walk away and contains several congested blocks of little shops, primarily Hispanic. I wouldn't venture out onto Broadway at night, but during the day, you're fine if you keep your street sense about you.

Pink's

709 N. La Brea Ave.
323-931-7594
www.pinkshollywood.com

I had heard so much about this unique landmark beyond downtown that I could not wait to see and eat firsthand. The drive to Pinks takes you through a bit of Hollywood; then you turn onto nondescript North La Brea Avenue, and there in front of you is Pink's. It was not even 11 a.m., but people of every variety were already queuing up to place their orders.

Pink's opened in 1939 and apparently hasn't changed much since then. Famous for its variety of chili dogs, I decided on an "almost-loaded" concoction, full of taste and artery-clogging possibilities. Still, I ate every bit of this monster. Pink's is very reasonably priced but accepts cash only, and the lines can be long. I found it well worth the wait.

BEVERLY HILLS

Beverly Hills's much-touted **Rodeo Drive** (www.rodeodrive-bh.com) is actually only three blocks long. It purports to be the most famous shopping district in America and the three most expensive blocks of shops in the world. Well, if you say so.

Bijan

420 Rodeo Dr.
310-273-6544
www.bijan.com

Bijan is supposed to be the most expensive boutique in the world, requiring an appointment just to shop there—even if you are only in the market for a $50 pair of socks. Still, much has changed since Julia Roberts traipsed down the famous drive in *Pretty Woman*. Many of the fancy stores are still there, but so are the same chain stores that you can find in Kalamazoo.

A creatively designed mall called Two Rodeo is a recent development.

Two Rodeo Drive

9480 Dayton Way, Ste. 200
310-247-7040
www.2rodeo.com

Essentially an upscale, small, outdoor mall, with tenants like Tiffany, Valentino, Cartier, Jose Eber, and others, Two Rodeo has small shops, various restaurants, and no bargains, but it is still very attractive.

Driving Diva Tip: "Gently worn" used, upscale clothing can be found at Rodeo Drive Resale in Sherman Oaks (not Beverly Hills).

Rodeo Drive Resale

13727 Ventura Blvd.
713-777-0390 or 888-697-3725 (MY-RESALE)
www.rodeodriveresale.com

The selection is quite large, and "100% authenticity" is guaranteed. Their website is excellent, and you can take advantage of the fabulous collections.

Beverly Wilshire Hotel

9500 Wilshire Blvd.

310-275-5200

www.fourseasons.com/beverlywilshire

This grand hotel is not far from Rodeo Drive. Hollywood's stars and history over the years have added to the property's reputation. As a tribute to the hotel's construction, it has withstood three earthquakes and served as an air raid shelter during World War II. There have been many owners over the years, but Hernando Courtright and his group of investors brought the hotel to elite status and made it an enclave for the Hollywood crowd. Pennies have never been pinched as it is continually being updated, the latest renovation being a $35 million makeover in 2005. The restaurants are excellent, but if you have to ask the price, then . . . well, that should give you a clue.

Driving Diva Factoid: The Beverly Wilshire uses black dinner napkins so you don't get bits of white linen on your dark clothes. Excellent. I was told they were the first to use black napkins. Very considerate.

RIVERSIDE

Fifty-five miles east of Los Angeles, Riverside is the navel orange capital of California. It's charming, with its Victorian homes and the very unique Mission Inn Hotel & Spa.

Mission Inn Hotel & Spa

3649 Mission Inn Ave.

951-784-0300

www.missioninn.com

Built in 1876, the Mission Inn Hotel has grown in many stages and is now the size of an entire city block. Its turrets, domes, circular stairs, art collections, bell collection (largest in the world), wedding chapel, and Tiffany windows all evoke the feel of a Spanish town. No two of its 238 Spanish-themed rooms are the same.

The inn contains **Kelly's Spa** (800-440-5910) and five restaurants. **Duane's Prime Steaks & Seafood** is baronial in atmosphere and serves a fine steak. **54°** at Duane's offers wines and tapas in a modern setting. The **Mission Inn Restaurant** (951-341-6767) offers more traditional fare. Adjacent is the **Spanish Patio**, the perfect place for alfresco dining. **Las Campanas** features Mexican cuisine and outdoor dining in the garden. The **Presidential Lounge** (888-326-4448) was at one time a four-room apartment used by eight U.S. presidents, and Richard and Pat Nixon were married here. It now has live jazz on Friday and Saturday, and the menu is casual. Another gastronomic addition at the Mission Inn is **Bella Trattoria**, which offers southern Italian cuisine: pasta, pizza, pressed panini sandwiches, and more. The ultimate for every sweet tooth is **Casey's Cupcakes**. These cupcakes of many varieties won *Cupcake Wars* on the Food Network.

Driving Diva Factoid: The inn participates in Riverside's spectacular annual Festival of Lights, which lasts from the day after Thanksgiving until the end of the first week in January. Some 2 million lights adorn holiday decorations all over the property, aided by frequent live singing of carols.

LONG BEACH

I'd say that the beach community of Long Beach has a lot of potential. It's a little funky in places and chic in others, but it also has a city aura, perhaps because Los Angeles is so close.

Note: You can take the metro from LA to Long Beach.

Driving Diva Factoid: The post office had bulletproof-glass windows!

Queen Mary

1126 Queens Hwy.

562-435-3511 or 877-342-0738

www.queenmary.com

A famous Long Beach landmark, the Queen of the Seas is permanently docked here and is now a hotel. Checking in, you board the *Queen Mary* just as if it were about to sail, and then you are shown to your cabin.

The *Queen Mary* not only transported the elite "across the pond," but during World War II it served as a troopship, transporting over eight hundred thousand soldiers and traveling over six hundred thousand miles. After the war and some 1,001 transatlantic crossings, the city of Long Beach had the foresight to purchase the ship in 1967. After extensive overhauling in 1972, the Hotel Queen Mary was opened.

Everything is as it was on the original steamship, except some of the engines have been removed. There are many places to dine and imbibe on board, from the elegant **Sir Winston's Restaurant & Lounge** (562-499-1657) to the **Promenade Café**, the **Observation Bar**, and the **Chelsea Chowder House & Bar** (562-499-6695). Since I was on board, a lot has been added in the way of entertainment, such as **Tibbies Great American Cabaret** (888-484-2243) and **Vamp: The Lounge** (562-499-6625). There is also an annual Art Deco Festival as well as other special events.

Obtaining passage on the *Queen Mary* is a unique way to have a shipboard-hotel experience. Accommodations start at around $190 and up, and no Dramamine is needed!

Scorpion

1126 Queens Hwy.

562-435-3511

www.russiansublongbeach.com

The *Scorpion*, a Russian submarine of the Foxtrot class (to be tediously precise, a Povodnaya Lodka B-427), is docked next to the *Queen Mary*. Open to the public, the *Scorpion* is in near-operational condition.

Driving Diva Plan: On your next trip to Long Beach, take the ferry to special Catalina Island.

CARLSBAD

Less than one hundred miles from Los Angeles is Carlsbad, but don't let the distance fool you: It took me almost three hours to get there in typical Southern California traffic.

La Costa Resort and Spa
2100 Costa Del Mar Rd.
760-438-9111 or 800 854 5000
www.lacosta.com

My visit to this feature of Carlsbad coincided with the Acura Tennis Tournament, so the place was jammed, and much of the hotel was closed off since it was undergoing a $140 million renovation. While the staff definitely could have used a little help managing the crowds, getting my car parked and checking in was not a problem. Bellmen take you and your bags around in golf carts since La Costa's terrain is hilly (but scenic). As with many such resorts, there was no real signage, so I had to make a mental note of landmarks so that I didn't get lost among the hills. But even with all the construction and the tennis tournament, I was pleased to see how well everything was functioning.

The accommodations were most attractive and the view from the porch outside my room wonderful.

La Costa features a beautiful golf course, many tennis courts, inviting swimming pools, and even a center for children. Eating options include **Legends Bistro**, a pleasant way to start the day sitting outside amid the beautiful scenery, but the breakfast buffet was ordinary. Blackbirds made themselves right at home on my chair and even on the table. (This was not a problem; in fact, it was rather nice.) Since my visit, **BlueFire Grill** has been added, and from what I hear it's wonderful.

In addition to the Spa at La Costa (800-729-4772), where I enjoyed a very good treatment, La Costa is home to the **Chopra Center for Well-being** (888-424-6772), founded by new age guru Deepak Chopra, "which offers programs in mind body medicine, yoga, self-discovery, emotional wellness, meditation and personal empowerment."

From all I experienced here at La Costa, KSL Resorts has a gem of a Carlsbad property.

Driving Diva Munch Discovery: Pei Wei Asian Diner (pronounced "pay way"; www.peiwei.com) uses the freshest ingredients, cooked to order and sensibly priced. Enjoy! Find one and go enjoy.

Out and about in greater Carlsbad and on into Rancho Santa Fe and Encinitas, one finds lots of upscale neighborhoods, small boutique shopping areas, and places to stop and snack.

Sheri Designer Resale
920 S. Coast Hwy. 101, Encinitas
858-481-3843

Carolyn's Designer Resale
1310 Camino Del Mar
760-943-1556

Carolyn's has top-quality designer clothes at reasonable prices. Just down the highway is Thrifty Threads.

Thrifty Threads
607 S. Coast Hwy. 101, Encinitas
760-753-0028

This is an eclectic, colorful shop.

DANA POINT AND POINTS SOUTH AGAIN

The following discoveries are not listed in travel order due to scheduling and reservation availability.

Heading north from Carlsbad, my next destination was Dana Point, specifically the St. Regis Monarch Beach Resort.

Driving Diva Humble Confession (a First!): I had already driven almost six thousand miles, so perhaps white-line fever was finally getting to me. Anyway, I pulled into this impressive entryway to be met by a very efficient doorman and bellman, the latter of whom whisked my bags away. Upon checking in, I was presented with the news that I did not have a reservation. I quickly took out my confirmation letter and realized that I had just done something totally "blonde": I was in the lobby of the Ritz, not the nearby St. Regis!

St. Regis Monarch Beach Resort

One Monarch Beach Resort
949-234-3200
www.stregismb.com

There's one word for the St. Regis: "splendid." This is not just another impressive property. I felt as if I were in a palatial *Arabian Night*'s setting—though the hotel information says the interior design is Tuscan inspired. The decor begins at the reception desk and continues throughout, with commissioned paintings, formidable mirrors, ceiling murals, and glass art by Dale Chihuly. Yes, it is a museum of sorts, complete with a listing and description of each piece of art.

The view from the lobby is of the huge pool and then the magnificent Pacific Ocean. If you walk to the far end of the pool and look back, the splendor and magnificence of the property are easy to grasp. I found the accommodations everything you would expect—excellent in every way.

There are three pools: the Main Pool, the Lagoon Pool, and a three-lane lap pool at the **Spa Gaucin** fitness center (949-234-3367) in the spa. At the Main Pool you can rent a fully equipped cabana with a private patio, flat-screen TV, DVD video system, CD stereo, fax machine, cordless telephone, ceiling fan, and Internet access including Wi-Fi. Oh my! I could have just stayed there.

The private six-acre beach and **Monarch Bay Club** (949-234-3330) are available only to registered overnight guests and are accessible only by the hotel's tram.

There are many half- and full-day activities for children, and include studying seashells, building sand castles, riding waves, playing tennis, taking etiquette classes, doing yoga, and more. The experienced babysitters at the St. Regis are also trained in CPR, first aid, and child care.

Dining options at the St. Regis include **Motif** (949-234-3272), which offers a "small plate," with many (perhaps too many) choices presented rather haphazardly. (I don't like to have to ask for bread and butter, for example.) Sunday brunch at Motif is expensive with or without champagne, but the restaurant does offer forty different types of pancakes. Reservations are a must. The private **Club 19** (949-234-3685) at the Monarch Beach Golf Links offers breakfast—at which I queried the stated freshness of the orange juice—and a full lunch at the **Lobby Lounge** (949-234-3309) provides seating inside or out with an ocean view. Here you must order this decadent delight: truffle butter popcorn. So good! The **Monarch Bay Club** served me what I can only call a perfect dinner: scallops on a bed of spinach with a thin sauce to start, a Caesar salad, and a steak entrée.

At the tiny shop **Crust** (949-234-3471), you can get breakfast, sandwiches, all sorts of coffee, and other delicious treats if you don't want to sit in a restaurant.

I have been told the **Stonehill Tavern** (800-722-1543) is only fabulous. It had not opened when I was there.

Then, of course, there is Spa Gaucin (949-234-3367). As you enter, the scent of fresh flowers fills the air, as does the sound of the spa's three-story waterfall. The toss of a coin into the "Well of Desires," to symbolize your leaving all cares behind, begins your spa treatment. There are many treatments to choose from, but I enjoyed every split second of an orange frappé lathering. Orange, honey, and yogurt were spread over my body, which was then wrapped in steamy, warm linens. This fruity treatment was then followed by a scalp and face massage and a citrus mist of my entire body, followed by a shower, followed by a cream orange lotion massage. (I've gone limp just writing about it.) A very relaxing stay by the pool in the spa area capped off the afternoon. There is a very healthy café at Spa Gaucin.

The town of Dana Point itself is quiet and charming, encompassing only 6.5 square miles with a population of about thirty-five thousand, including Monarch and Capistrano bays. This is obviously a savvy, affluent community.

ON THE ROAD

There are two "on-the-road" gastronomical beacons this Driving Diva adores. One might refer to them as hamburger joints. Call them whatever you want; just know they are deliciously fabulous and not pricey, and their other items are equally good.

In-N-Out
800-786-1000
www.in-n-out.com

This establishment started in 1948 with three very simple criteria: highest-quality foods, friendly service, and sparkling-clean environment. You'll find hamburgers, cheeseburgers, french fries, milk shakes, Coca-Cola classic and other standard drinks, plus iced tea, coffee, and milk. There are many locations. Look for this delight and park and enjoy.

Ruby's
30622 Coast Hwy. 101, Laguna Beach
949-497-7829 (RUBY)
www.rubys.com

Ruby's advertises "the Best Burger in Orange County" and just may be right. Also delicious are the sandwiches, soups, salads, fries, shakes, and other wonderful food. These 1950s-style diners can be found throughout California. They also serve breakfast and lunch/dinner. Ruby's burgers and sliders have zero trans fats. Ruby's is a must. The atmosphere, decor, and music all blend so well that you might want to get up and Lindy Hop.

LAGUNA BEACH

Due to its topography and proximity to Hollywood, arty and attractive Laguna Beach was a haven for stars and starlets. Walking shoes are suggested.

SAN CLEMENTE

Just down the coast and (in)famous as the residence of President Richard Nixon, San Clemente is also a popular spot for tourists, as the many rental properties along the beach indicate. I managed to find one thrift store, and there are probably more.

Toby's House Thrift and Gift
110 S. El Camino Real
949-361-7721
www.tobyshouse.com

Proceeds go to help abused women, so of course I bought something.

LA JOLLA

La Jolla (pronounced "la hoya," meaning "the jewel") is further south. It's a dressy place. I don't mean fancy—just neat and not sloppy. There are lots and lots of shops and eateries but few bargains.

Deli-icious: The Locals Deli
1237 Prospect St., Ste. J
858-456-6235

This was a definite find with nothing on the menu over $6 (then). It was delightful and felt very good to sit down.

CORONADO

The San Diego–Coronado Bay Bridge proves the old adage that "getting there is half the fun." This spectacular, two-mile span is, at one point, 243 feet high to allow large ships to pass underneath.

Driving Diva Tip: Try to avoid the bridge during rush hour. I made the mistake of heading to the island at 5 p.m. and got stuck for longer than I wanted.

Just a bridge away from the hustle and bustle of San Diego, Coronado is thirteen square miles of paradise, and the weather is about as perfect as it gets.

There are lots of wonderful shops and places to eat in Coronado, especially along Orange Avenue, Coronado's main street. A favorite of mine is Stretch's Café.

Stretch's Café
943 Orange Ave.
619-435-8886
www.stretchscafe.com

Billing itself as the "healthy alternative to fast food," Stretch's is small, cozy, deliciously friendly, and sensibly priced.

Hotel Del Coronado
1500 Orange Ave.
619-435-6611
www.hoteldel.com

The centerpiece of Coronado is this historic and grand hotel. The rare and extraordinary Del Coronado has something for everyone and in every price range.

Every time I've arrived, I've been greeted promptly by cordial, able attendants. Walking into the Del, whether it is your first or umpteenth time, is impressive and breathtaking. Keeping the 688 rooms organized is a mighty task, but the staff manage brilliantly. The accommodation options include the historic Victorian Building (my preference), and the newer Ocean Towers and California Cabana. Regardless where you stay at the Del, you are just a short walk from practically everything.

Since its opening, the Del has hosted presidents and other dignitaries, and Hollywood has come calling for more than just an overnight stay. The hotel was the set for the 1958 Billy Wilder movie *Some Like It Hot*, starring Marilyn Monroe, Jack Lemmon, and Tony Curtis, as it was for the lesser-known 1980 film *The Stunt Man*, starring Peter O'Toole and Barbara Hershey.

Dining at the Del is consistently good, whether you have an artichoke-spinach dip, peppered shrimp, or a salad. At **Sheerwater** (619-522-8490), an exquisite setting for dining, dress is casual but correct. Sheerwater is open for breakfast, lunch, dinner, cocktails, and light fare throughout the afternoon. The **Babcock & Story Bar**, named for the hotel's founders, is attractive and inviting. The award-winning **Crown Room** (619-522-8490) serves a famous Sunday brunch. Be sure to learn the construction details of this unique room. **1500 Ocean** (619-522-8490), beautiful surroundings and upscale dining, has been receiving superb reviews. Several outside eating stops include the **Sun Deck Bar & Grill, Splash Bar & Deli**, and **Cabana Bar**.

The Del also boasts a collection of pricey but wonderful shops. I suggest you visit **Del Coronado Jewels** and get a crown (symbol of the Del) pin or pendant as a souvenir.

The gardens throughout the grounds are exquisite, as is the wide beach and outdoor pool.

The latest addition at the Del is **Beach Village** (866-433-3030, www.delbeachvillage.com). You can have your own oasis—your home away from home—at one of the beautifully appointed and totally equipped villas. Mesmerizing and magnificent is the view of the vast Pacific Ocean. Call for details.

Note: KSL Resorts is at the helm of the Del and other exceptional properties, the Homestead in Hot Springs, Virginia, and Carlsbad's La Costa Resort and Spa.

Loews Coronado Bay Resort

4000 Coronado Bay Rd.
619-424-4000
www.loewshotels.com/CoronadoBayResort

I have not (yet) stayed at this special property, but I had a delightful evening and superb dinner at Azzura Point Restaurant, which is now **Mistral**. I enjoyed probably one of the best veal chops I've ever had. In my experience, chops—even those prepared by the best of chefs—are more often than not served dry as dust. Not here, at least not this night. Dessert consisted of a delicious dollop of ginger ice cream. I was told all ice creams are homemade on property, and the ginger is from the garden. Chef Patrick Ponsaty is diligent about using one of the eighty-five herbs grown on property whenever appropriate to the dish. One of San Diego's favorite sommeliers, Kurt Kirschenman, will answer any of your wine questions. This is a must-see property. I am told that the boat marina and other sporting facilities are state-of-the-art and the accommodations exceptional.

IN AND AROUND SAN DIEGO

Pacific Beach

This local destination boasts on its website, "It's all right here . . . California cuisine, wheel alignments and spine adjustments all in one place." However, many of the suggested discoveries had either moved, gone out of business, or were really quite frumpy. Alas, Chamber of Commerce, I'll give it another try next time I'm in the area, but I did enjoy that tagline.

Gaslamp Quarter (a National Historic District)

In the heart of downtown San Diego, the Gaslamp Quarter (www. gaslamp.org) offered no disappointments. This collection of restored, architecturally important historic buildings is now home to restaurants, shops, theaters, and more. I recommend taking the Gaslamp Walking Tour.

Gaslamp Quarter Historic Foundation

410 Island Ave.
619-233-4692
www.gaslampquarter.org

The tour lasts about one and a half hours. The ticket also allows you to visit many different sites and attractions. It's a good deal.

U.S. Grant Hotel

326 Broadway
619-232-3121
www.usgrant.net

At the foot of the Gaslamp Quarter, you'll find this small, attractive, cozy, quiet, yet glamorous hotel. With fewer than three hundred well-appointed and most inviting rooms, the U.S. Grant Hotel is not overwhelming but a gem, with its special use of different woods and complimentary decor. After my stay, the hotel enjoyed a multi-million-dollar renovation providing many upgrades and added amenities. For fine dining, there is the **Grant Grill** (619-744-2077, www.grantgrill.com), and for more casual fare, there is the **GG Lounge**. There is live entertainment Thursday through Saturday. I enjoyed my stay at this 1910 property and look forward to returning and seeing the renovations of all varieties.

Horton Plaza

Horton Plaza in the Gaslamp Quarter is most attractive and, in some ways, unique. Though designed like a European market, it is intended "to function like an amusement park for shoppers." There is a lot to see, do, and enjoy.

Note: Trolley travel is a definite consideration.

Bazaar Del Mundo

4133 Taylor St.
619-296-3161
www.bazaardelmundo.com

Located on the corner of Juan next to **Casa Guadalajara Restaurant** (619-295-5111), this fun, colorful, unique, eclectic, wonderful spot is a must-visit, with many Mexican-style shops and shops of all varieties. You can very easily spend the day here, eat, go home, realize you saw something, and go back the next day. There's so much to see, and it's so much fun!

Paradise Point Resort

1404 Vacation Rd.
858-274-4630
www.paradisepoint.com

This forty-four-acre resort in a tropical setting on Mission Bay has recently been refurbished and upgraded. From all reports and what I have seen on the website, the property is only magnificent. When I was there, Noble House had recently purchased Paradise Point. It's been my experience that after taking over a property, Noble House works magic. And indeed they did.

Update: As of this writing, the property is now under Destination Hotels. Here at Paradise Point, you feel as if you are in a private oasis—and you are, sort of, as you are just a few minutes from the heart of San Diego. There is much to do here, especially for the sports enthusiast, not to mention anyone who wants to escape and enjoy a respite from the hubbub of life. I look forward to returning and seeing all that has been done to special Paradise Point. Without a doubt, I suggest you visit and escape to this oasis on Mission Bay. You do not need a passport.

San Diego Zoo

San Diego Zoo
2920 Zoo Dr.
619-231-1515
www.sandiegozoo.org

I could not fit in a visit to the San Diego Zoo, but if time—and you will need quite a bit—permits, do go. It is a magnificent collection of four thousand individual animals representing eight hundred species, as well as sixty-five hundred species of plants. It is pricey, but you get a lot for your dollars.

LEAVING SAN DIEGO

Major's Coffee Shop
28870 Old Hwy. 80, Pine Valley
619-473-9969

I left San Diego early to miss morning traffic. About forty miles east of San Diego traveling on I-8, I saw a sign announcing Major's Coffee Shop. I turned off and found myself in Pine Valley. Little did I know I was to experience a real and delicious serendipity. Major's was right in front as I drove into "town." I entered with a smile and seated myself at the counter. Promptly I discovered a very friendly staff, decor featuring 1950s memorabilia, and a place that seemed bigger on the inside than it looked on the outside. I took the most attentive waitress's suggestions: delicious juice, light and fluffy pancakes, and perfect coffee. I don't know why, but I rate this Major's breakfast one of the best I have enjoyed.

Sidebar: An added bonus at Major's was the presence in the restaurant of one of the best-looking men I have seen lately—a real hunk.

DEATH VALLEY

Who would have thought that one of the Driving Diva's favorite places would be Death Valley, California? A flat, maybe slightly dusty, hot drive of about two hours from Las Vegas will take you to a most unbelievable place. The drive to Death Valley requires more than the usual preparation. Be certain to gas up and check all your car's fluid levels, and let someone know your schedule. The heat is severe, so have water with you and make sure your cell phone is fully charged.

The official *Visitor Guide to Death Valley National Park* advises:

Check your car gauges frequently. Radiator water is available from storage tanks along park roads. If your car develops vapor lock, wrap a wet rag around the fuel pump and line to speed cooling. And if your car breaks down, stay with it.

Death Valley contains a hundred or more abandoned mines and associated structures. Many have been closed but it will take years to close the rest. Use extreme caution in driving and walking around mines and watch carefully for openings. NEVER enter abandoned mines. STAY OUT and STAY ALIVE.

Austere desert beauty and borax mines (as in 20 Mule Team Borax) highlight the drive to Death Valley.

Marta Becket's Amargosa Opera House and Hotel
PO Box 8
760-852-4441
www.amargosaoperahouse.com

Marta Becket grew up in New York City, and by the time she was nine, there was no question she was a budding artist, dancer, and pianist. As a young woman, she performed in several Broadway shows and at Radio City Music Hall. During a road trip west in 1967 with her then husband, her car had a flat. A park ranger directed them to have it fixed in Death Valley Junction. While her husband tended to the tire, Marta poked around an abandoned complex of offices, stores, a hotel, and a dining room constructed by the Pacific Coast Borax Company for its employees in the 1920s. Behind the Amargosa Hotel, she discovered an old opera house with a debris-strewn stage, fabric hanging at the windows, and crude benches. It was love at first sight. The next day she agreed to rent the theater from the town for $45 a month. After refurbishing the place, Marta gave her first performance in 1968 to a packed house of twelve. By 1974 the audiences were larger, and Marta began to apply her artistry to the interior, painting an entire audience on the walls. After her husband decided to "move on" in 1983, Thomas J. Willett, a man described as a natural comedian, arrived in her life and became Marta's stage manager and occasional costar.

The hotel's fourteen rooms are filled with Marta's art, including a special dedication to Red Skelton in Room 22, where he stayed a number of times. (In the painting a ballerina dances on a ball, and acrobats perform.) The modest rooms go for about $50 a night, and while they have heating and air-conditioning, by tradition there are no telephones or televisions. Though there is a vending machine in the lobby, the closest restaurant is seven miles north on the Nevada border at the Longstreet Casino.

Longstreet Casino
4400 S. Hwy. 373, Amargosa Valley
775-372-1777
www.longstreetcasino.com

Driving Diva Factoid: The 2002 film *Amargosa* was an Academy Award finalist for best documentary feature.

Near the top of my must-do list is a return to Death Valley with a stop at Marta's.

Death Valley, one of the driest and hottest places in the world, is isolated by nine mountain ranges. As a national park considered an "outdoor museum," everything is protected by federal law—even the rocks. The national park comprises over 3 million acres, and there's no sign of civilization until you get to the heart of Death Valley, where tall palm trees greet you against a backdrop of huge mountains.

Furnace Creek Inn and Furnace Creek Ranch Resort
Hwy. 190
760-786-2345
www.furnacecreekresort.com

This way out-of-the-way, wonderful hideaway is a charming AAA Four Diamond property with all the amenities. There are 66 rooms at the Inn at Furnace Creek and 224 at the Ranch at Furnace Creek, the latter being the more family-focused property. You can enjoy an eighteen-hole golf course—the world's lowest at 214 feet below sea level—as well as tennis and horseback riding. The spring-fed pool is naturally heated to a silky 85 degrees. To me, the water's texture was smooth—if water can feel smooth. The night sky is the blackest of black, and the stars are so thick and seem so low, you feel as if you could reach up and grab one. The winds do blow in Death Valley in December and March. To visit this outdoor museum is an awesome experience you will treasure. The inn is open from October to May, and during the rest of the year, all operations are consolidated at the ranch. The accommodations at the ranch are many, including cabins and both deluxe and standard rooms.

The dining opportunities are many. The **Wrangler Buffet** serves all you can eat for breakfast and lunch. At night it becomes the **Wrangler Steakhouse**, with table service, for steaks, chicken, and seafood. The **49'er Café** also serves breakfast, lunch, and dinner.

The **Corkscrew Saloon** serves snacks, lunch, and dinner, and the **19th Hole**, adjacent to the Golf Pro Shop and open only in winter, serves burgers, hotdogs, and sandwiches.

Scotty's Castle
123 Scotty's Castle Rd.
760-786-2392
www.nps.gov/deva/historyculture/scottys-castle.htm

Another feature of Death Valley is Scotty's Castle, a two-story Spanish villa built in the 1920s by Chicago insurance magnate Albert Johnson and named for Walter Scott, the talented con artist and pseudo gold prospector he was financing. Scott duped Johnson with promises of hitting the mother lode in his worthless mine. The castle, which includes a huge pipe organ, antiques, and so much more, was taken over by the National Park Service in 1970. You may tour other castles, but none quite like Scotty's. Tours are available, which I consider a must. Go early in the morning when it is cooler, and remember you are in Death Valley.

China Ranch
PO Box 61, Shoshone
760-852-4415
www.chinaranch.com

While traveling in Death Valley near Tecopa, California, visit the privately owned China Ranch. Just eighty-five miles west of Las Vegas off California Highway 127, in the stern Mojave Desert near southern Death Valley, is a lush piece of land with a wandering stream. Date palms of the best varieties grow on this small family ranch. I have not been to this oasis, but I have received some of the China Ranch's delicious products: dates and date bread. I have become an advocate of this most healthy, sodium- and fat-free (and so much more) product of nature, the date.

View the China Ranch website and check out the gift shop, where you'll find not only local items, custom-made soaps, jewelry, canned jams and jellies, but one-of-a-kind items on consignment! Whether you are online or on-site, this gift shop could be a one-stop total shop, so bring your gift lists. Thank you, China Ranch.

You will have had a wonderful, unique time in Death Valley. You may experience a departure pang or two, but what memories!

CONTRIBUTORS

Kodak: The Kodak Easy Share V610 duel-lens digital camera is fantastic. It has helped me keep track of all I have seen. I recommend it and acknowledge that it can do more than I know how to take advantage of. It is the world's smallest 10x optical zoom digital camera. Given how quickly products develop, I am sure a new model is on the scene. Regardless, it is a gem of a camera, and I hope mine lasts for many more projects. Thank you, Kodak.

GM: The Rendezvous that GM loaned me to drive round-trip, coast to coast, was an interesting vehicle and totally surprised me. In my mind's eye, I did not think the Rendezvous, a Buick, would have a youthful ambiance. How wrong I was. Not only was it comfortable and roomy, but I had OnStar on board. What technology! OnStar gives you a consoling feeling as a real, live representative is with you and knows where you are, at the push of a button. Fantastic! I enjoyed introducing, explaining, and hyping OnStar as I traveled cross-country in the Rendezvous. Thank you, GM and OnStar, for the experience.

Magellan GPS: Thank you for introducing me to your product. This was my first GPS. Not being GPS savvy, it was a bit confusing for me, but thank you for the experience. I am sure all sorts of upgrades have been made. I appreciate your interest in my project.

Garmin: Thank you, Garmin. I got this GPS to work, and it is amazing. I used it up, down, and around the eastern seaboard over thousands of miles. What a helpful driving companion!

LifeHammer: Every car should have a LifeHammer. It alone can save your life in an accident in the water or on land. This special seven-inch item has two precisely machined steel hammerheads designed to break a side window. The razor-sharp safety blade will cut through a seat belt. Thank you, LifeHammer, for your support. For more information, visit www.lifehammer.com.

Buckwheat Pillow: All-natural, nonallergenic, buckwheat-hull-filled Makura pillows come in various sizes. They are the perfect pillow, conforming to your head and neck without compressing or causing strain in your neck. This pillow should be on every bed and in every car. They are ideal for when you stop and take a short snooze. For more information, visit www.theoriginal makura.com.

My Car: Over and over I am asked what car I drive. I have and am presently driving a Ford Edge, which is serving me well. It is a little challenging mastering (or even understanding) all the new, state-of-the-art features, but you are glad to have them. A Ford has gotten me from coast to coast and border to border— one hundred thousand miles and more. Thank you.

People: More people than I can list (or count) have contributed to my projects. Each has been a valued, appreciated contributor, and I repeat: Thank you!

INDEX

12-12

CPSIA information can be obtained at www.ICGtesting.com
Printed in the USA
BVOW032247011211

277346BV00006B/3/P

9 781589 796393